46 NOT OUT

46 NOT OUT

R.C. Robertson - Glasgow

Introduction by John Woodcock

CONSTABLE · LONDON

Published in Great Britain 1985
by Constable and Company Ltd
10 Orange Street London WC2H 7EG
Copyright © the Estate of R.C. Robertson-Glasgow
Introduction copyright © 1985 John Woodcock
First published 1948 by Hollis and Carter
printed in Great Britain by
St Edmundsbury Press
Bury St Edmunds, Suffolk

British Library CIP data
Robertson-Glasgow, R.C.
46 not out – (Constable cricket classics)
1. Robertson-Glasgow, R.C.   2. cricket players
– Great Britain – Biography
I. Title
796.35′8′0924   GV915.R6

ISBN 0 09 466710 1

To Elizabeth

CONTENTS

ILLUSTRATIONS

between pages 82 and 83

INTRODUCTION

Raymond Robertson-Glasgow was among the most skilful and entertaining of all writers on sport. I am not at all sure that this is sufficiently well known, so the reappearance of *46 Not Out*, although not exclusively about sport, may make, for many, a delightful discovery, as well as a welcome renewal for others.

"Crusoe", as he was universally called (see page 108 for the reason), was a good enough cricketer to play four years for Oxford, regularly for Somerset, and once for the Gentlemen against the Players at Lord's. As a writer on the game he was highly original, invariably generous, and effortlessly erudite. He was a classical scholar with a hilarious imagination. When in good health he was marvellously and infectiously genial; when not, he was still wonderfully good fun. Although he played it keenly, cricket had to be enjoyed. In the 1930s it must have been a job to know whom to turn to first to lighten one's day – Neville Cardus in the *Manchester Guardian*, "Crusoe" in the *Morning Post*, whose correspondent he then was, or C.B. Fry in an early edition of the *Evening Standard*.

In Australia, on the MCC tour of 1950-51, I drove from state to state with "Crusoe" and his wife, Elizabeth, to whom this book is dedicated. They had met when she nursed him through a bout of depression, and she kept him going, much more in the sunshine than the shade, for another seventeen years after *46 Not Out*. We were under the command of Jim Swanton, whose car it was. Elizabeth fed, watered, and occasionally gently reproved us, while "Crusoe" lifted the spirits of everyone we met. Such was his 'touch' that Australians, however far into the outback, took to him instantly. They laughed and laughed together, for with "Crusoe" laughter and people were the breath of life. Cardus wrote of him, "Tall and handsome and agile ... he was charged with brain and wit." "Crusoe" covered that tour for the *Observer* and a group of Australian evening papers, as well as for *The Times*, whose correspondent had fallen ill on the outward voyage. *The Times* job he did out of kindness, and when they produced a booklet of his Test pieces, his own book, which he had nearly completed and in which he was to have incorporated them, had to be scrapped. This was a sad loss to the literature of cricket.

The game is a thread, no more, in *46 Not Out*. "Crusoe" could never, anyway, bring himself to be concerned only with cricket, even in his match reports. It would have been a waste if he had. When, towards the end of his life, he got out and about much less, he wrote in fact about the countryside. *46 Not Out* is a charming book. It conveys, without a hint of vanity, the pleasures of the Oxford of the 1920s and the sporting life of the 1930s.

"Crusoe" was particularly strong on character: he had a rare eye for it, as anyone who has read his two volumes of *Cricket Prints* will know. So, in much the same way, did Ben Travers, dramatist, lover of games and, like "Crusoe", a Carthusiasn. "I have always cherished 'Crusoe's' company," he wrote in his own autobiography, *Vale of Laughter*, "since that luncheon interval early in his cricketing career when he had spent an exhausting and unprofitable morning (good bowler that he was) against Hobbs and Sandham at the Oval. On the way up the pavilion steps he lingered a moment to issue a brief confidential report. He said, 'It's like bowling to God on concrete." I can hear, as though I had been there, the bellow of laughter and the slap of the thigh that followed it.

JOHN WOODCOCK

"AUTOBOGRAPH"

THIS sort of thing should be done in the flower of life, before age has brought either the cynicism which smiles so irritatingly on all human endeavour or the complacency which sits back and awaits the opening of the golden gates.

It is a common mistake of biographers to assume that because a man is great therefore he must be interesting. The truth is, the story of a life is never written at all, because a life consists in the things of the spirit which may not be uttered and the affairs of the flesh which it is imprudent, or illegal, to print. In essence, everyone is a total stranger to every one else, and falls to be misjudged on the few and occasional fragments that he or she uncovers to hurried and self-interested companions. Even Boswell, ablest of his kind, touched but the fringe of his subject. We are given an idea of how Johnson talked and talked. But, like the rest of mankind, the mighty Doctor went down to the shades as a mystery which a thousand volumes, at a guinea each, will never unlock.

So biographers are driven to invent, like Frank Harris on Oscar Wilde, or to re-write, like Guedalla on Wellington and Rosebery on Napoleon. There is another method, the research on the trivial, which is very much esteemed in the United States and has gained ground of late in this country. It consists in squeezing a little dust from a subject which was long ago milked dry, and then arranging the particles over many hundreds of folios. We are gravely informed that the Christian name of Wordsworth's cook was not, as supposed, Maria, but Clementine; that Dickens preferred haddock to plaice, and that it was on 21 April, not 22 April, that Nelson said to Emma Hamilton, "I wish we had some asparagus."

To me, everyone is something to wonder at, and I thank heaven for a taste so catholic and vulgar; wonders of knowledge and ignorance, of fatness and thinness, of activity and inertia, of beauty and ugliness. I object to the narrow and mean distribution of what the world calls fame. I refuse to accept merely what

newspapers and the radio try to palm off on us as important. I
know an old man with a beard who is far more interesting than
Mr Bernard Shaw. He doesn't write plays or send tedious letters
to *The Times*. He *is* a Play, in numberless acts. He sits and tells
lies about himself with a merry twinkle. He drinks his own beer
and other people's as well. I know as great a General as Julius
Caesar. He is a grandfather, with three orphan grandchildren.
He gets them up in the morning, sees they wash, cooks, provides,
mends, protects, advises. He's not in *Who's Who*, and, when he
dies, he will not be in the newspaper obituaries, not even in a
couple of lines under the widow of a Commercial Baron. But
the triumphal music will be waiting for him on the other side.

Yet, just as there are books which I could not enjoy alone on a
desert island—Malthus on Population, the Poetical Works of
W. H. Auden, and Kant's *Critique of Pure Reason*—so there are
two species of the human kind that fill me with perplexed silence,
namely, Progressive Young Men and Motor Mechanics. In the
matter of the P.Y.M., I take no blame for the allergy. I don't
think they love even each other. Then there are actors. Them,
I cannot out-talk. But I got actors all wrong in early youth.

I used to haunt a certain theatre in a southern watering-place,
resort of a touring company which, to me, was as brilliant as
any which gathered round Henry Irving at the Lyceum. Mostly,
they acted melodrama, and the heroic parts were taken by a
young Apollo in whom were nightly combined an astuteness of
intellect, a strength of body, and a tenderness of heart which
placed him far apart from other men. I decided I must have his
autograph. I already had Melbourne Inman, the billiards champion, and S. F. Barnes, the Test cricketer, by post. The only
signature by personal interview that I sported was the hotel
manager's, who had remarked "that'll be ninepence," as he
signed. The stage-door took some finding and, when found, was
strangely disappointing; nothing like so big, or so clean, as the
swing-doors that led to the box-office. It was faded and musty;
and someone had chalked a few words on it. I stepped forward
to read them, when a fattish woman, wearing many rings and
smelling of scent, walked almost into me. "Hullo, young Lochin-
var," she said; "starting early in life, aren't you?" "Is Mr Ashley
Drummond coming soon, please?" I asked. "You see, I want his
autograph." "Ashley Drummond, who's he? Oh, you mean

Charlie. He's just having his third. Back teeth awash. Not worth while asking him to sign. Doubt if he could do it. But there's nothing like trying. So long, Sunshine." And she prinked off on high heels. I stayed, meditating on this information. She was trying to be funny, of course, and women's jokes were always hopeless. I wondered who she was. Some barmaid, probably. The doors swung again, and an old man, bald except for some grey hair above the ears, and wearing very light brown shoes with bulbous toes, walked out with a sort of stiff and dignified gait which I had seen used only by those who collected the offertory in church. Ah, he might know. He seemed to be allowed inside. So I asked him if Mr Ashley Drummond was coming soon. "He has come, young sprig," replied the man. "He's here and at your service. Mr Ashley Drummond or Mr Charles S. Jones. We are one and the same." A whole world fell to the pavement and broke in pieces. But I wasn't going to retreat now. I pushed the little red notebook and pencil at him, and asked. He signed just as he walked, slowly and stiffly, Ashley R. Drummond. "Like the little show?" he said. I said I did. "Good," he said. "Dukes didn't. But Dukes doesn't know a damn. I've told him so, often." And he strode thoughtfully away, leaving me to the mystery of Mr Dukes.

Actors, some say, should never be seen off the stage, just as commissionaires should never take off their uniforms, or chimney-sweeps wash their faces. Likewise, only more so, radio stars should avoid appearing in public among their fans. They should remain airy spirits, disembodied voices. I have had proof of this from one who has held millions with his golden tones. He was present, he told me, at an extensive garden-party given by the B.B.C. to some London children. He had performed, he said, many social duties and had, if I know him aright, talked to many strangers with his incomparable air of knowing who each one was, when a small girl detached herself from her companions, ran up to him, and said: "Are you Mr . . . 'oo broadcasts?" "I am," admitted the golden voice. And the small girl, after a long and gimlet stare, just said, "Aow," and retired.

CRAIGMYLE

ANDERING through the Crow Wood at Craigmyle with my brother is about the earliest thing I remember, and nothing then was any better than that. In season it was full of anemones; in and out of season it was full of rabbits, who were shot and reproduced themselves in their yearly thousands. Many times I have used that wood since, in reading or imagining stories, or just to recollect it in the hour before sleep.

I have used the Crow Wood, Aberdeenshire, as it was in summer, for Robin Hood's fight with Little John. From behind its trees, he and his green men have ambushed their portly clerical victims; which is very impolite to Sherwood Forest. In autumn, I have had the Boscombe Valley Mystery solved among its leaves, and chosen the very tree behind which the tall murderer waited with the stone in his left hand, while his right held the cigar whose Trichinopoly ash gave away the show to Sherlock Holmes. Into another tree, a gigantic oak, I have often disappeared by a secret door in the trunk, worked by a secret spring, when pursued by armed bandits of hideous ferocity, or, more stealthily, by solemn psalm-singing men of the Cromwellian faction. I blush to add that I have used a private lift in the tree to take me down to a room stocked with food and drink of the most luxurious sort.

Beyond the Crow Wood came the high-road to Aberdeen, twenty-three miles away, and the telegraph-posts, which were good to smell and to put the ear against. We thought the buzzing and throbbing were the telegrams going through. Here, on the railway-bridge, we stood waiting for the family's first motor-car. The excitement was terrific. Mr Henry Plumb, promoted from coachman, had gone in to Aberdeen early by train, and it was no certainty that he would reach home again. Then, round the corner he came, steering the bright new Panhard with anxious pride, and with my father in the back. We cheered triumphantly, and I had some extraordinary notion that they were going first

4

to Balmoral to show it to King Edward and Queen Alexandra.

Mr Plumb, who was English, used to clean the Panhard, which he called "she," with that purring whistle peculiar to coachmen and ostlers. He was a serious, patient, and dutiful man, who believed that cars, like horses, should not be pushed along too fast. "They won't a-stand it," he would say, and, when driving the car up hill he always leant forward against the wheel, clucking his tongue with tender encouragement, as if the engine were Snip, who was thirty-four and had gone to grass, or Tommy, who was a Shetland, and therefore fat and obstinate.

The 20-mile speed limit, which for years outlived its purpose, suited his sparing views, and to the end he suspected that every hedge concealed policemen with stop-watches; but they got no kick out of Mr Plumb, for he kept the speedometer dial at 19, rising to 19½. Often my brother and I urged him to take a chance at 21, and sometimes pressed a foot suddenly on top of his on the accelerator, which made the good man turn pale with shock and annoyance. I don't think he knew much about the engine, though he would explain the theory of propulsion with long words and tap the cylinders with an air of profundity. We were allowed to join in this, and, sometimes, to flood the carburettor. He disliked a too-generous flow of petrol, and was pure Aberdeen by adoption. But the magneto was sacred. "Fiddle about with that," he said, "and you're done." So we gaped at it with an ignorant solemnity which magnetos still inspire in the majority of mankind.

On Christmas Day he turned coachman again, and put on a cocked hat to drive us in the carriage over to matins at the Episcopal Church at Kincardine O'Neil. The snow-topped Grampians held the horizon. The sun shone out, as we clop-clopped along. In the church there was a real choir, with men and boys in surplices, and there were hymns to fill the lungs and raise the heart, and thoughts of presents at home to re-examine at leisure, and turkey and lighted plum-pudding. But on regular Sundays we walked down to the kirk at Torphins, where the choir was only women in their ordinary clothes, and the minister climbed up to the pulpit at the start and stayed there to the end, which was, oh, so very long in coming. Surely, I thought, God did not make men, far less boys, to listen to sermons for forty minutes. Yet the minister, I have since been told and find hard to believe, was a very good man, and more abstemious than his predecessor, who was a deep scholar and a deeper drinker. After a thick Saturday night, he would be assailed by qualms in kirk, and would close his eyes and grip the pulpit; but his timing was excellent, and he could cause these moments of pain to concur with silent prayer and introspection. Once, when his sermon-notes fluttered from his shaking hand to the floor, he leant forward and, in angry tones, requested the front pew to "pick up yon bits of dommed pappy."

To the north-east lay the Hill o' Fare, heather-covered and good at catching the sun or flying shadows. Adjoining its foot marched the estate of a rather mad Colonel. At his own shoots he fired on almost anything, in or out of range, and, when a bird rose some two hundred yards away, he surprised a guest by shouting at him, "Have a blast at it, man; you may never see it again."

Of other neighbours I remember nothing, except that they came to tea downstairs and went away again, without infesting the schoolroom, where tea was a business, not a convention. I don't think we missed them, or their children, who came soon enough, at school, when privacy flies, and part of you becomes a stranger for ever, even to your own parents. A common mistake among parents is to push their children into a premature gregariousness. A boy, if he is one, will learn whither and with whom he wants to go.

Few and fleeting are the years of uncivilized society, when you can talk without wisdom or regret, quarrel without estrangement, and make love without committing yourself. You wake to no business but the daily wonder of life. Sleep wraps you like a familiar lover. You are an accepted visitor in the kitchen. Your clothes are outside fashion and criticism. Your questions need no answer. You write letters that are not for the post. For the first and only time, pretence is better than reality. You are rich on a few cardboard counters, a musician with a drum and trumpet, a winning general with a hobby-horse and wooden sword, an accountant with a row of coloured beads. Tuesday was our day for photography. The camera was a biscuit-tin, covered with a red table-cloth. The results were ready on Friday. I have some of them still, unflattering, and signed by the author.

But Bertha Greub was an interruption, a nuisance, a plague.

She often said she loved me—"Raymond, you would look so nize if only you broshed your hair"—but in her harassed heart I think she took me, perhaps rightly, for an adenoidal little beast. She was a Swiss-German governess, with a wide, white, solemn face, pale blue eyes, and no laughter. Whenever I see a crossed continental figure seven, I think of Miss Greub and her sums on the blackboard, which never came out wrong. Stupid figures; how I loathed them, and loathe them still. What a mess mathematics make of man, damming his generous currents, frowning on joyous fallibility, pursing the dry lip at admirable error. They say that Einstein employs underlings to handle his figure-reckonings. That must be why he can still enjoy human intercourse and can smile without a dry creaking sound.

So there I sat at the sums, and looked across at brother Bobs, who didn't care whether he had them right or wrong, for he had the measure of Miss Greub, and she knew it, and gave up that battle early. But I had some futile idea that I ought to please her, a feeble propitiator. In the silence of miscalculation I called up rescuing thoughts, which took me, unseen, to Mr Crawford in his hot-house, or down the leafy lane past the house of Mr Greenhill, the bearded gamekeeper, where I found six eggs in a nest. Take one; that leaves five. Those figures again; and back to Bertha Greub who was writing a letter at her desk. I wondered if it was to Otto Keller. Otto lived in Hamburg, and she told us he was a wonderful man and that he was going to marry her. May the Gods forgive me, but even then I wondered why. She talked of him without restraint, with an awful directness and certainty. One morning we opened a cupboard in the schoolroom and saw an electric-blue dress hanging. It was her wedding-dress, and Otto liked the colour. Soon afterwards, in early summer, he came over from Hamburg, and stayed in the little Torphins hotel. We had days of holiday. Then he went home; and the news, swift like all evil, reached us that Otto had jilted her. It was my first knowledge of the inconstancy of man. In the stories that we knew, no one who had asked a woman to marry him broke his promise. There was no help to give. Only I tried harder at my sums and brushed my hair again and again. As for poor Bertha, she soon went back to Switzerland with her electric-blue wedding-dress. I wonder if she ever put it on, and for whom?

We did not call my father by his christian name, then or ever.

Not that it matters much, but to do so is, surely, a rather feeble hypocrisy; for thus, either the father is willing to be thought as young, and interesting, as his son—a very human fellow, you know, nothing pompous about him—or else the son likes to be thought as important as his father. We knew the forbidden times and places, and our love suffered nothing from being dipped in awe. We learnt when to "run along", a useful knowledge in wider fields than home. Lunch, at the long table, with a sprinkling of false aunts and with milk in the christening-mug, was one of our appearances in society. Colonel Thompson was often sitting opposite me, and he made sprightly talk. I don't remember lunch without the Colonel. He was a guest *sine die*. He had a white moustache and drank claret. He ate very slowly, to try to keep pace with me. Even so, I was always last, and got into a muddle with my knife and fork, and my father would say, "Shovel on, bubba." After lunch my father chased us upstairs, pulled off our shoes, and helped the ascent with sounding bottom-slapping. Other medicine there was none.

He fished, shot, and managed the estate, and, as I came to know, did all of them supremely well. In August 1914, when we were boys on school holiday, he walked back into the army, from which he had retired when his father died. He was about to go out to Gallipoli with the Royal Scots Fusiliers when he was taken ill, and, being transferred to the King's Own Scottish Borderers, spent the rest of the war in the depot at Berwick, where he found a havering Colonel in nominal charge. The Colonel was a weird revival. He had no head for soldiering. He drank little, but that little was too much, and when, at night, a suggestion of bed was raised, he would put his hands on the arms of his chair, as if he expected to be prised out by violence, and say, "No, no; I won't get up; I'm intoxicated; no, no; certainly not." He should have been in the muddle at the Crimea.

My mother, who came from a Suffolk rectory, was tall, dark, slim and, I will add, very beautiful. She neither spoilt nor scolded us. In the matter of our wrong-doing, she used no vain repetitions, but said: "Really, you must *not*", and sometimes we did *not*. It needed no son to know that she was someone quite different. I suppose an adult mind would analyse that difference as born from grace and intelligence, seasoned by a learning and humour almost masculine. She was perfectly suited to a world

that had no need to mistake agitation for action, where designs
were unfolded in security.

She had, too, what no learning can give, the art of telling a
story; and many a time, after prayers at night, we held her back
and listened till the easy drawling tones merged into forgetfulness. When she read to us, it was not the books that we might
handle moderately well on our own, Hans Andersen or Grimm,
but something just a little above the head, with new long words
to be explained and new countries to be imagined. But book or no
book, just to be near her was enough, in her own sitting-room, or
boudoir, as the fashion chose to call it. Even lovers do not know
this happiness, for it is without the hint of mortality. It did not
change; though the time that we spent together had to be counted in days, not borrowed freely from eternity; and it was I that
had to tell her, in her bedroom, about the people in the world
outside; till the shadow came, and the inescapable Fact.

When I was about five, and still wore the hermaphroditic
clothes of Edwardian childhood, I found myself on a visit to
London, for what purpose it was not for me to inquire. If we
visited the Tower, or watched them changing the Guard at
Buckingham Palace, I have forgotten it. I have never taken much
interest in the accepted sights and shows, and I prefer the faces of
mankind in one living street to all the Picture Galleries in the
world. Inspection of pictorial art gives me the dumb chills and an
increasing pain around the kidneys. The women of the Italian
masters are disgustingly fat, and their babies on the verge of
apoplexy. But even pictures are moderate heaven compared
with Museums. And the lowest hell is an exhibition of Pottery.
Have you ever noticed that Curators in Museums grow like the
things that they curate?

Most vividly from that first London visit come back the German bands, and the vulgar habits of the town dogs. The musi-
cians from Germany were "Frank Reynolds" Germans, comic
and genial, and probably always on the verge of pulling a string
of sausages from the pocket. They stood in the gutter in their
peaked caps, and the euphonium would step forward during the
lighter passages to collect the tinkling pennies. They were
hirsute and amenable, and showed no resentment when they
were requested to pass on and play their brassy waltzes in the
next square. The Kaiser might be rude to his Uncle Edward and

prepare armaments, but it was not easy to connect war with these fat old gentlemen and their trombones.

It was about now that I had ambitions to become a postman. It was an ideal life. He had a uniform, and an enviable helmet, not quite so fine as a fireman's, but a fireman's life must surely be very dull between fires, just sitting about and waiting for a call. Postmen must be men of great strength, for people talked about a regular postman's knock. Besides, a postman could read all the letters, having a sort of world-control of correspondence; and he walked everywhere alone, without being fussed at. He could step in puddles if he felt like it, and, best of all, bang all the knockers in the street. I made inquiries about the age when you began to be a postman and whether apprentices were taken on. The answers were vague and disappointing; and someone said that postmen were often very poor. I asked why someone didn't give them more money, then. The answers were vaguer than ever. I was told that I'd understand, one day.

Then another puzzle arose. Someone said that the cook was no good, and would have to leave. I disagreed, and said that she was a very nice cook and that I liked her, even loved her. I believe she stayed, not through my intercession, I fancy, but because we were soon going home again. I have no doubt that she drank and was in collusion with the tradesmen; but it was a serious and unfathomable matter that anyone should be bad at a job, for degrees of ability or incompetence had not till then entered my consideration. If you were a cook, you were a good cook; otherwise, why be a cook? If you were a soldier, you were good at fighting; if a fireman, at putting out fires. Anyhow, as to being sent away because you were bad at something, it was unheard of. The world was growing very complicated.

We went to a kindergarten, which is one of the few German words that, even in the middle of a war, seems never to give offence; because, amid the hate and fear of war, love settles as a last hope on the children; and the news of Nazi children informing on their own parents was more despairingly terrible than the story of Judas.

At the kindergarten we had milk and *petit-beurre* biscuits at eleven o'clock in the morning, and once a week we took our pumps along for dancing, on which art I shared the views of Mr Bultitude when requested to do a sailor's hornpipe. The girls were extremely dull, and appeared to have taken a vow of silence. Also, they worked too industriously, and were for ever sharpening pencils or rubbing something out. I fancy that the ladies always tend to use these physical activities merely as an outward symbol, and I later noticed that the undergraduettes of Oxford aimed to take down every word of the lecturer, starting from "Good-morning, ladies and gentlemen", and ending with "and there, I fear, we must stop for to-day." In the afternoon, we had the freedom of Kensington Gardens, seeing how long we could sit free on the twopenny green chairs, envying the boats that didn't capsize on the Round Pond, and walking round the Albert Hall from opposite directions.

We travelled back to Scotland by day. I had worked myself into an excitement over the Forth and the Tay Bridge; but they proved too much for me. I snatched one look at the water of the Forth from a corner seat, then took my sinking stomach to the floor of the compartment. I was ready for the Tay, and went to ground some miles before we reached it. To this day, my worst dream is of a tidal wave on the Serpentine.

We left Craigmyle. My father had meant my brother to have it one day; but finance, and my mother's uncertain health, quelled that plan, and it was sold to "Tommy" Shaw, who became a Law Lord, and took to himself the title of Baron Craigmyle. Never again did the whole family spend more than a few weeks together. My mother travelled much abroad, and we began a nomad life of hired houses, hotels public and private, and apartments beside the sea.

III

CARUSO AND AUNTIE BUG

T HE Wabe, Reddington Road, Hampstead, stood, and may stand yet, on the top of Hampstead Hill, and from our bedroom window we could watch the lighted legs of the Flip Flap rising, crossing, and sinking each night in the Earl's Court Fair. Once or twice, but unluckily only in the day-time, the monster stuck, and it was said that the passengers who had thus perched reluctantly in its cages were compensated for their experience. It seemed an easy way of making money. I thought I saw a man with the bag of money ready in case we stuck. We would be rescued by the Fire Brigade, of course, who spent their lives driving at top speed to such emergencies.

It was at the Wabe that I first heard people talking about drains. A sudden sickness seized the house, and, as it was improbable that everyone had simultaneously eaten too much, the blame fell on the drains. This theory, not always confirmed by science, is common among those who rent otherwise desirable residences from invisible and extortionate landlords, and are afflicted by unexplained smells, sore throats, or a general sense of decline. Sometimes a man arrives and takes notes. He always wears an overcoat, even in a heat-wave, probably to show that he is not the man who is going to do the work, and possibly because he is wearing something very moderate underneath.

These were the last years of music, before melody and words were conquered by noise and nonsense; and the first of a long line of gramophones entered the home, with a great green trumpet and hopeful intimations about changing the needle. It was the rich, if autumnal, age of those songs that came somewhere between "Knock 'em in the Old Kent Road" and "Your Tiny Hand is Frozen," and might be sung, as an encore and a permissible condescension, by Ben Davies, at request, before an intimate audience, or howled by the love-lorn amateur, shining in pumps and hair-oil, into the resistless ear of a future mother-in-law; songs that tended to ask sad, if rhetorical, questions about a future state—"How can I leeve without you? How can I let you go?"—and it seemed that at any moment the singer might burst into fragments and his audience into tears. Doubtless, they were cheap; but they were warm, with the warmth of life; and they have lasted; unlike their modern substitutes, which are coldly vulgar, like cats approaching an amour under a wintry moon.

It was also the meridian of the incomparable Enrico Caruso. I once put on his "On with the Motley" ten times running; and only he could make the china ring on the shelves, and, even with a cushion stuffed into the horn, he was stronger than all the rest. Besides, he could laugh or cry while singing. The Italian words, by iteration, took on queer shapes and sounds, like some universal language. There were such unexplained phrases as "Humptee Dumptee, Frequento"; and "Dona Maria sine botoamo." Then he would rise into a crescendo of French, with "Arrivez avec moi-oi." But, for a rainy afternoon, nothing touched the duet from *Il Trovatore*, where, after the plaintive woman had coo-ed melodiously enough, Caruso burst in with a roll of thunder that might have split open the very gates of his prison, and even of heaven itself. Now, surely, they would be free together and live happily ever afterwards. But the accursed bell would toll them back, till, shouting despair and love to the last, they parted, and, after a new needle and a brisk winding up, would give their infinite encore.

Among lesser lays, "I like you in Velvet" was very delicate in the pseudo-Gallic style. It dropped in by some happy chance on the radio the other day, to fill an idle space, and it brought back my Aunt Bertha, listening to it with a smile on her broad face; for she looked her best in velvet, so I used to think. Years before, someone else had thought the same; but it remained just an idea.

She was one of the "good aunts that understand"; no blood relation, but so very much more real than real aunts, who probably have children of their own, and have heard them compared, audibly and to disadvantage, with the nephews and nieces, and the fat is for ever in the fire. The best aunts are spinsters; for then they see in the children the likeness, perhaps the image itself, of what might have been their own. It is an unhappy, even an irreligious, thing to defy a father or mother, but he who quarrels with a spinster aunt is for ever damned.

Aunt Bertha Tacon, commonly and without question known

as Auntie Bug, was my mother's oldest friend, and they had been brought up near each other in Suffolk. The Tacons had come from Spain, and Bertha's father, Sir Thomas, had received his knighthood for public, that is to say, private services, having agreed to relieve a certain Duke of a large slab of landed property in Wales of which His Grace was making a considerable muddle. Other speculations had prospered, and Sir Thomas settled at Eye, becoming a Justice of the Peace and a director of the Great Eastern Railway, with its blue engines and steadfast unpunctuality. He was short, but he weighed a full twenty stone, and at Liverpool Street Station it took two porters, and sometimes the silent influence of the stationmaster, to lever him, as directors should be levered, to the platform.

Auntie Bug was a fine figure of a woman, in the days before women aped boys and suppressed their bosoms and beams. She had a bust that Melba might have envied. But she could dance out three encores of "The Blue Danube" and then come up, after a glass of wine and a few flicks of the fan, for a polka or a barndance. She was shrewd in business, but had that smiling vagueness which is fatal to umbrellas and handbags. The latter were always stuffed to bursting, for, though naturally generous and honest, she had a jackdaw weakness for collecting notepaper, especially from the drawing-rooms of hotels, and she would write from Paris, Montreux, or Rome, on paper headed *The Metropole, Brighton*. Her letters ran three words to the line, four lines to the page; so this came hard on the management; and harder still when she was moved, as she often was in spring, to write verse. Then the stationery would be raked in from Hydros far and wide, and be stuffed in the bag, only to flutter to the carpets like Sibylline leaves.

She did not easily pass sweet-shops, and would glue her face to their windows like any schoolboy, trying to persuade herself and us that she did not often do this sort of thing. "Really," she would say, fixing her favourite chocolate creams with a look of dreamy avarice, "really, I have never seen anything quite like those before; run in and ask them how much they are for a half pound," as if the information would be denied to any adult. So we would run in, and find that these novelties were actually for sale, at a price to make you turn green to-day, and we would have our commission. She also smoked "Splendo" cigarettes, two shillings for fifty, and had a flutter on the principal flat-races, without previously studying any form whatsoever, but winning as often as the wisest punter, and saying, triumphantly, "Of course, it was bound to win with a name like that."

She dabbled in theosophy, not unaided by my mother; and what field-days she would have had with the neo-Georgian astrologers. From theosophy she strode on to spiritualism in its simpler manifestations. She sought no contact with the dead, preferring inside information on contemporary affairs, and we would be invited to seances at a table on which was set a tooth-glass surrounded by the letters of the alphabet. This method by-passed the need for a medium. On one occasion, the spirit, after giving satisfaction for some time, turned suddenly obstinate, causing the following sort of passage:

Q. What is the matter?
A. I cannot go on.
Q. Why not?
A. Someone is working against me.
Q. Someone in this room?
A. Yes.
Q. A man?
A. No.
Q. A woman?
A. Perhaps.
Q. Who is it?
A. You must find out.

So we pushed the tooth-mug around, and it spelt out the word JELY. Auntie Bug was asked to leave, in the cause of science. She refused, utterly; and the argument concluded the seance.

Humorous, fantastic, and kind, she yet had the power of attracting opposites, and her later days were beset by a family of sepulchral aspect and Calvinistic views. Among them was an elderly man, one of nature's widowers, who seemed to have lost all contact with the world. He just sat in a room. I was about to burst in on him one day, when Auntie Bug said hastily, "Don't go in there; Mr Kooey's nerves are very bad to-day. He wants to be alone."

One day at the Wabe, Miss Morris arrived. She came to teach us French and Geography, and introduced her subjects by re-marking that the Hampstead Tube lift was the deepest in the

world. Confidence being thus established, we tried a little learning, and, at her departure in the evening, went up to the flat roof
and threw down to her an informal letter which on one side
announced that we loved her and would continue to do so for
ever, and, on the other, was covered with symbolical gum. Nothing has weakened those early vows. Soon she was to be severely
tested. The Wabe was unexpectedly required by its owners. No
other house appeared to be conveniently empty. The drains
suddenly re-asserted themselves. I was violently sick during the
signing of the register at the Great Central Hotel. A bleak look
came over the face of the Reception Clerk, and Miss Morris said
to him, "Poor little chap, he's been like that ever since the boat
left Dieppe."

IV

TIME THE BOYS WERE AT SCHOOL

UNACCOUNTABLE manœuvres brought parts of the family, and Miss Morris, to rest at the Croft, Stanmore, Middlesex; an address which I wrote, with a spider-flourish, on the fly-leaf of my barren diary, on its Insurance Policy against death by accident or nature, and on any book, never mind whose. The Relation Who Never Gave weighed in surprisingly with a prayer-book about now, doubtless out of old stock, and had to be thanked; a nuisance when it is not the thanking season.

Many times since, I have seen the Croft, but only in fancy; for it was a perfect setting for murders and all deadly crime. Thick trees hid it from the road, and on such a closed-in park, under a gibbous moon, might have prowled Dr Grimsby Roylott's cheetah and baboon in fearsome vigil. Here, too, a year or so after we left, I had Dr Hawley Harvey Crippen rid himself of a tiresome wife; down in the cellar, under the floor. At Stanmore, too, not, as he would have us believe, at Godalming, "Sapper" placed the nursing-home of the infamous Henry Lakington, in one hand the syringe, in the other the document to be signed on the dotted line.

About now, the Zetterstein family arrived on a visit, father, mother, and a baby of recumbent age. It was the first boom in massage, a practice which the Swedes cornered and for years held on to with all the tenacity of that money-loving race. They were supposed to have the secret of strength with tenderness.

Mrs Zetterstein certainly had the strength. She was a whacking blonde, sunburnt in all weathers, and with a temper like a rocket. Invincibly stupid, too, and with a voice like an iron gate on rusty hinges. Worst of all, she was proprietary, an orderer-about. She was not asked to run the household, but made it understood, short though she was in the English language, that everything was far better done in Sweden; especially the cooking. This delusion led her into conflict with Mrs Henry Plumb, queen of the kitchen, whose vegetables had come up for criticism. The

Zetterstein said there was a way of doing brussels sprouts in oil.
Mrs Plumb said there wasn't, and that she would like to hear
about it. With pitying condescension, Mrs Zetterstein expounded
the recipe, and Mrs Plumb, seizing her chance, served up a dish
of sprouts floating in oily foam and mysteriously undergirded
with string, of a nature so vomitously repellent that even the dog,
an omnivorous mongrel, slunk shaking from the room. But Mrs
Zetterstein, unwilling to allow that she had been defied, swallowed two or three mouthfuls, and turned a dull red under her perpetual tan. She came to words with Mrs Plumb over this, but her
Swedish was all a dead loss, and the glad tidings reached us that
Mrs Plumb had called her "a foreign bitch", and that Mrs
Zetterstein, recoiling from her culinary defeat, had vicariously
blown up her husband who, apart from marrying, wearing a
bow-tie fixed on a stud, and cleaning his nails at table, was a man
without guilt.

As to the Zetterstein's baby, Mrs Zetterstein would contem-
plate this innocent creature with a flat stare, confidently supposed to represent maternal tenderness, then walk off muttering
and, doubtless, praying to some hygienic god that it would not
grow up like one of us. It came near to never growing up at all,
for, one morning, as it lay all unsuspecting in its perambulator,
my brother and I decided to enter that vehicle for a race with a
bicycle round the kitchen garden. It was to be a handicap, the
Zetterstein baby to receive two paths and one corner start. It
proved to be a very close-run thing; but, at the last corner, the
perambulator, when leading by two lengths, hit a stone, and the
baby was shot out. It lay seemingly happy and quite unharmed,
among the cabbages, gazing up at the heavens whence, so the
poets say, it had come. We were scooping it out of the greenery,
when Mrs Zetterstein began to bellow from afar. The baby,
rather unsportingly, decided to join in, and the welkin rang. So
many emotions simultaneously tore Mrs Zetterstein that she
spoke in a sort of Esperanto. "It is not," she ended, "a thing to be
apologized upon. It goes beyond." Later in the day, my mother
sent for us and explained in her quiet way that perambulators
should not be raced against bicycles, nor should babies be pitched
into cabbages. It was bad for the baby, and the cabbages. We
must somehow soothe Mrs Zetterstein. Then she returned to her
writing. So we apologized away to the bone; but the lamentation

continued, and Mrs Zetterstein would not be comforted. Soon afterwards, they left; and Miss Morris, who had been off duty during the race, said it was just as well.

We were to go to school in September; and in August Mr Henry Plumb taught us to bowl. "If you're going to school," he said, "you'll want to know cricket, and the start of cricket is bowling." On any science or art he took the simple view that it was there and could be learnt. Progress, variation, degrees of excellence, these had no place in his syllabus. If you couldn't do a thing, it was because you hadn't been taught. "I know 'rithmetic," he used to say; and when, some years later, we showed him such algebra as we had gathered, he said "It's all my eye and Fanny Adams, and where is the sense in mucking about the alphabet without coming to any words at all? There's history," he admitted, "and the Kings and Queens of England; and there's geography with the principal capes and towns. I've done 'em; years ago."

He taught us bowling in the stable-yard, far away from the house, with a tennis ball, against a broom, under the gilt-handed clock, which had stopped at twenty to nine. I always reckoned it was the pigeons sitting on the hands that stopped it. It was raining on the first morning's lesson, but Mr Plumb took no notice of that, and showed us an Over with his fine high action. "Keep your hand high," he said, "and brush your ear with your arm." With his second ball he hit the broom-handle, and down the wicket went with a clatter. So we went at it, morning after morning, Mr Plumb in gaiters and shirt sleeves, zizzing through his teeth, as if cricket, as well as motoring, were only a natural projection of his old ostler's art. We didn't go in for any batting. Perhaps he hadn't done it. Only thunderstorms stopped play; and then he would take us in to see the new Jackson car. It had one cylinder, and a hood that took ten minutes to put up.

So bowling was all the craze. Stamps, bicycling, plasticine, Sherlock Holmes, all went to the devil. We saw wickets everywhere, as lovers see each other in flowers, and round unexpected corners. Phantom-batsmen presented themselves and were summarily dismissed. I bowled unchanged down Regent Street one morning, from Oxford Circus to Swan and Edgar, Miss Morris feebly objecting behind. Jostled old gentlemen damned me and shook their canes. But who cared about being damned or shaken at? It was dottiness in excelsis.

One morning, the School clothes list arrived and the shopping began· It was a three-day campaign, under the generalship of Miss Morris, the objective being John Barker of Kensington. It was August, and the newspapers, still clinging obsequiously to the delusion that only five hundred families in London matter at all, had observed that town was empty and parliament in recess, unmindful that only in August is London alive with people, instead of being occupied by compulsory dummies. It is then that England comes to her capital. Mrs Mutton Fat receives her clients from Manchester and Birmingham, and purses her lips over the extra latch-key; John Widdecombe gapes at the pigeons in Trafalgar Square; Sandy Sauchiehall loses his penny in the weighing-machine; and the eternal sailor plants his stepney-wife in the taxi-cab to visit St Paul's and to investigate the colour of the beer in the Cheshire Cheese and the Cock of Fleet Street.

We began in the tailoring department of John Barker, and my brother gave a punch in the stomach to a perfect youth with fair hair and sightless blue eyes which rocked him on his waxen legs, and a young Mr Kipps, upheld by the high stiff collar of the day, winked and enjoyed the assault. But a floor-walker, knowing his enemies and their season, advanced with razor crease and polished tread, and Miss Morris, her hat already somewhat askew, drew us rapidly away to the hosiery. There we were required to have stockings measured round our dubious fists and, at the next counter, selected those Eton collars whose frayed edges once sawed so mercilessly at the necks of the young and whose bland surface offered itself irresistibly to those behind for noughts-and-crosses and topical illustrations.

Thence, up in the lift to the boots and shoes, where we found the Sportive Assistant. He was old, perhaps forty; but years of measuring feet, lacing football-boots, and stretching from ladders, had not quenched his laugh or blunted his soul. He was still ready to join in. It was a pair of dark grey plimsolls, ripe for the gymnasium, that started it. They were thrown, and hit a young customer of some ten years, who had not been introduced, on the back of the neck. He, nothing surprised or loath, threw them back. The Sportive Assistant took them on the body. For an instant he hesitated between convention and desire, then gathering

a pair of check bedroom-slippers, hurled them, and the battle of
the shoes was on; no sides, but each man for himself; a battle of
thud and thwack and rattle. Exhaustion brought a truce; the
wreckage was cleared away; purchases were made; and, after a
little bowling in the High Street, we retired for lunch among the
Italian colony in Soho.

V

1908 - 1914

IN those days Hindhead was wild and free, though already the tentacles of civilization were feeling after it. The Huts was still an inn, dark within and without; a "deversorium", for the thirsty traveller to turn into after the long pull up from Thursley, between the Punch Bowl and the Gibbet Hill; on which, some years before Trafalgar, hung the bodies of two Irishmen who had murdered a young sailor for his fifty pounds, till their skeletons danced to the breeze. From that hill (900 feet) you can look over Sussex, Surrey, and Hampshire, and southwards the woods slope down to Haslemere and the hidden house of Aldworth, where Tennyson wrote plays and avoided the inquisitive eye.

A stone by the Portsmouth Road marks where a shepherd found the body, too soon for the murderers, in what was then a tangle of bracken and gorse; and, in the Huts inn, there hung on the wall the old gibbet chains and gloomy pictures of the progressive story; the meeting at the Red Lion, the crime, and the arrest at Petersfield. Also, to fill the cup of curiosity, postcards pressed themselves against the Stationer's window, with these daintings in miniature, set off by rough doggerel rhymes:

> Lonegan and Casey used the knife,
> Marshall begged to spare his life.

and, after a touch or two on the purple heather,

> That lad's blood, more purple real,
> Soon was flowing down the Hindhead hill.

The postcards, I fancy, have been withdrawn long ago; and the Huts is an hotel, clean and ordinary, with the inevitable saloon; ready for the charabancs and week-ends, beer and bananas.

An opinion, or, rather, an indescribable feeling that there were around us woods not to be visited, perilous copses and dangerous lanes, still persisted when I first went to school at Hindhead.

Ridiculous, perhaps, when cars were ousting horses from the high-
way, and a pioneer A.A. Scout sometimes appeared at the cross-
roads; but the smell of lawlessness long outlives the sight of it.

From the south-west rolled the valleys, deep and dense, along
which the smugglers had picked their muffled way, desperate
men and doubtless armed to the eyebrows. The squatters had
left a wicked name for violence against the trespassing landlord.
They had excelled at arson. A house being newly built, acres
newly bought, were cause enough for the heather and gorse to
break into flames. Justice made feeble gestures at them, and they
replied by setting a policeman on the coals of a domestic fire till
warmth brought wisdom. We wouldn't have known a squatter if
we'd seen one, but we lived in a sort of hopeful fear of encounter,
and on certain Sunday walks we were careful not to wander too
far from the road. One man in particular, whom we sometimes
met on these walks, was, I decided, a brigand, and probably an
outlaw as well. He scowled at us so horribly. Some years afterwards I discovered that he was a retired ironmonger of blameless,
if solitary, habits, whose strained expression was merely the
combination of very short sight with an acquired distrust of
schoolboys.

This romantic quietude had attracted to it men of a literary
and learned bent. Arthur Conan Doyle lived for some years in a
house near the Huts, sunken below the level of the wood, with
only its roof visible through the trees. He played local cricket, and
was a roughish determined batsman, with a vigorous design on
short and improbable runs, not always answered by static and
calm-browed partners. These games were waged on Squire
W.'s big field, now many years under the plough. There were
long and unquestionable teas between the innings, dashing
blazers, and prizes for the year's best bowler and batsman, who
received them to the accompaniment of homely irony. The
Squire was the junior partner in the family wine-business, and
was known as "the pauper brother" on x & y thousands a year.
But he was rich in kindness. He gave enjoyment and that which
makes enjoyment possible. New Orders, whether Left, Right, or
Middle, that leave out Squires, are only half-baked.

Conan Doyle left the increasing popularity and week-endish-
ness of Hindhead for remoter Crowborough, where, soon, he cut
the wires that connected him with the material world, locked

away Sherlock Holmes, Sir Nigel Loring and Rodney Stone, and
made room for one ever-present guest. His place in the sunken
house was taken by Thomas Selwyn, who in the 'eighties had
succeeded the mighty Thring as headmaster of Uppingham. He
appeared to us as a retired clergyman in a white tie and very low
collar, walking up and down the Portsmouth Road, arguing
with strangers, and as if weighed down with some knowledge that
he must, somehow, pass on to others. He may have stood high in
his own world and time; for the Selwyns have seldom wanted for
wit, learning, and a pugnacious intellectual thrust. But greatness, mediocrity, failure, are all alike to children, and, perhaps,
to their Creator. To us, he was the arguing walker.

Nature shielded the Punch Bowl from the enterprising builder.
Two or three paths, difficult to know, join, part, and meander
towards the Devil's Jumps. Two or three families occupied abor-
tive but sufficing farms, and entered the census with indifference;
but were often good for a glass of milk and a smile to the young
blackberry-picker. Most of the Punch Bowl was trees and tangle
and tuffeted bog, semi or total. Dr Scott Holland, the eloquent
divine, when he first saw this generous crater, shot his arms into
the air and rushed down the side in a pantheistic ecstasy. He was
a great man if he reached the bottom, intact, in that same posture of adoration. A good Sunday afternoon was to go down there
and dam the stream with great stinking clods of black earth,
trousers rolled up and Eton collars slung from a branch, and, by
crashing a boulder into the water, to baptize some heathenish
friend.

It has become unfashionable, faintly Edwardian, to recall
from school what was happy, what was fine in a person or lovely
in a place. The hosts of Misery prowl and prowl around. The
banner of the Juvenile Martyrs of Parnassus, wrought in lily-
white and black, would wave us down into sympathy, into a
little, just sometimes a little soul-understanding; their fugues of
self-pity would lap us into the hushed communion of despair;
their motto is: "I will count only the hours that were loathsome,
and I will count them over, every year, every one of them
apart"; and their coat-of-arms is: "Aesthete, Couchant and
Bloody, transfixed by the arrows of the Philistines." Fetch me a
basin.

I was just seven, my brother Bobs rising nine, Miss Morris admitting to about thirty, and Mrs Asquith set fair for another eight years in Downing Street, when the growler rumbled up the slope to Waterloo and strange adventure. Near the top, doubtless at the same point where the frantic Mr Bultitude had requested the porter to fetch him "a cab with a sober driver", I was seized with unforeseen horror. My liver paid an abrupt call on my boots, shiny and a little tight, and the growler had turned tumbril. This must cease. I had refused to stay at home without Bobs; and there he was, as calm as an elderly giraffe, with a wedge of Callard and Bowser's butterscotch in his mouth, and a *Chums* story by Andrew Soutar sticking out of his pocket. "Miss the train, if we're not careful," he said.

There were bad moments in those early terms, and why not? Unbroken happiness makes soapy remembering. My worst hang-overs came on geography afternoons in autumn, when cricket had gone and Christmas had not yet come up for anticipation. I used to look out at the sunset beyond the village, and imagine that Miss Morris was somewhere behind it. I was still free from that old fool, Reason, who could have told me that Miss Morris was in precisely the opposite direction, teaching girls in a Hampstead School, where three Scotch sisters used her brain and devotion and necessity for thirty years, then let her go, almost unrewarded, and died respected by many.

A school dormitory is man's first club, with self-appointed committee and a few difficult members. There was one who, from time to time, felt that I would derive benefit from a midnight dip in the cold hip-bath that each of us kept under his bed. Perhaps he was right. I hated him for one year, then, for three more, highly esteemed his company. He taught me the art of making paper jabberwocks and ink-bombs, how to bottle blaeberry wine and mix it with sherbet when fermented by burial, and how to hide conscious guilt under the mask of innocence. At belching, he was second only to the eldest son of the then Bishop of Salisbury, from whom I received tuition, as a favour, in the senior changing-room. But at expectoration he stood unrivalled for distance combined with accuracy, and from ten yards he could hit the picture of Pericles on the class-room wall three times out of four. A genial lad was William Bunnett. At sixteen he enlisted in Canada for the first World War, and was killed in Flanders before his seventeenth birthday.

Whatever came to me was always coming. I may have had a few casual wits, but I was underweight on tact; over-fond of society, yet a slave to monologue; convinced that if silence was golden, it was a bare nine-carat; and with an inquisitiveness that would make a cat puke with envy. All this descended, unmixed with more temporal legacies, from grandfather Holt-Wilson, the Reverend Thomas Daniel, who, having married for the third time, took the five children of that union, and his wife, to Canada in his sixty-ninth year. His courtship of his third wife, Miss Turner, is described in the ten-volume diary which he dictated to her. Riding on horseback to make his proposal, and further sunk in meditation on "the foolish obstinacy of the chairman of the Parish Council", he let his pony, which was doubtless lost in sympathetic rumination, stumble in a hole and throw him over its head into a stream which was "flooded beyond custom by the severe winter". Arrived at the house, he "cleverly contrived to see Mr Turner alone", and borrowed a suit of clothes from his intended father-in-law who was "four inches taller and two stone heavier than myself". Mr Turner expressed merriment and good wishes, but, "when I trailed in to see Miss Turner, whatever she may have thought, she did not laugh, and I felt that I could win her. Within three-quarters of an hour she was mine."

His activity was inexhaustible, his interest universal. Into each month of his life he crammed a year. He laughed at time and distance. To preach in his own church, teach in the Sunday School, carve the joint, try out a new pony, visit the cook's declining father, walk six miles each way to preach in another church, return to miscalculate his accounts and dictate the diary—this was just an average Sunday to him. He loved anniversaries, and the slightest of them could provoke him to celebration. "Three years to the day since the Men's Recreation Room was opened. Invited C—, who built it, to dinner, and we sat down twelve to table. Mr B— bored everybody with a long harangue on the decline of farming in East Anglia. Nearly all his facts inaccurate. The Madeira, which Cousin H— kindly gave us last Michaelmas Day, with high recommendation, proved most disappointing. Once again, I had severe pain round the heart during the night. I am giving up all wines for six months; but not my after-supper pipe." Family birthdays, to the remotest collaterals, were registered in his memory, and it was in remembering one of these

that he inflicted, on one of his own sisters, his only recorded act of
discourtesy. For some, probably pardonable, reason he resented
her and her artistic methods of resisting the invasion of the years.
So, on her sixty-ninth birthday, and well he knew it, he sent her
a postcard inscribed, "Many Happy Returns; to think that you
are seventy to-day." Ah, the difference.

I was nine when I last saw him. He was parsoning away in
Great Malvern, whither he had moved, "to try out the West
Country", before trying out Canada. During the visit, I fell
backwards down an area, for reasons still unknown. A futile, if
benevolent, decision was reached to keep from him the news of
this lapse. That afternoon he required my company to walk with
him up the hill and listen to long passages quoted from the Pick-
wick Papers. No me. People were had in, singly, questioned, and
found guilty of prevarication. At last someone said, simply, "Oh,
he fell down an area this morning." The truth was reached, and
grandpa rested happy.

Fifteen months later he fell dead, still talking, in the streets of
Toronto. The old pain had won. It was not the Madeira, nor the
after-supper pipe, but acute angina pectoris. Something just
had to burst.

Be grandfathers as they may, I was fresh, too ready on the
quack, and green, oh, very green. On the third day at school, I
walked into the headmaster's study, sat down in his best chair,
and asked him if he could sell me a second-hand tennis-ball. He
turned his head, like a grey lion in pince-nez, and said that he
would see, but that, on the whole, he feared tennis-balls were out
of season just then. But already I had forgotten tennis-balls, and
became very keen on his clock, a walking-stick with a whacking
great iron point, and a revolving book-case. Exhausting these in a
few seconds, I sat down again and, so he told me in later years,
asked him what he'd like to talk about. This was Mr Cyril
Morgan-Brown, the wisest and the simplest man that I have
known. He could solve the Torquemada cross-word, unaided by
man or book, between lunch and tea, and, when the school, in
earlier days, was on the verge of bankruptcy, he could give five
pounds to a charity and defend the gift with: "After all, we are
nearly the richest people in Hindhead", and mean it. He could
read and explain a boy's character as easily as a page of Xeno-
phon or an Eclogue of Virgil, and he could appoint to the staff

a man who was as well suited to his avocation as Bertrand
Russell would be to the Archbishopric of York.

He loved good things to eat and to eat them slowly, no matter
who or what was waiting: and three times a year, on the first day
of the holidays, he spread himself and a guest or two at a snug
little restaurant in Soho, ordering the second liqueur-brandy
with a knowing air. But he used self-denial as a habit and an
example, and in the Great War I, when the bread was potato
held in place by sawdust and the meat an amalgam of linoleum
and rope, he held back from his fair share of more palatable relief, and grew thin in the cause.

Mixed with his greatness as a Christian and, for those who
cared to learn, as a teacher, there was a vein of conceit, innocent
but invincible, which led him to call attention, quietly, and often
only by inference, to the neatness of his hand-writing, his im-
munity from common illness, and his deftness as a carpenter.
But few minded, and, if they did mind, he wouldn't have noticed
it. It was part of that "Cyddy" whom we loved, rather at a distance, and feared not a little, and whose walk we imitated, down
corridors, with infinite degrees of verisimilitude. For his feet were
as flat as they could be. Many reasons for this were current, the
most popular being that he had been bullied when a boy at
Marlborough by having play-boxes dropped on his toes, or that
he had been purposely shot in the calves when changing the
targets on a rifle-range. The truth was chronic rheumatism in
the ankles; an affliction which he derided with one of his favourite
saws: "For every evil under the sun, there's either a cure or
there isn't one; if there is one, go and find it; if there isn't,
never mind it."

His last illness began at Christmas time, and the doctor at
once put him on a flimsy and fluid diet. Old "Cyddy's" answer
was to come down to afternoon tea and help himself to a large
slice of Christmas cake. Then, whistling a few bars and making
other semi-musical clicking and popping sounds which he was
known to reserve for times of mutiny, he helped himself to another slice. It was about a week before the start of a new term in
the school, where I was now a junior master. After tea, it happened that he and I were left alone together. He settled into his
chair by the fire and humming away like a bumble-bee, beat the
nonsense out of *The Times* crossword. Soon, he nodded; and I

began to open some letters and to flick the envelopes into the fire. An intimation that untidiness was about woke him, and he said: "If you want to put the fire out, Raymond, you're going the right way about it," and knocked me back twenty years, into his study, and I was Glasgow minor; being called a casual and conceited ass, not to say a howling nuisance. For a few weeks he battled away against the last Visitor, and had his bed put where he thought he could see the school at football. "And be not conformed to this world, but be ye transformed."

He used to read those words in Chapel on the first evening of each term, and they bring back the smell of a clean surplice and ruminations during the second Lesson on the chances of secretly baking half-a-dozen conkers or of making a new bowling action work properly. We had two services every day, week-days and Sundays, and a sermon once a week, which was rather heavy going for the young. Sometimes I ached in the Litany; I felt lost in negligence and ignorance, liturgically overborne, paralysed by repetitive psalms; I grew exhausted in Lent by cod-fish and the *Miserere* and the difficulty of deciding whether to give up pepper or mustard. But, from all this emerged a nugget of Faith, a nucleus of Hope, some intention of Charity. I Believe—in a merciful God, and in the extraordinarily ordinary man whom He has created.

As the choir made ready in the vestry, with some scuffling for cassocks and position, Miss Mona's left hand used to come round the corner through the door, fix on a withered straw boater held in place by the school hat-band, and clap it casually on her head. The whole action was a protest against St Paul's injunctions concerning women in the Christian community. From the vestry she made her way to the organ with a rapid and rather nautical gait and, after a few words of encouragement and hope to the boy who hazarded the hand-pumping, she plunged into a sort of Voluntary with all the assurance of those comedians who whack arpeggios out of the Broadwood to prepare the house for the funny stories.

Miss Mona was Mr Cyril's youngest sister, and domestic head of the school; a woman of dauntless spirit, inexhaustible kindness and energy, and a flat disregard for customary opinions and appearances. She would meet prospective parents with a trowel in her hand and mud on her skirt, and they could make what they

pleased of it. Some fled, muttering, back to this world of convention; others took afternoon tea, and marvelled; a few came back,
year by year, and their sons after them.

Everything that you did with Miss Mona was fun, and "went",
whether it was Latin in the bottom Form, with Queens who
praised the Black Slaves, or roasting potatoes on the faggot fire at
the Selborne picnic, when she would crouch over the cauldron
like a beneficent witch, and we would crouch on the other side by
turns, sniffing and prodding in anticipation, then rush off to
toboggan on our bottoms down the slope in the wood. She never
fussed. It was not likely that she would fret at children and other
axiomatic nuisances of the world when she spurned away a
chronic asthma as something less than a common cold, going to
bed for three or four days in the year, to get back her breath, and
rising to shed light on the Second Declension of Nouns or to join,
on equal terms, in a game of Rugby Fives.

Guardians and teachers of the young, who are not utterly
trapped in the rut, often and naturally incline to court the notice
of the young by some exhibition of mental or physical prowess,
and to extract their affection by a deliberate breaking of routine
or by some sugary indulgence which would say: "You see, I am
not as strict as I appear." Not so Miss Mona. She had our love
without asking for it. It was an easy yoke, and she would have
made a kindergarten suck up Irregular Verbs like barley-sugar.

On Saturday night she used to read us to bed in her sitting-
room at the top of the house, where we would ooze into a known
corner, or push and wriggle for a carpet-seat in front of the fire.
A favourite reading was *At the Back of the North Wind*, as it
whistled fury and whipped the rain against the window-panes;
or *Treasure Island*; when that window was a port-hole and we
were snug by the fire of the captain's cabin in the "Hispaniola",
or listening fearfully for the tap-tap of blind Pew's stick on the
corridor that led, in daylight, to the biscuit-cupboard and the
junior bathroom. And there was the thought of more stories
ahead in the dormitory, where, as drowsiness came on, fiction
passed for fact, and William Bunnett found easy listeners for his
popular tale of how he had shot a burglar dead, and buried him
in the garden without the formality of telling the police.

Miss Mona was a suffragette, that hideous word which once
branded and now glorifies. Miss Mona did not burn golf greens,

press pamphlets on Mr Asquith at the gates of Palace Yard, punch holes in plate-glass windows, slap policemen's faces, or issue expressions of defiance from prison. Her attitude was more Gandhi-esque; and, except for persuading the domestic staff— Miss Chichester, the cook, dissenting—to accompany her for a twenty-four hour visit to London in order to avoid the Census, she was content to show by daily example that she was at least the equal of any man in her varied spheres of thought and action.

Her creed was service; and, when the young men, the best of them, went to the War in 1914, she was seized by some sympathetic nomadism, by a distaste of the life institutional and its conversations, with or without trowel, concerning Tommy's chilblains or Johnson minor's hernia. She decided to join a married sister of incurable eccentricity. At length the years cast up Miss Mona, kindly philosopher of a hundred battles, last of her generation, still supreme in the hospitality of afternoon tea, in a small cottage by Frensham village, from which she wrote to me in June 1940: "My legs are like boiled macaroni . . ."

To the lowest game of cricket we walked, uncrocodiled and fancy free, through the village. On the left was Dr Lyndon's house, ample, calm, and discreet, like the doctor, who timed our pulses through the measles, listened to the lungs in a serious and benevolent way, and showed a fine understanding of life by suggesting "another day or two in bed, and then perhaps we'll see." Mrs Lyndon seemed always to be bicycling against the wind and giving out a preoccupied smile. She was a great hand, it was said, at parochial matters, at meditation on the bicycle between meetings and inquiries, and at speaking up for the accused as a magistrate at the Petty Sessions. On the right, just before the shops, was Miss Massy, who let rooms and made stays which she refused to call corsets, and had a cat which, in certain lights, she much resembled. She used to say, "that cat won't scratch you, not without you pull her whiskers first." The parallel must here cease.

The cricket won't be starting for half-an-hour yet; so we can press a cold nose against Mr Lloyd's window, where wristwatches, with their venal charms, were beginning to push the decent-living old "turnips" out of the best seats. The usurpers were mostly coarse, lusty brutes, unfit for the company of the ladies, who still tended to wear little silver watches pinned to the

bosom. This custom survives among a few grannies and Edwardian landladies, and recalls the time, worthy of a passing tear,
before women learnt to refuse the offered seat in public vehicles
and began to carry all behind them in trousers. For boys, Mr
Lloyd's favourite ware was the celluloid watch-guard, which
rendered the watch moderately immune and its face totally invisible in frosty weather. As to repairs, when he was feeling lazy,
which was always, he would say: "I'm afraid I'll have to send
this to Portsmouth", as if the watch was a ship that needed caulk-
ing or undergirding; and the young customer would clutch it
back, not willing to have it sent half-way to Spain, and not
minding if it ticked for only ten minutes in the term, so long as he
had it to breathe on through the long wait between courses at
mid-day dinner and to fiddle with during the eternal manœuvres of Julius Caesar.

On the other side of the road, in the middle of the village, as
befitted her trade and character, was the sweet-shop of Marion
Menzies, a Scotchwoman from Eskdale, who also dealt in china.
Broad was her bust, to make room for the generous heart beneath it. She had been cook in the school's earlier days at Hun-
stanton, and, when the embassage to the proposed new premises
in Surrey returned to report Mr Bernard Shaw as tenant, and
other desirable features about the property, Marion began to
make jam for the great emigration. It arrived, jar upon jar, all
smashed; and she stood by the van and greeted the soil of Hindhead with her tears. After a few years she retired to her shop,
which she called Edinburgh House, and sat by her well-filled
window, spread out and smiling, as we walked down to games.
Sometimes, as you straggled, tactically, behind the master, and
passed her window with musing gait, one eye on the sky, and the
other pretending sorrow and emptiness, she would knock and
beckon you in and feed you free. But this Act had to be as subtly
handled as any in *Hamlet*. Deviate from the script, and you were
floored; and one boy wrecked the whole term's market by misin-
terpreting a slight palsy of the head, which she called "the dother-
ums", as an invitation to the bull's-eye and the butter-ball. Late
in life she was afflicted by diabetes, and was told that abstinence
from all sweet stuff would prolong her life for so many years. Her
answer was to gather up an ample sum of money from the re-
cesses of her house and pay a visit to Belgium. Returning in

high spirits and with the mortgage of at least five years of her life-allowance, she answered a polite inquiry with: "I didna care for the cathedrals, but the iced cakes in Bruges were just gra-and."

From the open door of the next shop would come a burst of laughter; then a mumble of monologue, and another burst. Mr Johnson, the hairdresser, at work. Let's take a liberty here and look ahead and back at him over twenty years, the last twenty in his life of clipping and laughter. He sported a stud of tandem-cycles on which he and his wife or his son and heir, when he reached the years of endurance, used to pass mobile Sundays. The calves of his legs, like his tyres, were pneumatic and set off by cycling breeches à la Du Maurier. He was short, with long body and big head above, a fleshy aquiline nose, a shiny receding fore-head that stretched to the intellectual as baldness hurried on, a gleaming face and eye; the whole man framed for bank holidays and badinage; rescued, but not easily, from charlatanry by a good heart, good humour, and good trade. On the wall of his shop, where the patron's eye must fall, were cards exhibiting specimens of hair before and after use of Damschinsky's In-fallible Dye. In the window was an elderly lady, sawn off at the bust and waxenly simpering at her disreputable past.

After shop hours Mr Johnson bicycled around and worked private, thus gathering his knowledge of affairs. "Down at Mr Lloyd George's yesterday evening," he would say. "A good job there, very good. A very affable gentleman. How was 'e? Ah, only so-so; prett-y middlin'. Worry, I think. What about? Didn't you read it in the papers, sir? Ah: perhaps it didn't get into yours; wanted to hush it up, I expect. There's been a quarrel, you see; him and the Prime Minister of Rumania. Mr Lloyd George found out what 'e was up to; trying to get out of a Treaty or something. Says he won't have him at 10 Downing Street again; not at any price. How's that for shortness at the back, Sir?"

Then the bell of the shop-door would jangle, and Mr John-son, whose ear was subtly attuned to know the difference be-tween public and private custom, would be in the corridor with two skips and an if-you'll-excuse-me-sir, and would thrust the confidential visitor into the back-parlour, from which would be thrown on to the mirror near the Damschinsky-dyed hair a glimpse of Mrs Johnson, reading *John Bull* on her black horse-hair sofa, or recreating her ideas on doing the ladies' coiffures.

And back Mr Johnson would glide with "Pardon my absence, sir; some special hair-cream for a gentleman at the 'Fox and Geese'; his hair has got very dry in the East. India. Aggerpatam, I believe. I attended the Rajah when he stayed a week-end at the Heathercrest a few years ago. You knew the Rajah? A very nice gentleman, if somewhat dark. Could have been a Maharajah if he'd wanted, they say, but was fond of travel, and disliked the responsibilities. Now, sir, there we are; just a little brilliantine? No? Something to keep it in place? I have the very thing!"

Past all this sort of thing, then, past Harry Sadler, who scowled at us when he was sober and grinned when he wasn't, we meandered towards the cricket field; the fanatics in front, making a pass or two with a bat that had been oiled to an early death; Mr Mayo "Spem" Druitt in the middle, blinking redly like a Wyandotte, pecked at and pecking at; the slave of the Biscuit Tin behind, carrying the hopes of Rich Tea and the moral certainty of Thin Lunch; and behind him yet, one straggler, in crazy hope that Marion Menzies would nod him to afternoon tea or that the sky would burst into cataracts of rain. That was Charlie Dodds, who hated cricket and its murder of his summer half-holidays. Long afterwards he recalled that procession with horror. "Who are these going to the Sacrifice?" Brave, witty, and generous Charlie Dodds. For thirty years he fought a losing battle for his breath, with intermittent and well-used victory, with chuckling mockery of himself, and no home-grown pity. On bad nights in the dormitory he would burn "incense", or smoke an asthma cigarette and hand round a couple more for companionship. From school at Westminster he went on to the London stage and was adept at Old Man parts; "they come natural to me, you see." But the regularity of the theatre needs health. So he tapped his musical vein and, turning librettist, struck out as an entertainer in the Corney Grain manner. His province was schools and the private "swarry"; his speciality, the light verse of A. P. Herbert set to his own tunes, himself or his like-minded wife accompanying. "Don't tell my mother I'm living in sin"; "Financiers have to be Fathers"; "I likes a bit of enjoyment on a Friday"—these, and many other Herbertisms, he presented with a skill and intimacy that are already quite prehistoric, and scarcely intelligible to a world emasculated by crooning and filed to nothing by wisecracks.

So I doubt if he had reached the ground when the captain handed me the ball and I opened with a trio of wides and, being advised by mid-on to "try a different run," bowled two more, and said "damn," so that "Spem" Druitt called the game into the pavilion, and said he didn't know what it was coming to, what *on earth* it was coming to, and a boy called Stukeley Lucas laughed, and was ordered back through the village an hour early, with the biscuit tin.

"Spem" Druitt had joined the school as a junior partner; but, as we then vaguely suspected and later came to know, the senior community did not too seriously regard this office, and he soon gave occasion for a series of privately performed tableaux, called "The Seven Ages of Spem," in which he featured, heroically and in turn, as a favourite pianist in a kindergarten, a University Oarsman with cheesy curls, and a lady-killer in a straw helmet on the Margate promenade.

As a schoolmaster, he was a farrago of opposites. His class-room alternately assumed a prim dignity and rattled with a wild disorder that was mostly of his own creating. His scholars, too, such as they were, see-sawed between calculated provocation and fear, real or mimic, of the thing provoked; for his punitive sallies were famous, and celebrated in traditional verse. In habit, he combined the extremes of laziness and energy. On the mornings when it was his turn to wake the dormitories and conduct the cold baths, he would lie in bed at the top of the house and clang a bell supinely; yet he would spend in the school grounds hours of his free time in collecting what amounted to rubbish. Much of this he devoted to the ruining of his own garden which might, if left to itself, have been a prime ornament of the neighbourhood.

His deep and private generosities were countered by open economies which seldom failed to defeat their intentions. When fuel was short, he set up a laborious factory of clay balls which, he had decided, were a substitute for coal. With these he would extinguish any fire almost as soon as it was lighted. He would hoard old examination-papers, then abruptly plant them on some young master who had ideas and was just printing off his own. He collected fir-cones by thousands, assisted by the forced labour of malefactors. Casual fragments of metal flew up into his pockets as to a magnet. String from parcels, tape from under-

clothes, anything from nowhere, all found in "Spem" an asylum
and a friend.

Though shrewd in business, and a cute student of the market,
he was yet born for April the First and its colossal hoax. Simple
forgery claimed him as a natural victim, and he had not long
applied for membership of the local Golf Club when his col-
leagues saw to it that he received from a phantom committee a
regretful black-ball, on the true grounds that he had won a
croquet tournament, albeit in good faith, with a false handicap;
and only when he was pumping up his bicycle to visit the secretary did the jokers intervene.

For boys it was an exciting game, because the penalty for
missing the bull's eye was not slight, as when a young Rabelais,
poring over his atlas, asked "Spem" whether there was not a
place called Belch in Western Alberta. "Anyhow," the boy added
with an assurance that still staggers me, "I have heard my father
say so."

At about fifty, he wearied of the moil and retired to a neighbouring house. Here his soirées, like his character, were a mixture of benevolence and quasi-Chinese courtesies. He loved to
set three or four tables of bridge in motion, which he could in-
terrupt with quaint refreshments; indefinable emollients in little
porcelain boats, delicate but inconclusive cakelets, trim segments of nougat, and always something new and vaguely terrify-
ing in the way of wine: "Try a little of this, Miss Tusher; my
sister has sent it all the way from Madagascar." And Miss T.
would try a little, and overcall her next hand, and not care when
she was frowned upon by her partner, who was rumoured to
read the bridge articles in *The Times*, and had stuck to still-
lemonade. Then the cards would be put away, and the host
would play his pianola very fast and loud and Liszt-like, or, more
horrifically, invite one of his uncounted cousins to oblige on the
violin, while the guests stuck it out in their chairs and secretly
saved themselves with the wine from Madagascar.

He was oddly good at games. He did not easily go under at
lawn tennis; he could harass and sometimes unhook the most
presumptuous batsmen in the moderate class; and at croquet he
was of that small and thrice-happy band who can cause the
Queens of the Lawn to cluck their lips and to tap the mallet with
impatient toe. At home-made Fancy Dress he had no local rival,

whether as an Andaman Islander or as a packet of Reckitt's Blue. At the piano, with "The Four-horsed Charabanc" and "The Choir Boy," he never missed a break-up concert.

"Spem" never knew that, in the matter of species, he was away on his own; and so he never played up to himself; unlike, say, Kipling's prince of sarcasm, Mr King, and a host of school-masters, real or fanciful, who have nourished their own myth in their own lifetime. He saw nothing strange in painting his finger with New Skin and so filling the classroom with a smell of bananas while his pupils struggled with that epileptic noun "Domus" and that dangerous substantive "Spes"; nothing faintly uncon-ventional in asking visitors on the cricket ground to wait while he polished the bench with disused underwear.

Shortly before "Munich" he engaged two elderly female ser-vants, called Fish and Fry; "they should," he said, "work well together, but I shall call them Fisher and Fryer. More dignified, I think." He was not long with them. He had been reaching up to adjust an ornament in his unique parlour, when he slid back and lay on the carpet.

One of my school heroes was Levett, the boot-knife-and-boiler man. True, he had hammer toes, but it was only in years long after that I learnt of this invisible flaw. There was a swashbuckling air about him, as showing there was no end to what he could do, if the world could pull itself together and give him the chance. He was a boaster, no doubt of it; but boasting presupposes bounds of belief, and I was not yet ready to draw depressing limits round credulity. The local carrier was a favourite object of Mr Levett's derision. This ramshackle old charioteer and his horse used to haul the school trunks to and from the station, four miles, in half-a-dozen relays. He looked like the old man in the early American films who stood blinking outside the saloon while the younger cowboys galloped about and shot each other up. Beer glistened on his moustache, and down below he was held in place by gaiters. This early Saxon and age had nothing in common, but popular opinion put him down at ninety-four, and Mr Levett offered to be able to knock down any ten of him.

Another, and more enduring, hero was Harry Scott Stokes, the finest intellect that I know, for rapidity and depth combined. He went to the first War from Winchester, returned after it to take up his scholarship at Oxford, discussed a few problems of

Free Will and the Categorical Imperative with the ingenious Mr
Joseph of New College, and broke off into commerce, to which
he has since applied an originality, vigour, and humanity whose
political parallel can be seen in his fellow-Wykehamist, A. P.
Herbert, M.P. He was head of the school when I was nearly
bottom of it, and, setting up a record for half-term examinations
with 740 out of 800, he was taken up by Mr Cyril to see the sights
of London. Scott Stokes was also an athlete. A vigorous mind and
a vigorous body like to go together, and I have found more bone-
heads among the "intellectuals" than among the games-players,
more fools in dubious shirts than in clean flannels, more natural
idiots around Bloomsbury than at Lord's.

The match of the term was against Sandroyd, near Cobham;
from our view, at least; for it meant a day out, and be damned to
the beating that we nearly always took. Sandroyd tried a motor
charabanc one summer in the adolescence of petrol-engines,
were shot out for 43 runs, then fielded for a long time. Well, it
may have been the charabanc that did it; or it may have been
our cunning left-hand bowlers, Guy Morton and V. H. Wells-
Cole. Morton was a strong natural gamester, who used a knotted
handkerchief as a cricket cap, and far too early retired from all
fields of play to write clever and urbane novels under the name
of Peter Traill.

Our journey to Sandroyd began by horse-brake, and the sound
of its wheels in mid-morning brought us with a bump of delight
from a gnarled Equation or sweaty Subjunctive. We ate our hard-
boiled eggs in the sandy pine and fir woods of Cobham, a little
over-travelled and hot, silent, and ruminative over the coming
clash. But C. P. Wilson, headmaster and founder of Sandroyd,
would view from his upper window this blue and white and
inquiringly hesitant cavalcade, and would cheer it back to
nature with welcoming shouts and the sight of his brown bald
head. Good, easy, manly master was "C.P." He was scholar
enough and to spare; had played cricket thirty years back for
Cambridge against Oxford, and Rugger and Soccer for England
in the larger days before football divided into unmeeting paral-
lels. When, yet again, we had lost, he would pick out and praise
the one of us who had nearly scored a dozen or almost shot a
goal, and warm us homeward with laughter and a whacking tea.
Once we beat them over there, beat that long, long walk out to

the wicket and the awe of white-coated umpires. For them, no doubt, it was an odd lean year among the fat; unmemorable, in a dead score-book. For us, it was triumph; for me, if pride be allowed and forgiven, it is still a festival in the wordless diary of reflection. I still believe I was l.b.w. first ball; the umpire's hand began to rise, then fell back into his pocket. A family man, I expect.

Behind us, sometimes with us, in these games, helping, praising, and blaming was Ivor Sant. He was junior partner to Mr Cyril, and resembled him in the essential view that learning and manners, both in the wide sense, were ends in themselves, not merely means wherewith to cut the right figure in the examination-room or in what is called "the world"—that mean and narrow miniature of what God so generously and vastly created. He resembled him, too, in refusing the interference of the maladies of life which most of us pretend to call trivial and hug as daily grievances. But Ivor Sant was the more sensitive, the more widely understanding, quicker to wrath as to praise; and he touched life by many wires which his senior had long since and deliberately severed.

His sitting-room was a harbour on stormy half-holidays, where we would exchange the hot water-pipes of the class-room for a real red fire, and divert our energies from catapults and conkers and face-slapping to puff-billiards and Dickens and bagatelle. On the walls hung pictures by his uncle James Sant, R.A., who had been born in the reign of George III and still had ten years of his span to go, pictures with beautiful hands and faces in the pre-Raphaelite style which once fetched money, and still hold the affection of thousands. It was a room of happiness, with that nameless air of things hopeful and humane. To the end of the Hitler War Ivor Sant still taught Latin and Greek; Ovid, as the latest Icarus roared over the chimneys; Virgil, as other Evanders waited in vain for their sons' return; and he sent his young scholars on their road to a world which grows yearly more impatient of knowledge that cannot be converted into money or into the ephemeral power of money, and where, if "Balbus Built a Wall", he'd get merry hell from the Trade Union.

> All the litanies e'er chaunted
> Shall not keep thy faith undaunted.

Such was the broad outline of our City State, and, if I have spent over long in its drawing, that is because I love this picture and have often returned to it for relief from the artful etchings of manhood. But, if memory holds the door open too long, there's the devil of a draught. I'll risk it for a few minutes more, and let in another guest; Guy Warwick, with his flaming red head and lusty limbs. He excelled at the part of Hercules in the *Frogs* of Aristophanes, and, in keeping with that hero's character, preferred his own methods to the institutional routine. He reckoned nothing of irregular verbs and washing for meals, but in all mechanical contrivance he was a second Daedalus, and he could whizz a propeller off its stick clean across the play-ground and over the fives courts beyond. He used to take me, as a sort of reluctant builder's mate, in the forbidden hours of winter darkness, to help him in the making of a hut out of heather and bracken and wooden corner-posts which he had acquired when the gardener, Harvey Newman, wasn't looking. He was killed when flying in the King's Cup race, hitting the side of Broadlaw in a mist. I hadn't seen Guy Warwick in years; but I missed him as if we had still been at school.

At the end of my last term, waiting for Bobs to arrive from Radley, I stayed a few days with Miss Massy and her cat. The newspapers said that General Leman was defending Liége successfully, and that the Germans would lose the War within three weeks.

VI

BESIDE THE SEA

THOSE who grow up at home miss far more than they know. When the cook in the Boarding House gets drunk and throws the plates around, it is agreeable to reflect that they are not yours. It is a free show.

Owing to my mother's variable health, Bobs and I spent much time, and as much money as we had, at various seaside resorts. There is something supremely apt in the word "resort". It implies a place to which people go when they wish to retire from the stale conventions, to wear peculiar hats, to get up when or to go to bed with whom they please—in short, in the words of our old drill-sergeant at school, to "act silly".

In this delightful world we passed most of our holidays. On and off, we touched at almost every port from Weymouth, where I suffered from the severest heat-bumps on record, to Newhaven, where we watched the boat leave for Dieppe. A full life. But Brighton was our headquarters; and it was there, on the pavement outside Sopers', that I was pushed violently into a gentleman in spats, and received some remarks about whose mysterious meaning I vainly questioned Auntie Bug. "Run along now," she said, "and don't be silly; I'm sure he never said that."

Childhood is the time for staying in hotels. You do not pay the bill. Draughts under doors, the absence of ash-trays in the lounge, and the presence of some one else's hair in the bathroom, alike fail to disturb your senses. You are not assailed by the desire to be somewhere else or the scruple that you should not be there at all. You are on easy terms with the staff, who are not meditating whether you will give them five shillings or just sixpence on your departure. Milk-pudding is an infrequent visitor to the dining-table. The grown-ups don't like milk-pudding. Even the reception clerk, who is trained to suspect everybody, smiles upon you, unless you are actually sick on the carpet in front of his desk; he loves

to gaze upon a child,
A young bud bursting into blossom.

We did not plunge at once into this *beau monde* but graduated
from such establishments as Miss Hemming's Private Hotel in
Preston Street, where the front door knocked against the hat-
stand and rattled the buckets and spades. Miss Hemming, who
was about four foot eight, sat on a stool at the head of her dining-
table, and carved the mutton. At the other end sat Mr Roberts,
who was always referred to as "poor Mr Roberts". He wore a
dark suit, and a high stiff collar, and he never spoke except to
say "have the goodness to pass the cruet"; so no one knew what
he thought about anything at all. He was rumoured to suffer
from indigestion; but he never got the most out of it; as he spent
much time and energy in suppressing what might have been the
the belches of the century. He was a very polite man. We never
found out whether he was retired, or had never done anything
by way of business, or tried to do something that didn't come off.
Poor Mr Roberts.

Rooms in Norton Road, Hove, were a step up from this.
Hove is Brighton's respectable brother, and dislikes being confused with naughty Brighton, and the only gaiety it got was when
the clock on the Town Hall played "The Blue Bells of Scotland"
at each hour. It was while staying here that we came, one morning, upon a small crowd on the sea-front, nodding and curtseying
towards a fattish man in an open car. "It's King Edward,"
someone said, "take off your cap." He seemed to enjoy it all,
and smiled affably over his beard.

Thence we rose to Stratheden Mansions Hotel, where the old
ladies bowed to each other as they came into lunch, and read
books during meals. In this room Franz held sway, and when we
asked him the meaning of "Kromesky à la Russe," he said
smilingly, "It is there to deceive." By the front door stood Emil,
king of hall-porters, bowing slightly in his courtly Austrian way,
ever ready with suggestions for the day's entertainment, pro-
viding change for sixpences to take on the West Pier and
spend on Brighton rock, automatic single-wicket cricket, and
the gentleman who would oblige by being publicly hanged
at eight in the morning. Emil was foster-father to all Hotel
children.

Uncle P. came to stay at Stratheden, and, having a heavy
cold, spent most of the week sniffing smelling-salts on a sofa in
the lounge. At last, he so far recovered as to suggest a visit to the

Aquarium, at 2d. a head. They were proud of having an octopus in the Aquarium, but it was only a twopenny squid, clinging rather dismally to a window, like a cross-section of a harmonica; a wretched disappointment after the pictures in *Chums*, showing an octopus sucking down a whole ship into the green Pacific, or goggling horribly at a diver with carving-knife on the bed of the ocean, while a few sharks and sword-fish waited their turns in the background. But the diver was going to win; or who would read the story?

There is no *Chums* to-day, with its man-eating lions, and gnashing crocodiles, its swarthy young men with fierce eyes and bulging muscles. Nothing has quite taken their place, unless you count the insipid stuff about aeroplanes and submarines which they palm off on the modern boy. We were well off for reading then; there were *C. B. Fry's Magazine* and the *Captain*, stuffed with information and adventure; the *Boy's Own Paper*, not yet whittled away to the size of a large postage-stamp; *The Scout*, for those who would be handy at lighting fires in the rain and tying curious and infallible knots. Boys still long for mystery and wonder; instead, they have to make shift with the doubtful wisecracks of sophistication.

Brighton never failed. There was no need to invent games; they were ready all around. You could watch the fat women in fur coats being levered into taxis outside the Metropole, or walk behind them on the front and wonder how their pig's trotters fitted into their absurdly high-heeled shoes. You could go to Muttons' and eat the best pork-pies in the middle of the morning. I used to think the old waiter there was Muttons in person, and sometimes said: "Good morning, Mr Muttons," and he would smile gravely. We would pick a particularly fine day, with strong sun and cloudless sky, to go to the cinema. The performances were continuous from 2 p.m. to 10 p.m. To-day, they advertise the word "Continuous", but cannot bring it off, giving way to intervals at the end of a set cycle of films. They also waste much time in giving "trailer" pre-views of forthcoming attractions. Then, they knew better than to lift the veil in advance; and they kept you on tenterhooks with "serials", in which the hero or heroine, or both, as good as died each week, but popped up, fine and large, to baffle the villain next Thursday. The show went clean on, and sometimes we would see it through twice,

finally staggering out into the evening like moles with cramp,
and Miss Morris would complain of eye-ache.

It was on the Brighton front that I saw the newspaper poster:
"Titanic sinking", and just couldn't believe it. It was the greatest
ship that had ever been, and was said to be unsinkable. Everyone knows the vivid and fearful story, which has been a fill-up
in weekly illustrateds ever since. One hour, they were dancing
and drinking; the next, they were singing "Nearer my God to
thee". Thirty years later, the sinking of a ship or the loss of a
thousand souls was to be only a paragraph. The value of a life was
still, as it were, on the Gold Standard. Murder, too, was rare
enough to be startling, or was it that the murderer was less often
caught? Whatever the reason, murder was rationed, and the
Press made much ado about their villains. Hawley Harvey
Crippen held the headlines for some months. I have seen it
written by an eminent criminologist that Crippen was, after all,
an insignificant and rather pathetic creature. Well, he murdered
his wife, and then chopped her up and concealed the fragments
under his house. A strange manifestation of insignificance.
Certainly he was a mild enough little figure in the dock; but
they nearly didn't get him there, for he was well on his way to
the United States when that youngster Wireless Telegraphy
caught him up.

We bought an ounce of the best tobacco, "Taddy's Imperial",
for sixpence; a pipe for a shilling; and began a life of nicotine on
the road to Telscombe. You went part of the way by the little
electric railway, over which the waves splashed on rough days.
At Telscombe, beyond Roedean, which they always said would
one day fall into the sea, I completed my bicycling lessons, and
peopled it, wrongly no doubt, with characters and tales from
Rudyard Kipling. I went and stared at his house in Rottingdean,
with a virgin autograph-book in my pocket. But I hadn't the nerve.

I shall always love Brighton, even to the distinct and varying
smells on different sections of the beach. I can no longer find
Muttons' home of the pork-pie, and Professor Severn is no more.
He left, if I remember, a smacking good sum of money behind
him, for he combined with phrenology an unusual charm and
worldly wisdom. Illustrious visitors seldom failed to offer their
heads for his inspection; no one could more tactfully ignore the
bumps of destruction and obstinacy.

Hove cricket ground, too, has been good to me. There was something in the sea-air which helped a swerving bowler, something very soothing about the bath-chairs which, to my distant fancy, conveyed many of the older spectators to their regular angle of criticism. Also, there was a cosy pub inside the gates, where the Sussex professionals could meditate over the day's play with pipes and a pint and vast silences. It was at Hove that I played my first match of first-class rank away from Oxford, and took ten Sussex wickets in the two innings; it was here that I played my last match for Somerset, and took no wickets at all. I should have had cheesy-haired Harry Parks, but second slip was dreaming of whelks or women.

Eastbourne was pleasant enough, but, oh, so very pure, and it seemed to say, "I thank God I am not as other towns," meaning Brighton and Hove. The landladies tended to icy respectability and facile dismay. We lodged with two old sisters there, in the dignified shadow of the Grand Hotel. They both wheezed when walking upstairs, and, when you came on them during this journey, they would say, "It is my tubes, you see," as if it were rather common to gasp in company and they wished to dissociate themselves from the vulgarity of nature. We had been fishing one day, and brought back, after much letting out and hauling in, one sea-weary rock-fish. This we wrapped in newspaper, placed it in the base of the umbrella-stand on the first floor, and easily forgot it. At nine o'clock the sisters were climbing heavily to their inviolate rest, when they stopped to poke this intrusive parcel, and we heard them both say in disgusted chorus: "Aow, it's *fish*." They went twice to church on Sundays, and presented enormous bills weekly.

Sundays were moribund in Eastbourne; no pictures, not even a tea-shop open; and the best solution was to go up to Beachy Head and admire the red roofs from afar, avoiding the sea-front, where you would run into that most miserable of social spectacles, the school crocodile. There were a hundred and ten schools for girls and a hundred and six for boys. But, during the week, there was little the matter with Eastbourne, except its smugness. Sometimes I would rout out Basil Patchitt, who was a boy at Charterhouse with me, and we'd go off to golf on the downs at Willingdon, or roller-skate in Devonshire Park. Basil was a fine natural athlete, and the sleepiest boy I ever knew. He was in the

First Eleven at Charterhouse for Soccer and Cricket, and, when secretary of the latter, he was prone to clerical errors. Few Saturdays passed without two or even three teams arriving to play us. When possible, he would palm off the over-plus on the Second Eleven, a move unpopular with the visitors. He became captain of cricket in our last year at school, and would change the bowling sometimes with the remark: "Let's see now, you've been on a good time, haven't you?" He walked out carrying a squash racket to toss for innings with the captain of the M.C.C., who never quite got over it. At Cambridge, he gave up cricket as being too complicated, but got his Blue for Soccer, and played a great game at half-back against Oxford. Once, during a round of golf at Willingdon, he hit an enormous drive which pitched some fifty yards over the heads of the couple playing in front of us. They were very testy about this—"Blasted schoolboys, oughtn't to be allowed . . ."—and they reported us to Mr Brick-hill, the secretary, to whom Basil said: "I didn't see them, sir; you see, they were camouflaged in the rough."

Eastbourne, being a glossy old maid, did not encourage eccentricity, but there was one citizen who lent oddity and colour to the even and colourless scene. He was known to us as Charlie the Trumpeter. He was a large fat man with a wide and waddling gait. He carried a stick, with which he gave each lamp-post a hearty whang as he passed, and every fifteen paces, he emitted a loud trumpeting sound. There was also, on the way to Willingdon, a strange shop which had been leased by a man who had suffered from an unlucky law-suit. Nothing in this shop was for sale, but the window was full of notices and pictures insulting to the legal profession, such as—BEWARE OF LAWYERS; AVOID SOLICITORS, THEY SUCK YOUR BLOOD; and in the middle there was a large black-and-white drawing that showed a spider in black clothes sitting at a desk and saying to his client, a fly; "and how much money have you got?" Charles Dickens would have enjoyed it; but I fancy that the local inhabitants were shocked at this unseemly tilting against so respectable a profession as the law. It was an affront to a place that found its safest expression in the Grand Hotel, where, after a six-course dinner which their livers had done little to earn, the rich old pussies would settle their amplitude into vast armchairs and, with podgy hands, and tempered enthusiasm, clap the music provided by M. Van Leer (violin) and his orchestra. In due course, M. Van Leer gave place to Mr Albert Sandler, who saw and performed to the same people under different names, and elicited equal applause for Schubert's "Serenade" as for the "Cornish Floral Dance".

Sometimes we descended upon Margate, where the magnificent air was set off by the omnivorous flea. It was on a journey thither that we paid 13s. 6d. excess on luggage; a tremendous feat in those careless days, and only rendered possible by a great black trunk full of books, mostly uncut, which Auntie Bug had foisted on us boys with smiling persuasion.

Margate had a perpetual sun and the best sands, Jersey excepted, to be found on any summer holiday. We spent August days in a bathing-slip and turned oriental in colour. Chocolate and toffee were for ever to be bought from gentlemen in white ducks, who wandered about the shore crying "Devona," and "My Queen". Solids were washed down with drinks of bright red, yellow, and green. Shrimps and prawns abounded, and, best game of all, we raked the rocks at low tide for the eating crab. Sometimes we dressed and went in for high life at the Queen's Hotel, eating devilled kidneys in the dusk and listening to the *Tales of Hoffman*. It was a surfeit of this dish that put me off Offenbach for years. Or we went to the new Winter Garden and heard Miss Carrie Tubb, so aptly named, challenging the roof with "O, Ocean, thou Mighty Monster"; though we could enjoy fine singing for nothing in our Boarding House; for Harry Dearth was a friend of Mr Matthews, the proprietor, and would wake the drowsy midnight with Coleridge-Taylor's "Onaway, Awake, Beloved". Here, too, we played many sets of lawn tennis with a left-handed Polish gentleman of a very serious disposition, who used to say "Advantage to myself," and, when beaten by a fast one down the side-lines, "No, I cannot; points to you."

In this house, as on the sands, every one spoke to every one else. There were no introductions. Like the early Christians, we had all things in common. One morning, as we lay on the sands, munching "My Queen" and contemplating the shimmering sea, one of those well-meaning men in anonymous blazers, who enjoy a temporary kingdom at the sea-side, came up and said, "Would you lads like to play in a cricket match this afternoon?" He named a place and time. We walked miles with our fasces of bat-cum-pads, and at last came on some men playing cricket in an erratic manner. He of the blazer walked over to us and said: "The boys are going to play Podex." Bobs, always capable of sudden and powerful decision, said: "No. We've walked four miles to play cricket; Podex be damned." So we trailed home. I have never heard of Podex again. The next day there was a Railway Strike. I believe it was the first of its kind. We attributed it to the heat and the porters' objection to handling heavy luggage. I can't say we worried. No one worried at Margate.

At Littlehampton, where, rather rashly, we rented a whole school for the summer holidays, nearly everything went wrong, mostly for me. First, I slipped on a bank and put my bare foot and leg into a wasps' nest; then, I fell off the step of a bicycle on which we were jointly propelling ourselves to Worthing, to spend a half-a-crown, and severely cut my knee; finally, when about to help in opening the innings for the Visitors v. the Residents (under 15), I fell on the stone steps of the Pavilion and broke my left arm; greenstick fracture of the lower end of the right radius, according to Dr C. E. Last, who used to bring me sweets and, sometimes, a comic paper. I connect this accident with a remark which, though kindly meant, I value highly for its fatuity. An elderly clergyman, as I rose with my left arm in a strange shape, came up and said: "Which arm do you bowl with?" I said, "Right." "Well," he replied, "that'll be all right, it is luckily the left that you have broken."

In this same August, Colonel Cody was killed while flying. Illustrious airmen could still be counted on the fingers. Their deaths were of national significance, and were accounted as a set-back to the art of flying and, by many, a judgement on man for trespassing beyond his element.

Mine were not the only contributions to domestic misfortune, for, in the middle of one night, the cook and the maid had a quarrel which brought the plaster from the ceiling. The cook, certainly, seemed at fault, for, in the absence of a window-blind, she had taken the maid's walking-out dress and fastened it to the window-frame with a pair of scissors. The maid had turned the scissors against the cook, who prepared to defend herself with hat-pins. A lively scene. Peace was restored, and, the next day, the maid absconded with some rings and other jewellery. She was caught by a constable, but my mother let her depart without prosecution. Next, the mother of the light-fingered lady arrived, and, after denying the possibility of what had already happened, remarked that "she felt as if she was falling through space." But these incidents interrupted rather than marred the joys of Little-hampton, among which must be highly rated the bombing of passers-by with raw onions, and the successful fishing for bream at the mouth of the River Arun.

From Littlehampton, I might work along the coast and tell you of the Bohemian excitements of Southsea, where we learnt to roller-skate on a stone floor and watched old men watching old ships through old telescopes; but we have dallied long enough side by side by the seaside.

VII

"FARTHER FROM THE EAST"

I N my last term at Hindhead I had won a scholarship at
Charterhouse, largely on an allowance for extreme youth and
because of a geography answer in which I had traced the
course of the St Lawrence River with inhuman accuracy. It was
not to be known that I had done half-a-dozen St Lawrences a
week earlier as an imposition for "Spem" Druitt, awarded for
buffoonery. The examiner asked me if I had ever been to Canada,
and I replied, unctuously, "No, sir, but I should like to go there
some time."

I had not wanted to go to Charterhouse and told my father so,
but, as I could only cite the same unspecified dislike that his
enemies felt for Dr Fell, my amendment that I should wait a
year and try for Winchester was over-ruled. So over to Godalming I went on a bitterly cold morning at the end of May, clutch-
ing a geometry-box which was as much use to me as to the Punch
Bowl past which the taxi was hurrying. On that first afternoon,
House-matches of cricket were in progress, and, as I stood for a
vacant ten minutes watching some Titan hitting the ball around
the field, a couple of olive-faced and oily-haired louts came and
stood near me, and one of them, nodding towards me, said to the
other: "Look at that pretty little thing in the straw-hat." I
walked away from the cricket, boiling with rage and perplexity
at this double error of judgement and taste. A few years brought
me a more exact understanding, but that night I told my pal,
Sylvester Gates, how I hoped by all the gods that I failed in the
scholarship. This, of course, was bravado, and an insurance
against probable failure. The election news came at the end of
lunch on a Tuesday. Within ten minutes I was half-way to the
dentist at Haslemere, pedalling on air, not caring if he drew all
my teeth and put them in again upside-down. I burst into the
surgery, sat down with a whack by the green spittoon, and shouted at Mr Wiley Ditcham's back: "I've got a scholarship."
Slowly he turned his flat and melancholy face, and said: "And

50

I've got indigestion." Never keep an American dentist waiting.

For fourteen out of fifteen terms at Charterhouse I worked, and was worked, like the devil. The scholars came under the authority of men who taught all things well except idleness. I was one of the exceptions who go to prove, or disprove, the saying that hard work never did anyone any harm. It did me harm right enough. I suffered from a restlessness of mind and body, from an abnormal competitive instinct, which some call ambition but which I know to be mere vanity, and from a strong appetite for the sort of and amount of food which, during the first European War, never or almost never reached the tables of those whose future duty, so we were to be told, was to build a new heaven upon earth.

I went to Charterhouse, as it were, bald. None of our name had been there before, no uncle or brother to chuck me in ready-warned against the nature of the beast and ready-schooled in sentimental and unbreakable traditionalism. I was callow and a stranger; and when I heard a fat-chapped man in the train say, "You could have cut the atmosphere with a bloody knife," I thought he used the adjective picturesquely to express that slitheriness which liquid imparts to surfaces in general. I soon found willing tongues to put me right, also a new boy, a London merchant's son, whose silence found rare relief in the use of that short old English word so popular among His Majesty's forces, and in a request to pass the margarine for religion's sake.

In the middle of the war against Hitler, a Mr Muff, a Socialist Member of Parliament, was a guest for some days at Charter-house, a visit that produced much mutual pleasure; and he after-wards wrote a letter to *The Times* which must have been an eye-opener to those of his party still willing to open an eye and capable of believing that the modern public schoolboy is neither snob nor drone, in spite of those so-called journalists who feed them-selves and their public on the sour bread of envy and hold up a tinsel and distorting looking-glass to catch dirt and ugliness. But I wonder what Mr Muff would have made of Charterhouse thirty years ago. Plutocrats, or their sons, abounded; no doubt of that, but, how far it was a privilege for them to be with us or for us to put up with them, and whether it was a privilege to be old enough to feel the war but too young to take part in it, these are matters open to doubt.

The change from the first school at Hindhead was abrupt, colossal, and for the worse. It was not that I had been "somebody", as they say, and now was just one of the herd, and *what* a herd. I didn't care a damn how many pairs of shoes I cleaned, or how often I jumped up from breakfast to carry the Odes of Horace to a study on the third floor. But I longed for some thing or some one to take pride in. I mean that intimate and mutual pride which is the unspoken contract of friendship. I could admire J. Pollock on the football-field, the toughest tackler in the school; I could wonder at V. J. Seligman's wing-collar and grown-up dignity as Head of the School; but these were Olympians. Even so, their very altitude permitted them to step down, at their own whim, without loss of status or caste, whereas the rest of the House occupied descending terraces of social and sartorial privilege as intricate as a suit in Chancery and so ridiculous in retrospect that I sometimes believe the whole thing was a dream, or a story from the *Boy's Own Paper*. Anyhow, the Third Table, who were allowed a "clock" in their socks, looked down on the Fourth Table, who weren't, and regarded them much as the draper's wife regards the woman across the street who takes in washing. It was "not done" for the fags to visit other Houses except by way of business, and something that was "not done" was not done. School Rules might be broken, not etiquette. Friends made in form-work or in games were strangers once they had returned to their House, and you would no more have thought of walking in for a chat and a glass of water than the Prince Consort would have meditated forcible entry into a convent.

There was a dank fustiness in the House which, in that first winter, went in at my mouth, oozed down my body and legs, and settled like an unpaying guest under the shoe-laces. The Long Room, where we lived, ate, chattered, wrote dubious Latin verses and fagged, was a fitter place for a Dinosaur to say his farewell to old age than for a boy to greet his adolescence. The windows, built on one side only, looked no further than the vegetable-garden of another House, where the Rev. E. E. Bryant could be espied, tilling his ground like a crop-headed Cromwellian, or trying to stare his hens into less quixotic notions of production.

"Eb," as we called him, was my form-master for the first year, a Spartan with a brain, a Tartar with a heart. Rumour, than which Virgil found "no swifter evil," but which remains a faithful and necessary friend of sentient man, poured into our young ears the news that "Eb" was a man with a past. On this intelligence various interpretations, all agreeably wild, were fixed. One view was that "Eb," though you mightn't think it to look at him, possessed Herculean strength, and that he had nearly killed, in fair fight, a blacksmith who had tried to elope with his daughter; an incident that had persuaded him to take Holy Orders and a life-long vow of celibacy. Another and less Gilbertian theory was that, when he retired behind the blackboard, doubtless to enjoy a rest from our faces, he was having a fight with the devil. Be such things as they may, he was fond of telling us that Satan lay ever ready for boys who had not prepared their lesson, and, like the old Egyptian taskmasters, he would cry: "Ye are idle, ye are idle." Then abruptly he would burst away from this attacking mood and publicly castigate himself with the whips of self-depreciation, muttering, "Who am I to apportion blame and to find fault? Bryant, you have been a sinner yourself." At those outbursts no one either laughed or was dismayed. They were accepted with the superb acquiescence of the schoolboy who, if a green hippopotamus with a mauve tin-hat were to come in during the Latin hour, would ask him what House he was in and whether he had half-a-crown about him till the first of next month.

Within dour and self-imposed limits "Eb" was a fine instructor. He scorned the showy and the sentimental in man and in the works of man, and, one morning when we were reading Tennyson's "Ode on the Death of the Duke of Wellington," he came out with bitter railing against the stanza about the funeral horses, asking the reader: "Well, child, isn't that horrible? How it offends me. One more line, and he'd have been writing about the undertaker's top-hat." He married in late middle-age, and retired to bee-farming in the West Country. There were still years of teaching in him. I fancy that some social injury, real but exaggerated, went into him like iron—"How it offends me." But, if these pages should meet his retired eye, I should wish him to know that here is one out of not a few who with gratitude recall the discipline of that rare man in a world of humbug, the practising puritan.

At six o'clock p.m. work in the class-room ended and work in the House began again; work for the mighty; toasting, or again carrying two books up three flights of stairs; work for the stomach; trying to satisfy it with a kipper and two rounds of bread which, as the German submarines increased, relapsed into an alloy of potatoes and sawdust; work for the nose; trying to keep it away from the stinking shirts of the buttery-boys whose method of cleaning the table was to roll the cloth into a ball knotted with all the fragments and scourings of the meal; work for the eyes; trying to read three hours' work in an hour and a half by a gas-mantle with St Vitus's Dance; work for the brain; trying to understand the aforesaid work, as a scholar should. Day after day, no rest, no surcease; worst of all, no privacy. For what is a man, or boy, better than sheep or goat if he can never be alone? In exchange for one waking hour of loneliness in the twenty-four I would have given a half-pound pot of raspberry-jam; any little box with a chair and a table would have done, anywhere away from the clatter and chatter of the sheep-pen.

Yet no one thought of complaining. Schoolboys are miracles of tolerance and survival. Like dogs, they hope and forget. After a month or so of this, I walked up from a lunch and/or dinner that a plumber's mate would have thrown back at his wife's head, to cheer and yell for Charterhouse against Repton. We beat them 3-2. Heroic figures float back from the scene. Emley at full-back, tackling his wing like blazing fire; Winterbotham in goal, foiling a desperate thrust in the last ten seconds. Besides, you can't complain to a system; it's like objecting to the personal appearance of the Albert Memorial. That system, now dead, but once common to nearly all Public Schools, was that the Housemaster received no fixed salary for being a Housemaster, but was expected to make profit from his House. That is not quite how the Governing Body expressed the contract, but never mind. And, if the Housemaster should be a married man with children coming up for care and education, well, he might be the best of shepherds, the kindest and wisest of providers, but what? Charity begins at home.

The Governing Body looked very well on the printed School List with their letters, titles, and preferments, but what Charterhouse needed far more was a Central Catering Office run by a man from J. Lyons, or the Express Dairy, who had learnt his own job and other people's jobbery. Also needed, was some copy of the "Dame" system as successfully practised at Eton. The "Dame" amounts to a boy's Welfare Officer, relieving the House-master's wife to a great degree, sometimes totally, of the neces-sary, if indefinable, duties of observation and advice. The in-fluence of such a woman on the incoherent years of adolescence is beyond price or estimate, and had such a system enjoyed a wider vogue in English schools, one third of *Tom Brown's School-days* and the whole of *Eric, or Little by Little* need never have been written. Each House had its matron whose duties lay chiefly with the medicine-bottles and the linen. In general, they were like our own incomparable Miss Stallybrass, women of kindness and devotion; but, if you take my sense, it was we who went to them, not they who came amongst us.

So, the seemingly impregnable tradition of middle-men and muddle-heads still prevailed, rooted in the power of the fools who say: "It was good enough for us." At those roots Frank Fletcher had already swung his axe; but, though the trunk was rotten, the roots were strong and deep; and the day was not yet when the whole tree should crash to the ground, and be hauled away and supplanted by the sapling which grew in its place, and now flourishes to the sky.

1915 rolled in. The first European war, paradise of profiteers, thickened in the Flanders mud. So did the casualty lists. And the tradesmen went on trading, on ignorance, necessity, and ostentation. There was no Lord Woolton. And, at school, we worked and drilled and plodded and drilled and played and drilled our way along; and ate what happened to be eatable, and borrowed without usury.

F. R. L. Wilson assumed the housemastership in my first quarter; Charterhouse call a term a "quarter," Eton call it a "half"; let's call it a day, and avoid idiosyncratic expressions and the need for a glossary; "Willow" or "Fiery Fred" took over from the benevolent and credulous Mr Moss, and on my first shop order, for a bottle of hair-oil, he wrote the word "odourless," shouted "unnecessary," let out a short laugh like fire-irons falling on the grate, wheeled round, cannoned off a Windsor chair, and gave the door a slam that brought down flakes from the gas-mantle like a flurry of snow. That was the visible "Willow," without fear, favour, grace, or delay; richly imitable, and perpetually and hilariously imitated, no mimic reaching quite the standard of George Delaforce. But within, within was a brain, shrewd, wide, rapid, fiercely witty; a warm heart ("damned fool, talking about hearts"), a friend, constant through years, shooting away the bull's-eye with advice and hospitality. He was bound to accept the prevailing economic system of the school, but he accepted it, as did the kindly Mrs Wilson, because there was nothing else to accept. Good wishes don't knock down the wall of tradition. *Il faut vivre.*

"Willow's" workshops were the science laboratory, and his garden; in both, his knowledge was deep but, at times, hard to follow. In the laboratory, which he pronounced with an emphasis on the first syllable that might suggest another place of reflection and disappointment, he had the services of an adult assistant with the highest drain-pipe collar in the district; on this questionable surface, it was said, "Willow," who had an uncertainty of vision, sometimes scribbled a rapid note, some formula or inchoate thesis. In the post of deputy-assistant alchemist there came and went a succession of youths, alike in reluctance and incompetence, varying in pimpledom and sniffle. Most of them were born droppers, especially of glass. They seemed to like the sound. I fancy that "Willow," who was a deceptively able man, had fewer failures than is customary among experimental chemists; fewer, certainly, than his neighbour, the Rev. F. Forder, from whose room would come dull booms and crashes, indicating that once again he had got the mixture wrong, or that, while demonstrating the principles of Latent Heat, he had forgotten to allow for the subsequent contraction of metal spheres. "Willow" had his minor set-backs, but he over-rode them with a sort of casual ferocity. Once, having heated one end of a long test-tube in a Bunsen burner and having failed to note that the other end had been warming up in another Bunsen burner, he put what he reckoned to be the harmless end into his mouth. With sizzling lips he cast the offence from him, and glaring at the class, said: "Fools; don't laugh; didn't burn; too hot to burn; ought to have known that if you had any sense." More wonderful still, in a world of smells, he could detect the pungency of hair-oil. The offender was sent out to purge himself, or, if an experiment should be boiling up to its crisis, he would be summarily sluiced under the tap, in the sacred cause of purity and learning.

At the end of January, 1915, I picked up whooping-cough, and rumbled down to the Sanatorium in the "dead-cart", a mouldy and celebrated old four-wheeler, driven by a mouldy and anonymous old party. I was excited at the idea of a different life, and didn't mind if half of it would be passed over a basin or spittoon. Anything for a change. It was to prove an odd existence. The matron in charge, a negligent and negligible little woman with red hair, divided her life between saying what she planned to do when she was off duty and showing how little she meant to do when she wasn't, except admire the figures of the older patients. I was too young to be interested, or interesting, but not too young, it seemed, to be taught by some genial sophisticates a baldly smutty parody of Basil Hallam's star-hit song, "Gilbert the Filbert." Basil Hallam Radford had been a boy in our House, Lockites, a few years earlier. He was killed while on Active Service with observation balloons, his parachute failing to open. He had suffered from a physical disability which prevented his earlier reception into the Services. So he was given white feathers by a few hysterical bitches of the London pack which had so lately yelped his praises.

So far, so not very bright. In fact, as the medical students of Edinburgh University used to sing and may still sing:

> Life presents a dreary picture,
> No one ever speaks or smiles;
> Mine's a cheerful occupation,
> Cracking ice for grandpa's piles.

I wasn't unhappy; quite the wrong word. Nor did I enjoy that most abject and clinging of drugs, self-pity. But I was puzzled. Reality had fallen whole acres short of anticipation. I suppose I had stuffed the back rooms of my mind with heroic and flamboyant ideas on Public School life. Well, I hadn't found the heroes yet. I was many foolish things, but not prude, nor prig. It just happened that I came from a prep. school that didn't deal in juvenile sex-muck, and from a father who thought it bad manners to swear in front of women and children, reserving his generous and Rabelaisian wit for the smoking-room and our adult ears; and I found "bloody" this and "bloody" that just bloody monotonous. Monotony. That was it. Monotonous work; monotonous football; monotonous food; monotonous language; monotonous rifle-drill for a monotonous war.

Summer was to come.

I can see now that the school, like the society around it, was in a state of silent convulsion. There was a struggle being fought out between an old idea and a new, of which, at Charterhouse, the respective champions were Frank Dames-Longworth and Frank Fletcher, the headmaster. Conservative v. Liberal; Trinity, Cambridge v. Balliol, Oxford; champagne, if you like, v. tea. They were united only in their love of classical learning, and both were scholars of the first order. But they differed utterly and from the roots in their conception of scholarship. Fletcher loved learning because it was learning; Longworth loved it rather because it was something without which no gentleman was quite complete, a polite adjunct of the finished social article. But Longworth would have learning come without its poorer relations, inkiness, grubbiness, the signs of ugly toil. Brain must not interfere with manners. Like my Lord Chesterfield, he would have kept at least one door between himself and that dusty Dr Sam Johnson.

Longworth's appeal to a schoolboy was obvious and natural. He had presence, bluff geniality, the warm kindness of an Irishman, and ample means wherewith to express it, as in his oyster lunches on Sundays, a prelude and set-off to the Greek Testament which followed. He had three times been amateur champion at Rackets, that grand and somewhat exclusive game. His dress was that of a county squire. He used no turn-up to his perfectly creased trousers, and shot his cuffs approvingly over Horace's Odes. "Odi profanum vulgus et arceo"; "And why did he hate them? Because they stank." We liked him, too, because he used no sarcasm, attacking us head on: "You're talking b—l—s, my boy, absolute b—l—s, and you know it's b—l—s." And once when a young and timid scholar, seeking to render from Greek the lamentations of Medea, said: "Woe is me for the children I begat!" he shouted: "Sit down, boy, for heaven's sake, till you can get your sexes right. Women don't beget; they bear; a fact of which you may one day become cognisant, to your cost."

He excelled at Latin verse, and often his Prize Versions would appear in the old Saturday *Westminster Gazette*, and, when they didn't, he was apt to write to the Oxford don who judged those nice affairs, and tell him what he thought of his miserable misjudgements. One morning he was explaining to me some intricate point of prosody when the class-room door opened, and a friend of mine, a young Scottish mathematician who regarded Latin verse as immaterial to worldly advancement, walked in to prepare himself for the next lesson, and I winked at him. This wink, though only a little one, reached Longworth, who tore my exercise-book in two pieces and hurled them out of the window, and told me that I never again need appear, with or without verses, in his presence. At the end of the next lesson he called me up and invited me to play rackets on the following day.

It was over a game of rackets that I first saw how clear-cut was the rift between Dames-Longworth and his headmaster. I was partnering Frank Fletcher in a four-handed game of moderate skill, and we were waiting for the court, which was occupied by Longworth, Gilbert Browne the professional, and the school first pair. They had played on for a full quarter of an hour over their allotted hour, and Fletcher "knocked" them on the door, twice, without result; the third time, he knocked in a way that meant, and received, notice. Out shot Longworth, noisily indignant about the "rights" of the school pair, etc., etc. "Well," said the headmaster, with habitual calm and icy clarity, "there are other players here, who may in their turn become the school pair. And, if they do, I hope they will observe the courtesy of the court. You frame the time-table, Longworth, but you take little notice of it." And the loser in this little battle rolled away, fuming in a swathe of silk scarves. And, as we walked into the court, Fletcher murmured, with a bleak smile, "Strange man, Longworth; can't bear opposition."

He couldn't. Probably, because he had known it so little. From Charterhouse he had gone as a scholar to Cambridge, then returned. He was the country gentleman condescending to that part of schoolmastering which befitted his caste; a little contemptuous, in a kind but magnificent sort of way, of time-tables and accuracy and time-table-ish and accurate pedagogues. He was more of the Eton and I. Zingari cut, and considered nothing so inexcusable as forgetting to be a gentleman. He liked what was honourable by the world's standards, upright, but not *too* good. He subscribed to Church and State, a well-heated church and a well-lined State. In this very visible, very tangible world he was a great man, and powerful.

Powerful, and most necessary, during the headmastership of Frank Fletcher's predecessor, the Rev. Gerald H. Rendall. This courteous and benign scholar was appointed headmaster, startlingly, towards the end of the last century. He was like the White Knight on a bucking young horse; and, after two or three falls early on, he trotted along beside his fractious mount, which visited and cropped where it listed. A few masters, of whom Longworth was one, formed the executive *de facto*. But the scandal grew. Long week-ends were taken by boys who felt the need of a change and the improbability of their being missed. Dozens each morning would rest in bed during early school, on medical grounds, then change for football or cricket in the afternoon. Rendall, courteous as ever, preached in chapel well-turned sermons on morality and, inaugurating a social evening of a Godalming Working Guild, began with "If you open your Euripides." At last the Governing Body, sensing, perhaps, their own misnomer, looked round for a rescuer. Frank Fletcher was invited to accept Charterhouse. For him, happy and successful after eight years in the Mastership of Marlborough, the idea of Charterhouse was scarcely inspiring. But he went, and stayed for twenty-five years. Of these years he has himself written the story; but he could not tell us, what those of us who had the honour to come close to him know, that he was great; an idealist with the will and the power to turn dreams into fact. Also, he was one of the few utterly unselfish men that I have known; not only in those more obvious and external matters which are all life to most men, well-being, comfort, advancement, leisure, but also in that Pauline attitude of attack which willingly, and without counting the cost, makes a host of enemies in battling to an appointed end; and Fletcher's end, beside which nothing worldly counted for much or for long, was a Charterhouse that was free but disciplined. In his quest he was inflexible.

There was much of Dr Arnold in him, and it is worthy of note that among Fletcher's early pupils at Rugby was one William Temple, who, like his master, was to be not gentle to plutocracy.

The Charterhouse that Fletcher found had too much money and sophistication; it was steeped in that vulgarity which considers learning the most vulgar of all things, and scholars the most ludicrous. One of the most senior housemasters had assigned to himself a time-table that consisted in teaching the same three propositions of Euclid in terminal rotation, and the master of another Form, when told by a pupil that time had been insufficient for attempting a Latin Prose Composition, satisfied himself with the dim sarcasm that, in such a case, the master would be spared the pains of correction. So Fletcher went to it; and, within a month, the first batch of boys took single tickets for home.

Certainly, he lacked the grace of conciliation; and he was often rude to those whom he had decided to regard as opposed to his system and ideal. He made enemies of some who, more graciously and deftly handled, were ready to have been important friends. Not all of the Rendallian era were won over. He often broke opposition, less often converted it. Pomposity, the weakness of the city-merchant and purse-proud parent, turned him to ice. Yet, for those who found it, his kindness was as warm as fire. I know what I owe to him, and to Lady Fletcher; and they will know it without my writing it down here.

In the summer of 1916, I captained the Under Sixteen cricket eleven against Christ's Hospital and St Paul's. The School first eleven had a great win, by 13 runs, over Winchester, and, in their match against the Artists' Rifles, I first had my eyes opened to what batting could be, by a beautiful 90 from D. J. Knight. He and his partner, A. Hartley of Lancashire, put up over 100 for the first wicket. Hartley was killed in France, a month before the Armistice of 1918. I have the fancy that Knight was caught in the deep off the slow left-hander, J. B. Beck. Beck played little cricket afterwards, but he reached eminence in golf, and it was his geniality and wit that welded together, in 1938, the first British Walker Cup team to beat the United States.

In 1917 I stood a chance of getting into the first eleven. I went as far as being required to practise in those nets set apart for the few; but, one afternoon, the captain found me batting left-handed, a method that was novel to both of us. He asked me why; and I, with foolish innocence, said that I wanted to find out what it felt like. I was not invited to experiment further, and my services were diverted to the second eleven. Our matches were played on the pleasant little ground called Wilderness, mostly against military teams full of non-commissioned officers in white ducks who, previously fortified by alcohol, tended to bowl very fast and before you were ready. Sound schooling.

In that same summer I took part, for the first and last time, in a stand of over 200. This was in a house-match, against Verites. My own share was only 57, but my partner, Eric Lavenstein, a brilliant athlete from Johannesburg, went on to score 193. He then laid waste the opposition with vast leg-breaks. The housemaster of Verites was Mr Alexander Hay Tod, who, as a boy, had come down with Dr Haig Brown from the old London Charterhouse to Godalming. In height, he was about equal to an average new boy. During the long stand between Lavenstein and myself, he appeared behind the bowler's arm, first at one end, then at the other, tilting his bowler-hat to every possible angle of menace, and twining one leg round the other in an ecstasy of disapproval. At football matches, he could come to closer grips with his opponents, and many a time, when I was keeping goal against his House, he would stand close behind the posts and utter words of discouragement and evil prophecy: "Ha! our for-wards have the ball; they are approaching; and I think a very awk-ward shot will en-sue. Here it comes. Yes; I thought that would be too much for your vigi-lance."

Summer 1917 marked the end of my year in Tod's Form, the Under VI Classical. Our love and fear of him were about equal; for he could be the very devil among the inkpots and dictionaries. He wagged a defiant head at life, and, if the three Furies had suddenly appeared in front of his desk, he would have sent them packing with a howling imposition. He carried a glass eye in that round little head. Once at least this eye was mislaid, and once it fell on to the floor of the class-room. It was after this latter event that he decided to have a duplicate; dupli-Kate, as he pronounced it. The loss of the original and natural eye was explained by ingenious and apocryphal narratives, the most popular being that he had been struck by snow-blindness when climbing the Matterhorn in the company of Edward Whymper.

I wish I could reproduce Tod's voice, which was a sort of militant and vibrating hum, low in tone, with a precision of diction often to be noticed in lecturers. In times of anger and penal affliction he pronounced each syllable with an awful clarity and a peculiar stress on the final letters. "You've neg-lected your less-*on*. Five hun-*dred*." Those were lines.

But the names of the villains in our history or reading he rolled with a sinister menace that fixed their wickedness for ever in the mind. There was "that rogue Tissa-phern-es, capable of an aband-oned duplicity scarcely parall-eled in anci-ent times." But even he gave place to "that monster Heli-o-gaba-*lus*, on whose debauched counten-ance was printed every sign of folly and vice." Here he would cast his Cyclopean gaze round the Form, as if expecting to find some rival in folly, if not in vice, then sigh, and mutter "Ah! not yet quite, perhaps."

To him words were almost living creatures, to be treated according to their station and condition. "My dear boy," he said to a hesitant translator, "it is only a conjunct-ion, a long name for a very small thing; a mere poor relation among the parts of speech; recognize it, raise your hat to it politely, then pass by, like the Levites, on the other side."

He knew the value of a little injustice, and taught humility as thoroughly as he taught Latin. During verbal answers, places were taken, up or down. Success was fleeting and favour in-secure. If the temporary head of the Form showed unwise signs of elation, he would suddenly assail him with a hail of questions and, before the answer came, pass each question on, till the victim had bumped to the bottom like a rattling stone. Then he would "number down from thirty."

He used old words, of which "shuffle" was the favourite. "Answer me now, yes or no, and don't shuffle." Shuffling covered every kind of equivocation, the bald untruth, the des-perate excuse, the supposedly perfect reason. Sometimes he would delight us by an insulting attack on the editors of our text. "Ha! that is a very stupid note. Take your pens and draw a line through it. I should like to know to which of our edit-ors we are indebted for that ridiculous err-or, whether Mr West-cott or Mr Hort." There was a fearful joy in annihilating the printed word.

In times of depression, when no one seemed to know anything, he would suddenly say, "Unroll that map of the Holy Land. We need a change of air. Put your hand on the Lake of Gennesar-et. Now show me Tyre and Sid-on. Ah! an unlucky conjecture. Five maps of the Holy Land, please, in different coloured crayons."

But, in spite of eccentricity, or because of it, he was a fine teacher; and, for all his tyrannies, he was loved; because he cared so much. Out of school, his hobbies were many. He was the best amateur photographer for miles around, and had a wonderful collection of brass medallions, which he would buy straight off the plough-horses all over the country. As a boy at Charter-house he had been in the Eleven at soccer, and I found to my delight an account of a match in which it said: "Tod put in much hard work, which was, however, largely discounted by erratic manœuvres in front of goal." Yes, erratic were his manœuvres, and from them was drawn, and chanted, the parody of the poet Cowper.

> Tod moves in a mysterious way,
> His wonders to perform;
> He plants his footsteps in the sea,
> And rides upon his Form.

He "rode upon" us to the extent of setting us to do Latin and Greek Composition, prose and verse, out of school hours. This meant four "copies" in our own time each week; undoubtedly too much for anyone, who, like myself, did not intend that a classical education should ruin a summer term. There were ways round this dilemma. I used the simplest, which was to "show up" to Tod verses and proses that were the work of previous scholars in his Form. The same compositions came round in a regular cycle, and "the market" was well-stocked. Tact was needed to reproduce these works of art in a shape that would not arouse comment. They must lack gross error as well as unnatural brilli-ance. In this, somewhat specialized, traffic, I held my own for some weeks. Then, one day, I made a fatal blunder. Tod had set us to turn into Latin Elegiacs the verses beginning—

> When the British warrior Queen,
> Bleeding from the Roman rods . . .

I went to my usual source, a friend of mine who happened now to be head of the School. He soon turned up the offending pas-sage in his files, and, with it, a Latin version whose confident splendour proclaimed it an obvious and authentic Dames-Longworth. I swallowed this dangerous but irresistible bait. A few days later, we received back our exercise-books from Tod.

Against each of "my" lines was written, in bold red ink, the initials "F.D.L." At the end of that hour, I had an interview with Tod, brief and, to me, unsatisfactory. I was referred to the Headmaster, who invited me to attend in the Green Room below the stage in the Hall. There was I executed; and, in the platoon-drill that followed this untoward event, I kept falling out to remove pieces of birch which had become enmeshed in my pants.

"*Suave mari magno.*" In short, it was agreeable to be in the Sixth Form, and sometimes to catch sight of Mr Tod breathing out memories of slaughter on his sauntering path to the Under Sixth. The Sixth Form were privileged to go into work three-quarters of an hour later than the profane herd. This time had been set aside for preparation of the classical authors; but not by us; and we used it mostly for repose and the exchange of that scandal without which no community is complete. Edward Pearce and I were often received at this hour in Saunderites, the Headmaster's House, where we offered unsafe advice on the *Georgics* to Christopher Green, who became titular head of the School, or to Basil Murray, who had inherited much of the intellect but none of the industry of his father, Professor Gilbert Murray, Regius Professor of Greek at Oxford. Basil Murray had charm of manner and an unequalled gift of escaping deserved punishment. Later, at Oxford, he used that city mainly as a stepping-stone to London, and no undergraduate of his day paid more frequent visits to the dentist. Thence he passed into journalism and irregular authorship. When the Spanish civil war broke out, he went out to lend what help he might to the Republican side. Basil hadn't the health to stay the course, and he died at sea. He was a genius in his kind; but he had no guy-ropes, no pole-star; and, of his own drifting choice, he passed most of his life in a society which, inwardly, he despised.

Edward Holroyd Pearce was, and remains, my closest friend. I first saw him as a small slight figure in black set off by red hair and a red ribbon of vaccination round his arm. It was our second day at Charterhouse, and I asked him the way to Mr Bryant's class-room; "the scholar's form," I added, with the pompous assurance that he belonged to some far debased society.

"You'd better follow me," replied this rufous pigmy, "I'm

going there myself." "Are *you* a scholar, then?" I asked. "I,"
he said, "am the top scholar." And so he was. By chance of
alphabet, a P and an R, we sat next to each other, and for five
years at Charterhouse, and four at Oxford, we lived and laughed
together.

Among those who sat in the Sixth Form at the feet of Mr
Irvine was Charles Graves, who seems doomed to be mentioned
in autobiographies, because he can be neither overlooked nor
forgotten. Younger brother of the poet and novelist, Robert
Graves, Charles is one of the most facile and determined journalists of the day, with a pachydermatous contempt for criticism and an unquenchable power of arriving. Tough and clever;
not deep, but eloquent. His feature in the *Daily Mail*, "Looking
at Life", was a clear and unflattering mirror for those who liked
to enjoy the reflection of what passed for London Society. When
the Hitler war came, he adapted his machinery to it as skilfully
as any Nuffield factory, and was among the first to produce read-
able books on the work of the Royal Air Force, which he followed
with a standard history of the Home Guard. In his Charterhouse
days, he already showed a sufficiency of Gravesian self-assurance
and obstinacy. He was a scholar, but not a particularly good one.
This did not hinder him from backing his opinion against Bentley
or Porson, let alone his immediate master, A. L. Irvine, from
whom he habitually, and often impolitely, disagreed on any subject from the art of Botticelli to the propriety of ending a pentameter with a word of four syllables. Graves was many things, but
never dull.

Nor was Richard Hughes; called "Black Hughes", in distinction from his red namesake who is now a master at Rugby
and an expert at mulling claret, when there is any. "Black"
Hughes set a new standard of dreaminess as Head of the School.
He was full of Welsh folk-lore, out-of-the-way reading, and
mysticism. In translation from the classics, he never allowed a
little ignorance to stand in his way. The dustiest passages of
Thucydides flowered under the Hughes treatment into something rich and rare, and he could have squeezed a sonnet from
Euclid's "Pons Asinorum." In the winter of 1917 he sat for a
Scholarship at Corpus Christi College, Oxford. He was suffering
from 'flu, and carried in his pocket a flask of refreshment, with
which to recreate his body and stimulate his notions. This over-

zealous attention to his health caused him to fall asleep in the middle of his Greek Prose paper, and he failed for Corpus Christi. But Oriel took him, on the strength of his Essay—he had. kept awake for this—in which he had quoted extensively from Chinese proverbs not seen before or since. Provost Phelps of Oriel, who was also a member of the Governing Body of Charter-house, liked his scholars to do credit to the College, but many a day he pulled his beard over Richard Hughes, who said that his Classical tutor was so dull that his pupils felt their pulses to see if they were still alive. Hughes took to contributing to the Satur-day *Westminster Gazette*, and wrote a Grand Guignol play, *The Sister's Tragedy*, which gave full scope to Sybil Thorndike's art. He was always looking for something new or different, working his passage on unlikely ships, deputizing for a night-watchman in a Paris cemetery, arriving at Mittel-Europa towns in time for mysterious revolutions, unearthing a sunken and ruined cottage in Wales and making it habitable for his mother and himself, and revelling in the limbo between fact and fancy. His parting gift to Provost Phelps was a Fourth Class in the School of English. A few years later, he published his *A High Wind in Jamaica*, probably the best written best-seller of that decade, and, in its power of describing the indescribable sea, not inferior to Joseph Conrad.

Leicester Irvine was master of the Classical Sixth at Charter-house from 1914 to 1946. Without absurd brilliance or eccen-tricity, he induced admiration of the ancient authors and knew what paths led to a scholarship at the University.

Omne tulit punctum qui miscuit utile dulci.

In all things he was meticulous, thorough, but was saved from pedantry by a dry and searching wit. He was Roman in a certain steadiness of deportment and solidity of mind, and would have made an admirable Aeneas. Indeed, he was the only man I have ever known who stood up for that somewhat portentous hero in his most unheroic treatment of Dido.

In the Easter term of 1918, I won the Gordon Whitbread prize for a study of certain segments of Homer and Horace. This was the direct result of pride. I did not mean to be beaten, and I read the authors in their required passages till the lines popped up even in my dreams. It was not scholarship, but self-imposed sweating. A foolish performance, which to-day I neither would nor could repeat. The lesson of relaxation is hard to learn.

In the summer, Pat Rucker put me into the first eleven of cricket, as an opening batsman and an inswerving bowler of the sort that likes a new ball with a big seam and makes the old gentlemen gobble away about the superiority of spin over swerve. Rucker himself was a slowish left-hand bowler with a lovely action and, at the age of fifteen, the promise of greatness. But, by some freak of circumstance, his skill declined a little each year, though it lasted just long enough to win him his Blue at Oxford in 1919. The action remained, but the deceptiveness of flight and the nip from the pitch deserted him.

My first school match was at Harrow, on their ground, and I can recapture even now a backwash of excitement. We batted first; a Press photographer snapped us on our way to the wicket. Five minutes later I was on my way back, bowled by "Fritz" Matson. "Fritz" was pretty fast, and took five wickets in this match. We won by 12 runs, Pat Rucker taking 7 wickets for about 30. We did not win at Eton, being shot out for 13 somewhat peculiar runs. This was the combined action of the tearaway Basil Hill-Wood, the fiercely inswinging A. C. Gore, a pitch on Agar's Plough which was hard underneath and wet on top, and our own abysmal incompetence. I was given out caught at wicket off my top shirt-button. Not that it mattered. For Eton, that beautiful bowler, Clem Gibson, was not called upon, but his pleasant conversation at lunch made me nearly forget the morning's disaster, and I recall the wisdom of his remark: "Examinations are all right if you know anything about the questions." When Eton went in, we had six of them out for 21. Then came the rain to make the pitch easier; some good batting by T. Bevan and some slap-happy slogging by G. J. Yorke carried them to 168. I took 7 for 77.

Winchester beat us by 3 wickets at Charterhouse. We scored 157, and when we had seven of them, including one Douglas Jardine, out for 120, victory smelt near. But Jack Frazer, a strong left-hander, scored 60 not out, and that was that. Jack went on to get a Blue for Cricket and Soccer at Oxford, but, soon after being appointed to a tutorship at Balliol, he was killed in a skiing accident. He was one of the very finest men that I have known.

Pat Rucker, too, is gone. He volunteered for service at the start of the Hitler war, and was killed in the early fighting in France.

As to that other War, for so long it had been a charnel-house of a deadlock that the mind had become blunted to it, and few dared to foresee the end in that last German retreat. The news of the Armistice came in the middle of the morning Physical Jerks. They stopped abruptly. A volume of cheering swelled and swelled around, mostly from voices of persons invisible; a mighty sound of four years' hope bursting its prison. The Union Jack was run up, and a small member of our squad, in his ecstasy, threw his jacket up into a tree, and left it there for several hours. That afternoon, Gilbert Murray talked to the assembled school on the tasks of peace, and outlined the scheme that was later to be called the League of Nations. We hung on his oratory, and he soon had us all convinced that war would for ever cease from all the world.

A fortnight later, some half-dozen of us set out to sit for scholarships at Oxford. Edward Pearce and I aimed for Corpus Christi. We lodged in Oriel Street, talked shop, and reckoned we were already undergraduates. Back at Charterhouse, I went to bed with 'flu and a resignation to whatever news might come. It turned out to be good. Dick Gregory, who had been a new boy with me and was now champion runner in the school, brought it. "Pearce and you," he said, "no one else." This was not quite exact, but very flattering. I sent a telegram to my father, though I knew he hated telegrams. But he liked this one, and whacked back a reply.

In January 1919 I became head of the House, which, on the first Sunday and third day of the term, caught fire and was burnt nearly to the ground. Fate likes to do things in twos; in March of the previous year, Mr Tod's House, Verites, had been burnt out, with Tod skirting around it, taking photographs, and breaking alternately into tears and oaths. In both fires, the cause was said to be electrical, and, as electricity means no more to me than Japanese poetry, I will leave it at that. It was at ten minutes past two o'clock p.m. that a young master, Mr Williams, otherwise unsung in Charterhouse history, walked into the Sixth Form during Scripture hour and said: "Lockites is on fire; can Glasgow go down there?" Frank Fletcher was discoursing to us on the Book of Job, and I had written the note: "The Book

of Job is not so much a lesson in man's patience as in the in-
scrutability of God's purpose." I found my housemaster, F. R. L.
Wilson, brandishing a bucket of water in a corridor. "Lock all
the doors," he said, "or in a few minutes there'll be six hundred
bloody fools in this house." And he laughed harshly. Neglecting
these instructions, I went at once, I am ashamed to say, up to
my study, seized some favourite books and lowered them, like
St Paul, in a basket. I then walked outside, and found the fire
was well away and the whole length of the roof blazing. Soon,
but not very, the Godalming Fire Engine, which worked on
steam, came chuffing up the long hill, dropping lumps of coal
on the road. The Brigade seemed to have made the most of the
Sunday joint and to lack tactical precision. Their hose, at last
adjusted, pumped a derisory stream of water well short of the
roof. The fun ripened.

The School Fire Brigade joined in with their late-Victorian
machine, which worked by hand and chance and a double-
pumping see-saw action. While the men of Godalming discussed
pressure down below, our own brigade began to scale the walls
on ladders, a perilous feat with the roof disintegrating. One member received on his helmet a falling slate which appeared to disturb his intellect, for he at once penetrated into a bedroom on
the second storey and threw thence a watch and chain, followed
by a large hand-basin. Other volunteers had reached the same
house-level and, seized by the lust of salvage, began to throw
down effects of every kind and size, of which mattresses were the
noisiest and the least appreciated by those standing underneath.
At the height of this mêlée the Southwark Brigade arrived,
having made the 32 miles from London in fifty minutes. They
pushed aside all opposition, cleared the house of helpers, and,
entering the ground floor with their hoses, blew the skylights,
which had so far strangely survived, whistling up to the clouds.

By 4.30 p.m. the House was a stinking ruin. Twilight came on.
"Better go now," said a spectator, "I think that's the end of the
fun." I went down the hill to the Sanatorium, where we were to
lodge for the next four nights, and interviewed the Matron about
ways and means. She flapped and fluttered. "I hope," she said,
"that all your boys have their indoor shoes; I don't want my
corridors spoilt." "No one," I told her, "has anything much
except what they stand up in." She belonged to that order

of matrons who like to have everything clean but never used, and who regard the death of a patient and a dirty square of parquet as equal misfortunes. She was also a philatelist, and purred when George Delaforce gave her the stamps off a letter from Oporto.

The School rented for us Farncombe Hill House, nearly a mile away. It had been empty for nearly two years. Many of our bed-frames had survived the fire, and the next three days were spent in carting these and other necessary bedroom furniture to the new home, which became semi-habitable. Our housemaster had 'flu, but fiercely refused to go to bed. He said he hadn't got a bed, and roamed in two overcoats round the School Hall, where his surviving furniture was stacked. We trekked down to the new Lockites on Wednesday evening, in column of fours, through slush and sleet, singing, "Katey, be-beautiful Katey, you're the only g-g-g-girl that I adore." No moon shone on the cowshed, and W. A. Nayler, our house tutor, a kindly man with a weakness for exaggeration, on entering the conservatory door, tripped over the water-pipes and measured his length on the cold bricks. It was an evil omen. The house was dank. Some windows wouldn't open, others wouldn't shut. Kippers were our inaugural supper, and the place stank of them and decay. Also, the wheels of excitement no longer revolved.

Frank Fletcher had given us leave off early morning School. But soon some enterprising idiot walked up the long hill and, poking his face into a class-room, mocked the sleepy students within, and our exemption was withdrawn. This same boy, who had itching palms, removed the telephone fixtures from the burnt-out House. He was arraigned and convicted, and I caned him, while he shouted, "Prove it, prove it," and, from a bending posture, called alternately upon me and his Maker.

The snow continued; the 'flu epidemic spread; and the School were granted an Exeat of a week. I went to Eastbourne, and, instead of roller-skating in Devonshire Park, worked nine hours a day for the Thackeray Prize. I read and re-read Lamb's "Essays of Elia", Keats' 1820 Poems, and Shakespeare's Henry IV, Part II. Competitive pride again; and something Scottish in the temperament. Back at school, I entered the examination in a daze of omniscience, rotten with knowledge, and won like an automaton. A shameful misuse of the glories of literature.

So to the last summer term. With belated wisdom, I thrust

nearly all work from me. Farncombe Hill House had shaken down to tolerable comfort. We prepared a tennis lawn, and there, on peaceful evenings, was to be seen Mr Wilson's unique service delivered from the reverse side of the racket. We revelled in our isolation, a democratic city-state. The sun came back, and cricket. My luck was in. I took 97 off Westminster and 100 off the Free Foresters, and bowled E. G. Wynyard off his instep with an inswinger. A perfect life.

It was now that I first came to know George Mallory. He was in his late thirties, but looked about nineteen. He took some Form in the middle of the school, where his charm and fastidious literary sense went for very little. He used to invite some of us to musical evenings with supper on Sundays, and Steuart Wilson would sing Elizabethan and Schubert songs. Arriving back from one of these soirées at about midnight, I found all doors of the House locked. My housemaster's head hung dimly over the porch. "Fool," it said, "you're beastly late. Good mind to leave you out there all night. Abuse of privilege. Better come in and have a glass of milk." I came. A few years later, Mallory was lost, with Irving, in their famous attempt on Everest.

Other pictures of Charterhouse float back; Colonel F. W. B. Smart, unique Commander of the O.T.C. on his calm-eyed white horse, absent-mindedly directing operations on Puttenham Heath; A. W. Tressler, walking rapidly with his bicycle, attended by a boy on each side, refusing remission from an imposition to one, and conducting a political argument with the other; W. R. ("Sweaty") Dykes, vainly asking boys in his French class not to sharpen pencils; a retired Bishop of Barbados, with only his pink forehead and white hair showing above the lectern, opening his sermon with the words: "My name is John; and I want all the Johns in this chapel to be proud of it"; Housematches of soccer, with the score at 0-0, and me watching the clock in agony from goal; a German Zeppelin floating high over the House in the moonlight; and a dark-haired day-boy called Wingate, walking about with his head down, deep in thought. About Burma?

VIII

DARK BLUE

To me Oxford is the Walled City, with a door of which in fancy I alone have the secret and the key, and I can go in there when I want to touch the hem of eternity. Our age clashes its cymbals in her ear, and still she dreams. The aeroplane roars past her spires; the shaven grass beneath catches the darting shadow, then rests in the silence of immemorial learning. It is August, by the Bridge; the clusters of sightseers, with their hot and explanatory guide, file into Magdalen, and out again, and are gone with their cameras, and facts, and assurance that they have done Magdalen College, and almost know Edward once Prince of Wales. And, suddenly, the years are nothing, and Keats walks out with his friend Bailey; *Endymion* is in the making behind his dark and lustrous eyes, or one of those letters to young Fanny, telling her of the abundance of clear streams about Oxford and asking her what she is reading; surely, the most loving letters ever written by a brother to a sister.

I love Oxford the more deeply because I did not go there to see what I could get out of it. It is not a mercenary friendship. Most undergraduates are working to a plan. Such and such a degree is necessary for the career that they have designed for themselves. Goodness knows, they are right, and, had I then stood still to take my bearings, I too might have come to some agreement with ambition. But I was never good at standing still. I meant, if I could, to take the highest possible degree in Classics and sometimes half-persuaded myself that I aimed for the Civil Service, Home or Indian, without any accurate or reasoned envisaging of what such a life would mean. I hated "arrangements" and loved improvisation; pushed aside the future, and swallowed the present whole. I meant to win a Cricket Blue, and, as with the Classics, I knew that I had it in me to succeed. Vanity was at work. I would enjoy the success for its own enjoyment. As for making success a rung in the world's ladder, I was quite vague and uninterested.

My own earnings were £160 p.a.; £80 being from Corpus Christi College, £80 from Charterhouse; both subject to good moral behaviour and a continuance in the Christian Faith. To this sum my father added an annual allowance of £150. I would have liked to whip it up to £200, if I could have hit on any convincing grounds for the request. But he used to send me a cheque each June, when the Oxford cricket team went on tour; adding, without fail, the remark that he couldn't understand why any one should want to waste money on a game like cricket. For fishing or shooting, yes. Cricket bored him; and he had never gone farther than "slogging about in the nets for exercise" at Uppingham, where, he said, the illustrious H. H. Stephenson made a very fat thing out of selling bats. Each year of four I sent my father tickets for the Oxford and Cambridge cricket match; but either he was going away fishing, or else he "hadn't been to London for years". He followed the scores from afar, and sometimes a letter would end with—"I see you took a proper knock from Kent last week," or "I see you got a few wickets at Weston-super-Mare. I lost two fish yesterday."

I made one or two passes at being a dry-fly fisherman, as I knew it would please my father. But it wouldn't work. The knots for tying on the fly baffled me, and the names of the various flies, though sounding well enough in an Izaak Walton sort of way, left me confused and irritable. My plebeian taste preferred sea-fishing from a boat for mackerel, plaice, and dabs. Most of all I envy those who operate in tropical seas against sword-fish, giant sting-rays, and the Leviathans of the deep.

I spent some bleak hours in practising casts on the river-bank at Newcastleton, just over the borders of Scotland, during the last summer holidays before Oxford. John Buchan and his brother Walter, who was Procurator-Fiscal for Peebles-shire, arrived for a night at the little inn. They were on a walking tour. Brother Walter retired early after supper, but John, though pale and peaky after a serious illness, talked half through the night with my father, and we left them discussing obscure villages in Ireland and the comparative merits of snipe-shoots in Scotland. The brothers were off again, northwards, while we sat at breakfast; I watched them from the window, Walter, rather lame and reluctant, a few paces behind John, who sprang lightly along, nosing the morning air. He asked me to come and shoot duck

with him at Elsfield, near Oxford. But I never did so; which was
foolish of me.

One more attempt I made at gentlemanly fishing; in Ireland,
on the river Lee, by Killinardrish, in April of 1920. This time
it rained, for ten days without a break. Each morning, we stood
at the window, which overlooked the river, and my father would
say: "River's risen a good bit." Each afternoon we would
squelch forth to verify this diagnosis. On the seventh day I wired
to a friend in Dublin, hired a jaunting-car to Cork, and took train
to the capital, where the jocular citizens were engaged in lifting
motor-cyclists off their saddles and confiscating the machines.
I could not tell you why. There is no "why" in Ireland. From
Dublin I went to the suburb of Dalkey, and picked up a few
rounds of golf. One of them was played with the worst golfer I
ever have seen. I suppose he was the worst in the world. He
kept a card, and holed out on every green, and he confided to
me, as he poured whiskey into the small hole between his moustache and beard, that he had never yet beaten 220. I made out
his handicap to be 153.

Corpus Christi was the nearest thing to perfection in a College,
though I doubt if the horsey sprigs from adjoining Christ Church,
who slapped their riding-boots and watered their dogs by Canterbury Gate, knew anything at all about that. Anyhow, Corpus
wouldn't have suited them, for there were no social distinctions,
and work came first; not self-consciously so, but of accepted
necessity; in which respect, Corpus had for many years been
ahead of its time. In classical learning, it was second only to
Balliol; but it bore its books easily, and was free from Balliol's
curse, the snobbery of the mind. Had George Nathaniel Cur-
zon gone to Corpus, not Balliol, he might have learnt the common touch and been Prime Minister. Certainly Balliol had
cause for its pride. The aura of "affairs" as well as of scholarship
still hung over it. Jowett was not forgotten. The last of Herbert
Asquith's sons was in residence. A. L. Smith, the master, was the
Head of his College, not just a prospective Labour Candidate.
Balliol, though we knew it not, was in the last days of her greatness, before she became the nursery of the *New Statesman and
Nation* and the Oxford branch of the London School of Economics. Indeed, the whole University, as our fathers knew it, was
near the end of her journey.

In 1919, as now, there were two ages of man at Oxford, those
who had been to the War and those of us who had just left
school. These war-veterans were just what we needed. They have
been painted as a generation wearied by waste, cynical, and dis-
illusioned. The pages of Siegfried Sassoon are full of vain heroism,
of high but shattered hope, of boyhood grown suddenly and
irrevocably old. If this is how they felt, they hid their feelings
from us. Perhaps our very youth retouched their own.

On looking back at contemporaries, it would be nice to be
able to say: "Aha, you could see the promise of genius and fame
in that young man!" In one, T. E. Lawrence, the genius was
already admitted and the fame already wide. He popped in and
out of All Souls; restless, and awaiting something commensurate
with his vast powers. Even in those days, Lawrence was invested
with the air of only half-intelligible performance. Rumour about
him was stretched to fantasy. He was the King of Arabia in dis-
guise; Lloyd George had offered him a place in the cabinet; he
was to be the next Grand Lama of Tibet. Oxford had known
nothing so mysterious since the launching of the Snark in Christ
Church, where now one Anthony Eden pursued the even tenor
of his studies. Eden was typical of all that is best in Eton; intelligent rather than intellectual; of society, yet sociable.

But Leslie Hore-Belisha, of St John's, was already the politi-
cian in miniature; something of a pusher, and not averse from
that publicity which the Press, with persistent naïveté, awards
to young men in a hurry at the Oxford Union. Here, he crossed
epigrams with Beverley Nichols of Balliol. Nichols, who bore,
or possibly cultivated, a likeness to Byron, was also something of
an author and a vogue. He had wit and vitality. In after years,
he did not grow much higher than all this; he remained, as it
were, a minor. But he kept his sense of the topical; and, when the
public suddenly discovered the charm of flowers, he led us up
his garden-path with his pretty notions and dexterous salesman-
ship.

On Boar's Hill, where Gilbert Murray divided his meditations
between Euripides and the League of Nations, Robert Graves,
an unusual undergraduate, ran a provision shop at some loss.
Graves already "had it in" for the world, which he blames for
its War and its social order. But he was far too intelligent for the
intelligentsia, too large for a party or a clique. Bloomsbury

whined; but Graves shouted. What he hated he attacked, with bare hands and broadswords, not with poisoned pins and mittens. He was a gale; not just a faint leak from a drain; a poet, often a fine one; not merely a nasty mind suppurating into verse; and there was no doubt whatever about his sex.

Among other Charterhouse worthies then at Oxford were Vincent Seligman and Richard Goolden; the former looked wiser than ever after his adventures as unofficial Secretary to Venizelos, which he had put into two books, *Salonika Sideshows*, and *Macedonian Musings*; the latter, armed with perpetual umbrella and inquiring smile, cracked whimsical jokes in that piping old voice which was to become familiar on stage and air.

But the narrower interest in School companions did not live long. University is more than a name; and I have never envied those who make New College an annexe to Winchester. "Where's the face one would see in every place?" Edward Holroyd Pearce and I set up together at Corpus, but our friendship was not coincidental on Charterhouse. It had somehow been meant from the start. We laughed at the same things, and such gifts as we possessed were complementary to each other. He could cook and I could eat. And we wrote each other's essays without our tutor being any the wiser, or the better pleased.

For a few days we looked up Charterhouse friends, and we told them where to buy ash-trays adorned with College crests, and superfluous cushions of striking colour and price. Tradesmen invited us to start accounts, and to enjoy the spurious wealth of payment deferred. Hubert Butler, who had been a scholar in our school, invited us to tea at St John's, but the whole thing somehow went wrong. The tea didn't arrive till half-an-hour after us. When it came, the buttered toast was withered and the tea stewed. The talk trickled on about Charterhouse, then dried up; Butler had not been happy there, and I had the weary feeling that he wasn't going to be any happier at St John's. Darkness came on, and, in his feckless way, he did nothing about it. Light and the conversation died. The melancholy knowledge came to me that poor Hubert had never been anything but a brain. The rest just was not. On our way back to Corpus we stopped at Buol's and had a subsidiary tea. A good one. Buol's is no more; absorbed in a multiple store of now familiar ugliness.

Tea with poached eggs at Buol's used to round off our Sunday golf on the Cowley Marsh, the less desperate parts of which were, a few years later, absorbed in the Oxford University Course at Southfield. Our match was a foursome, and began with the inestimable pleasure of being played without a green-fee. By local law, no play at all was permitted on Sunday mornings, to allow the steward, a genial and capable man with only one arm, to go to church if he wished. But, though the gate leading to the pigmy club-house was locked, there were gaps in the hedge through which a bicycle could be forced. Thorny twigs used to catch in the hammock-saddle of a Dursley-Pederson bicycle known as "The Forth Bridge", which was, at all immaterial times, the property of Alexander M. Wallace, late of Edinburgh Academy.

The match was played over two rounds of the fourteen holes; Pearce and Lock versus Hutchinson and Glasgow. Pearce lacked grace, his style suggesting a very muscular old man who had taken to the game late in life on medical advice. Lock, whose father was Lady Margaret Professor of Divinity, had a fluent and upright swing, and hit his iron shots higher and farther in the wrong direction than any golfer I have seen. Hutchinson's play was very straight, but so short that he might just as well have been crooked. On the whole, he was the most serious player of the four, and was apt to produce patent tees and other complicated inducements to excellence. He also studied the wind. The fifth or sixth hole—now the fifth on the Southfield course—ran parallel to the Barracks of the Oxford and Bucks, and sometimes we used to play mashie-shots with very old balls over the battlements into unknown military spheres. After this came "The Field", containing four of what were surely the worst and dullest holes in the world. Long ago they have been built over, and no golfer will grudge the resultant maisonettes. On the way home, there was a very short and blind hole over a hedge and a haystack; pleasing if uncommon obstructions. The whole course was infested by young bandits, who lived in the marshes, preyed upon the golfers, and enlivened the round with sharp chases and unsabbatical arguments. Our own match was seldom decided before the last hole. There was a hideous charm about old Cowley.

In the middle of the Corpus Christi quadrangle the sundial cast its shadow, though the railings are gone on which the gossipers once propped their idle backs. At night, I could fancy, other shadows paced their old haunts and conned with a satiric chuckle the plaques which, lining the cloister by the Fellows' Building, set forth in perfect Latinity the excellence of their character and the erudition of their researches. Anyone of a moderately romantic and sociable turn would have welcomed a short chat with the ghost of Cuthbert Shields. He it was who had told his friends: "When I am dead, I shall return as a bad smell in the corner of my room." He was a history tutor, of vast but disorderly learning, and of a habit of mind so discursive that, in a series of lectures on the French Revolution, he had only reached the Flood by the end of the term.

Not far from the memorials, and moving daily nearer to them, lived the Reverend Charles Plummer, the College Chaplain. With a dutiful but charming benevolence he invited each fresh-man to lunch once. Each guest received the same fare, simple but satisfying; cold meat, and commons of bread and cheese, washed down with water, and consummated by a "Mayblossom" cigarette from a packet which was not renewed till twenty guests had come in their turn and gone. Charlie P. himself had the same lunch, but no meat and no Mayblossom. Comparisons showed that the conversation varied almost as little as the lunch. He asked you where you had been at school, and where your parents lived; implying, by this latter question, the sacredness of the filial and connubial bonds, and the Christian authority of fathers over sons.

He was a deep scholar, and had written learnedly on the Irish Saints. One of the traditional duties of the young guests was to inquire how the Celtic Dictionary was proceeding. The manu-script of this unlikely work lay on a book-case between the table and a fire which was, like the chaplain, almost innocent of flame. It was dusted daily, like the other furniture, and one folio stuck out from the others, inscribed with the words: "Abae? Ears". I fancy the question was never answered. Celibacy cried out aloud in that room. But there were some who remembered having heard that Charlie P. once "had someone in view"; and the wits used to say that, in the days when he wished to marry, the College Statutes forbade it, and, when the Statute was revoked, his chance and his ardour had gone. But I doubt if there ever was a lady. He ranked Eve as a very designing woman. If saints on earth and saints in heaven are very near indeed, then, when his time came, Charlie Plummer did not have far to go.

President of Corpus was Professor Thomas Case, a Victorian who could keep pace with any Georgian; a scholar, but a man of the world; dignified, but playful; autocrat and servant of his College; abundantly liberal of heart, and immutably conservative in belief. He regarded Lord Palmerston as England's last minister of consequence; Disraeli had cancelled early promise by his fatal Reform Bill of 1867; "giving away votes," he said, "like a tip to the chamber-maid." He deplored female suffrage and the entry of women into competitive professions; "they should vie with each other, not with men; their only competition should be in beauty, motherhood, and domestic economy. Aristotle was right about women." Next to his wife Eliza, née Sterndale Bennett, Aristotle was Tommy Case's best friend, and he never tired of him.

When I went, in my turn, to see the President on my second day at Corpus, he was sitting at the piano in a dressing-gown that looked as if it had been made out of a quilt. "Sit down, Mr Robertson-Glasgow. What would you like me to play to you? Beethoven? Or some of this modern Jazz? Beethoven; very well. We'll have the first Movement of the Moonlight Sonata; it sounds so simple; but it's not; most amateurs avoid it, and pick on the fireworks, where they hope their mistakes won't be noticed." And he played, like some bearded patriarch of the keyboard. "And now, which would you like, a glass of port or sherry? You must learn to use wine, with control, like any other pleasure. Most teetotallers are cowards; they are afraid of themselves, and what the world will think of them. Don't be afraid of life. Sometimes the young dons ask me my advice on lecturing, and I always tell them: 'Before you lecture, brush your hair, and have a glass of sherry.' And now you'll have some cake, of course," and he drew a plum-cake from a cupboard and cut me a huge Thomasian slice. Then he opened for me the treasure-house of his wisdom, bringing out the world and men as he had seen them; a Nestor without conceit and with a humour as broad as the earth. "And now, as to the dons, don't annoy them. I often do; but you mustn't. And if you want to leave to go to London on pleasure, say it's the dentist; I always did. But you can't use him more than once a term." And he rolled on, with quotations from the ancients, a maxim from Aristotle, a tale from Herodotus, and a memory from Rugby, where he had been as a boy soon after Tom Brown and Flashman, about football games "when we played a hundred a-side, and you never saw the ball till you trod on it." "The Rugby game," he would say, "is ruined to-day. The introduction of passing the ball spoilt all the pleasure." Thence we passed on to cricket; he had been an Oxford Blue in the 1860's, and said he hoped to come and see me doing well in the Parks. And an hour and a half had gone like ten minutes.

He came to see me in the Parks in the following summer, and I happened to please the old man with some bowling against his own former County, Middlesex, and he wrote me a letter of praise in his flowing hand with its enormous curved C. I have opened it before me now, and am drawn back into an Oxford Summer Term. It is mid-June, and the trees are in their glory in Parks Road. Eleven in the morning, and I am on my way to the match. Bicycles are carrying men and women, willing, unwilling, studious plodders, brilliant idlers, to lectures, to the Cadena, to the river, to anywhere. A picnic-party emerges into the light with cushions and baskets and gramophones and laughter and bottles of beer. A bent old Grammarian in cap and gown passes into the Radcliffe burdened with books, loving learning even more than the sun.

Another day. The match in the Parks is over unexpectedly early. The College is empty, except for two bicycles. I mount the less battered one; down over Folly Bridge, across the railway, to tennis, some hilarious four, or sterner single. Back to Corpus dinner; there was no better in the summer; with gooseberry-fool ice and gooseberry-fool conversation. Then, I trust, to books. No, to the river, up the Cherwell to Elysian retreats, till the distant boom of Tom warns the sailor that it is time to come home from the sea.

Dr Ferdinand Canning Scott Schiller did not agree with the President's interpretations of Aristotle, nor with any Oxford philosopher. Schiller was a pragmatist. "It works," he would say, "therefore it is true." He lived in rooms looking south towards the Christ Church meadows, across the Fellows' Garden, where he would exercise his wit and his kidneys over strong and inaccurate games of Bowls. He grew lemons in his window-boxes, as an ally in his perpetual battle with indigestion. When the flatulence was gaining the upper hand, he would rise from his armchair and stand on the very tips of his toes, like an illustration from Edward Lear, till the enemy sank back into the depths.

He was a host in the old manner, and gave very satisfying breakfast parties, fried fish, scrambled eggs, bacon and sausage, and Cooper's Oxford Marmalade. He ate abstemiously, but he liked to see others at it. Schiller's charm, besides his generosity, was that he was modern in an old setting, without charlatanry or eccentricity. A former scholar of Balliol, he was not of Oxford only, and used to go to the United States to lecture, and later, to broadcast on social problems. He was a man of vast brain and almost inexhaustible information; he despised the mere specialist, and poked fun, in word and book, at the proudly obscure metaphysician. Intellectually, he measured up to Dr Inge and Bernard Shaw, though lacking Shaw's creative faculty and Inge's literary power. He should have occupied an Oxford Chair of Modern Social Ethics. As a tutor, he was not wholly successful. He suffered fools and idlers with a courteous gladness; but, when an essay had been read to him, he did not seek to improve it on its own lines, but brushed the whole thing aside and substituted his own views. As these were nearly always at variance with Oxford orthodoxy, the pupil became like a ship cut adrift from its slight moorings and tossing about on a sea of indecision and uncertainty. So Schiller was rarely a stepping-stone to a First Class in the School of Greats.

He had a keen sense of the ridiculous, and an almost boyish irreverence for pomp and office. About this time, the Reverend L. R. Farnell, Rector of Exeter College, was going through a stormy passage as Vice-Chancellor of the University. I have no doubt, looking back, that his disciplinary measures were necessary and fitting, but he handled his problems with a certain heavy and harassed solemnity which provoked both irritation and mirth. He had a particular dislike for "advanced thought", as then represented by the October Club, whose members were mainly recruited from Ruskin College. This body had invited Bertrand Russell to come down and address them. In those days, Bertrand Russell was considered to be very advanced indeed. He had not achieved the humdrum respectability of the B.B.C. Brains Trust. So, the Vice-Chancellor laid an interdict upon his address to the progressives of Oxford. This was unwise, and

My father   My mother

The author and brother Bobs, 1911

Above: A.H. Tod (left) and F. Dames-Longworth

Left: Edward Holroyd Pearce, Charterhouse, 1913

Opposite: the author (right) goes out to bat for Charterhouse, 1918

Left: the author

Opposite: Oxford XI, 1922
Standing: C.D. Knott, R.C.
Robertson-Glasgow, B.H. Lyon,
T.B. Raikes, M. Patten. *Sitting:*
R.L. Holdsworth, R.H. Bettington,
G.T.S. Stevens, V.R. Price, L.P.
Hedges, F.H. Barnard

Below: Hallows of Lancashire
scores off the author's bowling,
Oxford, May 1923

Above: Somerset XI v
Hampshire, Portsmouth, 1930.
Standing: Young, J.W. Lee, L.
Hawkins, Wellard, Hunt, P.H.
Mermagen. *Sitting:* R.C.
Robertson-Glasgow, E.F.
Longrigg, R.A. Ingle, C.C.C.
Case, A.G. Marshall

Left: Larwood, A.A. Mailey,
A.E.R. Gilligan, W.M.
Woodfull, Strudwick, W.H.
Ponsford, Hobbs, Tate,
Sutcliffe

Right: Hobbs and Sandham

struck at the ancient privilege of free speech in democratic
countries; moreover, the October Club was a private society,
and reckoned it could entertain private guests without leave
from any authority.

Soon after this episode, the Farnells received through the post
a box of chocolates from anonymous donors. They ate some of
them, and were, so it was reported, violently sick. The matter
became public, even famous; and the chocolates were handed
over to the eminent Oxford scientist, Professor Soddy, for analy-
sis. It was while the mystery was thus poised that Dr Schiller
held one of his Sunday morning breakfast parties. During the
meal, he asked me if I had heard anything new about the Farnell
case, and I was able to tell him that, according to the Saturday
evening paper, Professor Soddy had analysed the chocolates as
"containing some subtle Indian poison". Dr Schiller, who was
drinking black coffee, did what is commonly known as "the nose-
trick", and he rushed over to the fireplace to shake his streaming
beard into the flames.

Once or twice a term Dr Schiller played golf at Cowley with
W. W. How, of Merton College, part-author of the *Standard Com-
mentary on Herodotus*. It was a curious match. Schiller used only
two clubs, an enormous warped iron and a putter. After each
stroke with this iron he waved it round in a circle twice with his
right hand, and could be detected far away by this flashing Exca-
libur. Mr How took a wooden club for any shot above fifty yards,
aiming forty-five degrees to the left to allow for his slice. Late in
life, Dr Schiller married and settled in the United States. Official
Oxford never quite appreciated or understood him. He was
different.

In their first year, the Freshmen were housed in the Corpus
annexe, opposite Merton Chapel, whose turrets rushed wildly
across the clouds. My own rooms, ground floor, formed the
corner of Merton Street and Grove Road, a narrow passage
which was later called Magpie Lane. There must exist, somewhere, a society for changing the names of streets. They meet in
secret, and do their work at night. From my sitting-room windows I could see without being seen; hear, and laugh unheard. I
was on a favourite path towards the Christ Church meadows and
the river Isis beyond. Past me went old ladies in fruitless un-
answered conversation with their dogs; saturnine oarsmen, medi-

tating on correct leg-drive and clean finishes, galley-slaves, cut
off from freedom and the dear light of variety; Provost Phelps
of Oriel, in black straw-hat, talking and talking to the young
dons of his retinue, plucking at his beard, laughing at his own
jokes, and answering his own questions; sightseers, with the taut
aspect and puzzled acquiescence of their kind. Here, I was the
involuntary repository of many secrets, a sedentary Gallup-Poll
of Oxford opinion. Of all the voices, the clearest that returns
to me is an eager and rather pained one saying: "My dear fellow,
there is much to be said for a Platonic friendship, but I do draw
the line at anything more precise."

Our janitor, housekeeper, warden, and friend was P. Bancalari. He joined the Corpus staff in 1899, and now, though he is
past the allotted span of life, his hair is still as black and his wit
as fresh as when he sold me a second-hand kettle with the air of
a connoisseur parting with his last Sèvres vase. He attributes his
perennial youth to a life-time of smoking the blackest and strongest tobacco on the market. "Bancy" had been opening batsman
for Oxfordshire, whence also came Alec Bowell and George
Brown, who passed on into fame and the Hampshire team, and,
long after their retirement, were still referred to by "Bancy"
as "promising boys if they go the right way about it". In a small
and very warm sitting-room sat Mrs Bancalari, comfortably
smiling in black and an armchair. She would sew on buttons.
She chuckled at her husband's jokes, and seemed impervious to
his volcanic tobacco. A kettle tended to be sizzling on the hob.
Very homely and untroubled.

Corpus has a rowing tradition, and regarded rugger, soccer,
and hockey much as scientists regard poetry and painting, the
imbecile, if pardonable, toys of idleness. To me, rowing was like
mathematics; unintelligible, dehumanized, but seemingly necessary to some. Edward Pearce and I had been forewarned, and,
when the College captain and Secretary of Boats, men of otherwise considerable charm, visited us one evening with a little note-
book and a missionary light in the eyes, we were ready with the
answers. Edward, after a dubious bribe of coffee, opened with the
plain gambit that he didn't mean to "go in for rowing", as if it
were some tournament or competition. He supported his objection with ingenious rhetoric and a foretaste of that forensic skill
which is now so familiar to the courts of law. When he ceased, the

secretary said: "I'll put your name down, anyhow." It is the same policy that has caused the vacuum-cleaner to appear in millions of homes. Then it was my turn. Avoiding persuasion, I floored them in the first seconds with a weak heart. I regretted that this should be so, expatiated on the delights that I feared I should be missing, and even contrived to suggest that my thoughts, as I stood in goal on the soccer field, would often be slipping riverwards.

This weak heart, foisted on me by Dr Clarence Haig-Brown at Charterhouse, had done me well in the past. It had enabled me to play cricket, but had prevented me from taking part in O.T.C. route marches, during which, after an hour of light instruction of the under-fifteen platoon in the art of saluting and turning to the right by numbers, I used to eat a few ices at the School Shop, then play rackets with the affable Gilbert Browne and listen to the story of how he had been dethroned from the World's Rackets Championship by one whom he always referred to as "The Parsee". It was not likely that so subtle an instrument as this weak heart would fail me now, and the Slaves of the Oar retired, muttering that they would open the matter again. But they never did. The only Eight that I ever rowed in was that which the Oxford University Cricket Club put on the river in the Hospital Regatta. We were a heavy crew, with four men at thirteen stone plus, including R. H. Bettington and Brocas Burrows, more recently our military attaché at Moscow, who, however, discounted bodily weight by spiritual levity. We had one practice, rowing down to the Sanford Arms near Radley; there Bettington, in dismounting, put his foot through the bottom of the shell. We plugged the hole with yellow soap, and retired to a copious supper, rowing home some two hours later on an evening whose beauty was heightened by an altercation with a lock-keeper, in which legitimacy of birth was much called in question. On the day of the Regatta, we reached, by means of a Bye, the semi-final against the Association Football Eight, who, sensing defeat, rammed us amidships, and we sank with all hands.

The pride of Corpus was Leo Price; and, taking him all in all, he was as real an example of a man as I have known. He was magnificent in physique, shrewd but frank of mind, warm and liberal of heart; and saved from saintliness by a hot partisan

temper which could make him an opponent worth avoiding on
the Rugger or Hockey field. Fate took him, at the zenith of his
powers and task, to where praise means as much or little as
blame, and I can speak of him intimately, as we often spoke together, in those days, when, unconsciously, without sermon or
smugness, he expressed a way of life that was the delight and
admiration of those who knew him nearly.

At games, he had strength, speed, judgement of eye, dexterity
of hand; in these natural gifts I have seen him equalled and even
surpassed; but I never saw an athlete who could apply to a
given need or situation so immediate an exercise of these gifts.
So, at Rugger, he was not easy to place or to follow. For England,
he played in the back row of the scrum, so the printed card said;
but you would see him tackling an opposing wing-threequarter
who had judged himself set fair for the line, or, at need, he would
be found ready for a pass outside his own wing man in attack.
He was master of the unexpected, of the one move not included
in the book of tactics or in the mind of an opponent. Against
Wales, at Twickenham, he scored a try in the first twenty
seconds of play. England kicked off against a slight breeze; Leo
Price, following up, snatched the ball as it came down into the
hands of a Welsh player, swerved, ran a few yards, and dropped
at goal. The ball fell a few yards short of the posts, and, while the
full-back was still wondering what sort of a game this was, Price
collected it on the first bounce, and went over by the right post.

At hockey, he played many times for England at wing or
centre-half, combining skill of stick-work with a robustness
which often made opposing forwards wish that they, like the
goalkeeper, were wearing cricket pads. At snob-cricket, he had
no rival. This game we used to arrange in the little quadrangle,
hardly more than a back-yard, where the bicycles were kept,
and shamelessly borrowed. It was played with old golf balls,
a hockey stick, and a freedom from all care, giving much pleasure
to all but "The Archbishop of York", whose baptismal name was
Brown. He tended the High Table silver in a retired pantry
behind deep extra-cover, whence he would emerge, a second
Agag, with a dainty toast-rack or a few highly polished spoons,
and skirt the extreme limits of play like an old cat picking its way
through broken glass and heated bricks.

Leo Price, then, quite unconsciously, set the tone of the

College. He was our Admirable Crichton. He came from a home which put God and the family first. There are many who start from such a home, but they run into a society which is half-ashamed, half-contemptuous of the Christian way, a society which sometimes goes to Church to murmur lip-service to the Commandments, then admires the adulterer and ostracizes the aitchless. Leo went on as a master to Uppingham, having found time to gain a Second Class in the final School of Mathematics. From Uppingham he went to Christ's Hospital; thence, after a few years, as headmaster to his own School, Bishop's Stortford. How he fared in that office as an administrator, I do not know. I recall from earlier days a certain vagueness in practical matters which might not have appealed to a precise and official mind; but he had a disciplined understanding of youth, and a hopeful sympathy with youth's ambition, which, when he died, must have made many a Stortford boy feel that he had lost a companion from his own number.

In April of 1921 I first saw Westward Ho! golf links, and the dyke by the second hole, wherein, after thirty-seven holes had failed to part them, Abe Mitchell yielded to John Ball in the final of the Amateur Championship of 1912. No other links or course has so fully answered the measure of my expectation. The rough purr of the waves on the pebble ridge, connecting illogical fancy with that other Westward Ho! and the hero Amyas Leigh, the wild invincible splendour of the scene, which even Kipling sought to imply rather than dared to describe, these must stir the dullest heart and touch the hardest boiled of the Anglo-Indian officers cocking a fierce and retired eye from the club-house windows.

We were what is known, often by courtesy, as a reading-party; William Phelps, who was then Dean of Corpus, Leo Price, Walter Dalziel, and myself. From nine to twelve in the morning we pursued academic studies, Phelps, as ever, browsing peacefully in an enormous tome of Greek plays. I have run into many classical scholars, but, of them all, Phelps is the nonpareil. Had he possessed the inclination, or ambition, to publish, his fame would have been European. But he has kept his genius for the few, for his Corpus pupils and a handful of Oxford dons, who value not only his scholarship, but his wit and practical wisdom.

He carries his vast learning with a sort of supine ease. It is a thing of pencils and armchairs and comfortable talk. His temperament is superior to provocation or surprise, and the profoundest errors of prosody or grammar would elicit from him nothing more than: "A little severe, I think." He would transform a *Times* leader into Greek or Latin in the time that a practised debtor would take to compose a letter of regret to his tailor. Next to scholarship, his hobbies were golf and his automobile, and he would sometimes play in College cricket matches. As to batting, he held and expressed the view that no one should score more than thirty in a half-day match. When he had reached that number by moderately orthodox methods, he would give free rein to one or more of his theories, of which the favourite, to him as to us, was that any ball short of a full-pitch could be hooked; but the end would come before the proposition had been fully proved. He smoked pipes all day, beginning in his morning bath, and once, on the cricket field, when the opposing first wicket fell at 19, he drew a pipe from his trouser-pocket at mid-on and continued it without the help of a match.

We played two rounds a day at Westward Ho!, between early lunch and late tea, and sometimes, when we rather fancied some drive or iron-shot beyond our average, Phelps would tell us what Ernest Holderness, formerly of Corpus, had done at that hole when they had played together there some years before. We received these demonstrations with something of the incredulity of youth, which was to be corrected a few months later, when Holderness won the amateur championship, a feat that he repeated three years afterwards.

Sir Ernest Holderness provided a rare example of an amateur week-end golfer, who, for many years, could hold his own in the best professional company. As George Duncan, that keen and somewhat saturnine critic of his own and other people's golf, remarked of Holderness: "He plays his irons the same way that we do." Holderness, though he won both his championships between the Wars, yet belonged by temperament and instinct to the earlier age when games were still kept in their place. At golf, his dress had a slight Edwardian hangover, and his manner, cool but never impolite, implied a protest against vast ignorant crowds, searing publicity, and the indiscriminate use of Christian names. He avoided the easy ways to popularity, and, so far as was

possible, carried the seclusion of private life to the public occasion. He was no more likely to clap his opponent on the back than
he was to top a mashie-shot. Thus, on the course, he did not greet
either the easy match with any natural happiness or the deadly
struggle with any false assumption of hilarity. He went about
both tasks with a grey and purposeful solemnity, and not often
did he go about them in vain. He slew with the coldest and
sharpest of razors.

Holderness was the second amateur golf champion from Corpus, then the smallest in population of the Oxford Colleges; the
first was Horace Hutchinson. Just after the first World War,
came C. J. H. Tolley of University College and R. H. Wethered
of Christ Church, who between them were to win three British
Amateur Championships and, but for a careless backward step,
a British Open Championship as well. For Britain, in the Walker
Cup, they formed a pair which, at its best, may never again be
equalled in power and mutual understanding. Tolley driving
and Wethered playing iron-shots were things still left for golfers
to talk about during the long supremacy of the United States.

It seems but yesterday, to borrow an old man's phrase, that I
walked up and down the streets of Oxford waiting for the evening paper that would tell the issue of that terrific final between
Tolley and the American R. A. Gardner at Muirfield. Tolley
had been three up with seven to go, but, with three to go, the
gallant Gardner had squared. "Toothless Annie", who sold
papers at the corner of King Edward Street, and cared no more
about a golf match than French Grammar, became muddled by
the fuss and the snatching and the pennies on the pavement,
croaking out "One at a time, now, one at a time." But the first
snatcher called it out: "Tolley, at the thirty-seventh." There
was no Radio then to give us the Sports Bulletin down to the
two goals scored by Ballymena or against Distillery, and we
waited till morning to read how our champion, when America
lay stone dead for a three, holed in two from a distance that
varied, according to the whim of the reporter, from fifteen to five
yards. That was in the summer term of 1920. A year later, Roger
Wethered went up to St Andrews for the Open Championship.
After the first two rounds, he was of a mind to leave the golf and
join a cricket tour. He stayed, and, with two rounds of an aggre-
gate of 143, tied with Jock Hutchinson of the United States;

then he lost on the replay. A few days afterwards, while I was knocking about old Cowley, when, doubtless, I should have been un-learning my back-stroke at cricket, I saw Wethered drifting serenely round that appalling course in a single match with an elderly gentleman whose play was not adjustable to any known handicap; which explains Roger Wethered as nothing else could.

I watched the Oxford and Cambridge golf match on the Old Sunningdale course in March of 1920. It was the last to be decided in one day and by singles only. Oxford started favourites on the strength of Tolley and Wethered, who could but win two points between them. Had the match been played on the old and searching system of holes won, not even the futility of the Oxford "tail," and it was a ghastly futility, could have availed to avert victory. Tolley and Wethered were opposed respectively by John Morrison and C. P. Johnstone, both golfer-cricketers of distinction. Morrison, a Falstaffian figure of wit, width, and wisdom, was, moreover, playing on his native heath. In the morning, he held Tolley to the turn, but the great man came home in 33 strokes, and went into lunch 4 up. After that meal, he was irresistible. It was a match of terrific driving, but Tolley was much the straighter, and he won far from home.

Meanwhile, Johnstone was offering a stout fight to Wethered, whose iron play was a sight to see. At the sixth hole, in both morning and afternoon, Johnstone drove far and straight, while Wethered sliced his drive into the heather. But, each time, Wethered played an iron shot bang to the heart of the green. Johnstone never wilted, but Wethered drew inexorably away to win by 7 and 6. In the third match, Willie Hope of Cambridge beat John Beck at the 35th hole. There was never more than a hole or two between them. Hope was a little the longer player, Beck the more artistic. Cambridge's tail wagged vigorously; Oxford's did not. At least one Oxford player finished the course as if he were practising a hockey dribble; to the manifest delight of Mr Bernard Darwin, who has spent so many years in supplicating Oxford strokes into bunkers. Such were the limitations of the Lilliputians. But two giants of the game had entered their course; and, in the twenty-five years since, no Oxford, no Cambridge golfer has measured up to their heroic stature.

IX

DARKER BLUE

I AM glad to be just old enough to have known Oxford when the chief interest of the Heads of Colleges, with a few pleasing and comic exceptions, was still in their Colleges. The undergraduates liked it; in the same way that we like a King who not only opens Parliament, but cares for the people without whom there would be no Parliament to open. There has increased among very Senior members a tendency, possibly caught from their extreme Juniors, to use the University as a resort for short mid-weeks or long week-ends. They wish to be, or thought to be, public men. As Mr Lloyd Osborne so nearly said: a taste for the public service—as opposed to the public houses of their Stuart and Georgian predecessors—not promptly checked, has begun to sap their manhood. There is no passion more debilitating to the mind, unless, perhaps, it be that itch of public speaking which it not infrequently begets.

It is agreeable to recall men to whom Oxford came first, with Cambridge a poor second, and the rest of the world a long way round the corner. Since then, some have glided, not unremembered, from the warm circle of wit and decanters and firescreens; others, seduced by the radio or excited by rumour, have gone a little heretical; but all who could, when the need came, stood in for new and warlike, or for revived and academic, duties. Hostile and inquiring faces could be seen on College roof and battlement, like Trojans on old Priam's wall, peering down under helmets with a strange device. Others, slower of limb, but still swift to divide the mind this way and that, fought out the War with Hitler in chair and office, resolving problems which, after a myriad of essays on Truth and the Perfect State, were as easy as letting the peas roll off a polished knife.

The old learning, the love of a craft for its own sake, of truth not dressed for the party, of service with individualism, is hurrying away from the earth, and will soon be only a footprint.

The genius of Greece and the discipline of Rome limp together, amid fat-gutted jeers and fat-headed slander, into the mud of materialism. The world shakes under the feet of the Dunces. See, they come in pairs to their Dance—Speed and Din, with iron rattle and bloodshot eyes; False Charity, wearing a detachable front and smirkingly paired with Sickly Sentimentality, who dabs at the channels on her raddled cheeks; Honest Ignorance, who has arrived by mistake and clodhops a reluctant measure with hard-faced Learn-it-Quick; Temporary-Hero-Worship, eagerly clasping her Guide to Honours and Decorations and escorted by her wheezy old joy-boy, Mr Tufthunter, the present head of his ancient and, by reflection, illustrious family.

In the first copy of Latin verses that I presented for the inspection of R. W. Livingstone, he fixed, in the first five seconds, on a false gender. It was a healthy shock; rather as if Einstein had complained of a flaw in Italian Long Division of Avoirdupois. From the author of *The Greek Genius* and *A Defence of the Classical Education* I had expected, perhaps even looked forward to, a disquisition on form and style, a fair copy of his own version, and a tactful neglect of any grammatical solecisms in my own search after Beauty and The Eternal; and here he was, telling me in his own peculiar tones of dreamy firmness that a feminine noun-substantive was not to be regarded as masculine, even in verse. It was the same sort of surprise that must have seized the Victorian Bright Young Things, to whom, when they declared that their very souls yearned to be nursing the poor dear Crimean soldiers, Miss Florence Nightingale replied: "The strongest of you will be wanted at the wash-tub."

"Livvers" was, and, as Sir Richard Livingstone President of Corpus Christi College, now remains a practical idealist, the widest awake of dreamers, a scholar and a crusader in scholarship. He is a man who, having found much gold, calls upon the world, by speech and pen and radio, to share the discovery. In twos and threes the proselytes come in, and still he hopes for, summons, demands, the thousands, combining a faith that would have made Garibaldi raise an eyebrow with a labour which reduces all ants to the status of triflers.

In those days he received you, academically, in a room that looked across at Merton College on one side and down upon the bicycle-shed on the other. Somewhere on his desk there was always a glass of water, presuming to be hot, an antidote, he said, to indigestion. In judging work, he had a courteous knack of transferring the onus of opinion to the perpetrator: "Now what would you say of *that* line, Mr Glasgow?" and Mr Glasgow, who had known that line from its struggling, beastly infancy to its shallow, shoddy manhood, would hedge a little, and fidget in his chair, and "smiling, put the question by"; and the tutor would help him out by saying: "Well, *I* should regard it as the offspring of Necessity and the Dictionary."

But if, as happened three or four times a term, he found a line that pleased his fancy, he seized it and shared with you its most unexpected, most uncommon splendour. One such returns to my mind. In English, of course, it was ordinary enough; the sort of line that you may find by the hundredweight in Newdigate Prize poems and on the more untouchable shelves of those who have versifying relatives; something about

O gloomy lands and fast decaying realms!

this I shoved into Latin as:

A, populos tristes et tabescentia regna,

and was soon afterwards, I do not doubt, taking coffee and buns with Edward Pearce in the circular gallery of the Cadena and criticizing the clients on the ground floor. Next morning, Livingstone took this line and tossed it to the skies; or to be less romantic, he pushed the hot water aside and said it was the best line he had been offered that term. I repeated his flattering judgement to Maurice Regan, a Pauline scholar of the year before, and a gay good fellow as well, barring, or rather including, that comical prejudice of the men of Colet's foundation that from no other school doth any true hexameter arise. Regan, breathing heavily through his Effendina cigarette, the famous cult of the hour, admitted the chaste beauty of my six-footed ewe-lamb, but tore the wool clean off the others around it.

That might be enough about classical composition in verse; but the subject, as Franklin Roosevelt used to say, brings up memories. One of them is of Reginald Blaker, crouching over the desk under the House Notice Board at Charterhouse, and trying to force *"tempus in omne"* into the second half of every Pentameter that might conceivably be susceptible of this careworn periphrasis; another is of William Phelps receiving me in that most comfortable of studies in the Corpus tower, pulling at his pipe with backward tilt of the head and the familiar Phelpian look of amusement mingled with resignation, and saying: "What? Tennyson again? That's rather severe, isn't it?" And my answering: "Yes, sir; you gave me Browning, but I couldn't somehow manage it; you see, I have to translate him into English before I can put him into Greek." This by-passing of Browning happened more than once, and Phelps accepted my evasion with benevolent grace, though he once expressed a strong inclination to nausea at my choice of the passage from *Oenone* which runs:

Hath he not sworn his love a thousand times? . . .
Sealed it with kisses, watered it with tears?

I was purporting to pump this melancholy treacle into Greek iambics. The start was easy enough; fatally easy; but when I came to the line:

O death, death, death, thou ever-hanging cloud,

I was seized with a sudden devotion to the literal—something in my Scottish ancestry, perhaps—and wrote:

ὼ θανατ' ὼ θανατ' ὼ θανατ' ἀει μεταρσιον
νεφος συ,

and Phelps, hardly suppressing his inward frenzy, exclaimed: "I don't mind one θανατε, Glasgow, and two might just be borne; but I'll be damned if I can stand a third!"

It was about this time that Walter Lock and I brought off a win in the Problem Page of the Saturday *Westminster Gazette*, which, each week for many years till its sad demise, offered, and awarded, a prize for the best rendering of some English piece into Greek or Latin verse. Those who followed up this little corner became familiar with the initials of such frequent winners as: E.D.S. (E. D. Stone), F.J.K. (F. J. Kittermaster), F.D.L. (F. Dames-Longworth); and then one February morning in 1922 they might, if so disposed, have read that "Sphinx" had won the prize. That, as they say, was us. True, the learned judges had decided that "Sphinx" should share the prize with a gentleman, lady, or syndicate called "Pan"; but Sphinx's view was that Pan, while admittedly exhibiting a certain tortured and Teutonic ingenuity, had not deserved more than a passing, if honourable, mention.

> When shall I once again, O sea, behold
> Eurycome? She comes not; time grows cold.

Those were the opening lines in English. Not bad; not good. And this was the Lock-Glasgow rendering:

> *En, unquam Eurycomen anni, Neptune, reducent*
> *Qui desiderio consenuere meo?*

The hexameter is nothing; a little imitative cleverness, as demanded by the most psittacan and simian of all crafts. But the pentameter. There's glory for you! Worthy of a night of Elysian collaboration between Porson drunk and A. E. Housman sober.

I learnt of our elegiac victory as I stood by the solemn postcards of the vicinity in the shop of Messrs Slatter and Rose, stationers, and I let out, I am nearly ashamed to recall, a howl such as the Dog Cerberus must have let out when all three of his heads were pouched under the invincible arm of Hercules. A don, who was reading a book which, doubtless, disposed of his own standard views on the same subject, turned round with the air of a ghost surprised during meditations on haunting, and just looked at me. Even Mr Slatter—or was it Mr Rose?—who was some thirty years gone in Oxford tolerance, coughed a discreet but apprehensive cough, and altered the position of an all-steel pen. Then I was gone, down the High, on light regardless toe.

To return to Richard Livingstone. When Queen's, Belfast, acquired the status of a University, he went to it as its first Vice-Chancellor; then, on the death of Dr Allen, a man whose charm was always pushing out feelers, Livingstone was elected President of Corpus Christi. He continued, with increasing vigour, to combine academic duties with extra-mural interests, and, when England, in one of its "knowledge is power" moods, decided that pot-hooks and simple addition do not of themselves lead to political triumph and social success, Livingstone's rather tired, very persuasive voice would sometimes flow from the radio to invite the nation not to stop learning when they are fourteen or sixteen, or even twenty-three, but only "after this life's whim". At first, England, that perfect chameleon, took fright at such a notion.

Why, if Johnny goes a-learning instead of an-earning, where's
the money for the Pools, the Pictures, and the Pubs? But Mr
R. A. Butler had his way in Parliament, and routed, with the
sword of commonsense, the ranks of temporal apathy and of
Ecclesiastical crankhood.

The merchants and politicians are apt to feel the pangs of
envy and to affect the emotions of surprise when some learned
fellow leaves the groves of academe and shows them a wrinkle or
two in the House or on 'Change. They extend to him, at first, a
little natural courtesy, a little not un-snobbish interest. But soon
they are reminding us, and him, that brains alone don't make
"a House of Commons man" *et tout le bataclan du tra-la-la.* When
Sir William Beveridge made his great Report, and the World,
the Press, and the insurance companies fell upon it with shouts
or tears, there appeared a photograph of the author-producer,
standing calmly enough in an ivied archway of his home, the
Master's Lodgings, University College, Oxford. Bless my soul!
the man's a don; a professor, as you might say; one of those who
are scheduled to drink old port, think old thoughts, and live
pretty well, on old manuscripts. Well, Beveridge was persuaded
away by his mighty conscience. He left the dreaming spires and
went to "bluidy Berwick", as the defaulters in the King's Own
Scottish Borderers used to call that historic sandwich-boat of a
town. Fine work, Sir William. Oxford will no longer lose her
causes.

But will she keep her characters? By the foot of Pharaoh,
there have been some; men furnished with ability; living, not
always so peaceably, within their habitations; men who pursued knowledge for its own sake in their own way, referable to
no committee, no commission, only to their own unassailable
caprice; men who did just one thing superbly, whether it was
Greek Conjunctions, or claret, or obstruction, or rhododendrons,
or talking; magnificently various, but all partners in the dying
art of damning the world's eyes with or without courtesy.

There was the head of a most ancient College who was invisible, though his existence was never legally questioned. He
had a local habitation from which he was said to walk after dusk
to the pillarbox, and a name, which he presumably subscribed
to the letters to be posted. He was learned, but it is not on record
that he imparted his learning to any living person or embalmed

it in any long-buried book. It was said that he once put in an appearance at dinner in the College Hall; but I don't think so. Such an intention may have tapped at his brain, but at the crisis he funked it, and sent someone else along instead, a butler, or a brother.

At his own house, no visitor was seen to pass through the door. No one said to him, as a desperate guest once said to the whale-bone wife of an American President: "You have a very genteel assemblage here to-night:" for he allowed no assembling, genteel or otherwise. I have heard it told that a young scholar, inflamed by a wager, once rang the door-bell at four in the afternoon and, shooting through the hall into the right room, sustained a mono-logue, without punctuation, for half an hour, standing between the Unknown and the door. Then, in the heat of his oratory, the lad took an involuntary step to the left, and his host, uttering the one word "tea," was past him in a flash. Foot-work.

Across the road from Corpus was the talking Provost of Oriel. He would have talked the Sphinx off its plinth and back again. Dogs turned round, amazed. Gargoyles marvelled from their cornices. The leafy lanes shuddered. Rooks answered back once, then gave it up. I have often asked myself which of the two would have won if he had met Mr Bernard Shaw, who also has a beard. The sound began early, culpably early, when, rein-vigorated by what I am afraid was a cold bath, he drew a couple or so of young dons out for a sharp talk round the Meadows. It began early, and neither rose nor fell, jumping fully armed into an invisible meridian. He was a fairly able man and a most respected figure, with a special knowledge of the vagrancy laws; but few, when the wave of words hit them, swam safely to shore.

In the Corpus boiler-room there lived Mr Chandler, widely known as Jingles, or Swing-Foot the Tyrant. He shared his legal surname with the then Bishop of Bloemfontein, but his habit of deep meditation was considered to be not so much a sign of religion as of an inward presentiment that the boilers were shortly going to burst. Suspicion, and a preference for beer, were the driving forces of the kindly but permanently perplexed Jingles. He fancied that life was always on the verge of taking a liberty with him, and so he wore a mackintosh throughout the year. He was short and round, red-faced and strong, with cheesy curls in places. He was a former sculling champion of the

river Isis, but, when asked for corroborative detail in connection
with his triumph, he either said "which?" or unbuckled a metal-
lic sound locally presumed to be a laugh. Perhaps twice a year
he would be seen on the towpath near the Corpus barge, out-
staring a tree, or speechlessly confiding to the passing river his
private opinion of boilers, boots, and beer. But mostly he guarded
home, the College, proceeding very warily on flat feet, keeping
close against the walls, as if ready, but only just, to trust them.
At each corner of the quadrangle he stopped, raised one arm and
peered under it backwards; then, if satisfied with what he saw,
he took the corner by pivoting on the near foot and swinging the
outer one round in a slow arc. Sometimes his face only would
re-appear, like a luminous cat, taking final soundings.

Of the College servants, Chandler was the most mysterious
and the least intelligent. Perhaps the most entertaining, and
certainly the laziest, was Joe Coburn, who was for many years
"Scout" to the stair-case on the middle right of the quadrangle.
Joe never fell down stairs, but often up them, and, as the coffee
and porridge oozed past his boots, he always cursed the crockery
and its owner. A good Irishman, he despised, even resented, the
habit of drinking coffee or tea in the evening, and when, in the
cold, and for him remorseful, morning, he pecked away at the
debris of some teetotal soirée, he could be heard muttering,
"Another . . . mothers' meeting." Mauve and aquiline of face,
paternal in manner, generous of heart, he knew where his
duties ended, viz: at about the same point where they began;
and once, when a keen young scholar, who is now a pillar of the
Treasury, showed him a re-union of spiders near the ceiling,
Joe said: "Mr Hale, sorr, I don't reckon to deal with the likes
of they." In a long and interesting career Coburn gave and received notice at intervals of six months. This regularity was his
one concession to the Anglo-Saxon temperament.

Another "Scout" was The Corpse, so called because he appeared to have died young without admitting it. He stepped
around with grey side-whiskers and stygian gait, nor resting,
nor hasting, nor smiling, nor frowning, but doubtless pondering
on the problems of corporal survival. Judged, as he had no right
to be, by mortal years, The Corpse was younger than Walter
Salis, who was neat, short, bearded, as the social gossipers would
say. Into Salis's care seemed to pass, as if by kind arrangement

between earth and heaven, each occasional and envied clown who liked to forget the bogey of the academic curriculum through playing the ukulele, cards, and the fool, who seized and drained the beaded draught before life, prim waitress, should hand him her inexorable cup of cocoa across the dirty counter.

At the Corpus gate, guarding and, at need, controlling us all, sat the only Mr Wilsdon; tactful, humorous, and firm. He knew Oxford as Mr Samuel Weller knew London. For sheer memory, he was a Lord Macaulay; not only for faces, which is the habit of his kind, but for facts both bald and curious. One Saturday, when I fancied I needed the services of a stenographer and her office was closed, I found that Wilsdon knew not only her private address but her initials and her mother's maiden name. "It's five years now," he said, "since I saw them, but I daresay they live there still." They did; and so I was enabled to entertain the Pelican Essay Club with my original paper on John Keats, filched from the researches of Sidney Colvin.

On the Corpus gate might be found, and, by those who used microscopes, successfully deciphered, a notice signed G.B.G., suggesting that the Ancient History essay that week for those men who were reading in their last year for the School of Literae Humaniores was "Some Aspects of the Roman Proconsular System in the Second Century A.D. with special regard to Fiscal Problems."

Dr Grundy's pupils were regarded by him in three divisions: very able men, able men, and men. It would be idle to expect that this century will produce another G. B. Grundy. He was a very able man. He must have been, to have educated himself and to have reached Oxford, in the late 'eighties, by educating candidates for the Army in subjects which he learnt in order to teach, as he went along.

When Edward Pearce (an able man; a very able man, when he wanted) and I (a man) first entered his tuition, Dr Grundy was turned sixty and the best croquet player in Oxford. His handicap was $-1\frac{1}{2}$. There were one or two ladies in the Norham Garden district who fancied they could give him a game, but they couldn't, as a fact. There were some who criticized the champion's style on the lawn, saying that he held his mallet too low for elegance.

Now Dr Schiller's lectures on philosophy were full of sub-

jective humour. There was one fat negro who carried his umbrella into the class and used to roll about in his chair with
laughter whenever Schiller mentioned "the Absolute". But Dr
Grundy's pupils discovered in his lectures on Ancient History a
humour that was hidden from their author. These disquisitions
were full of sound learning, but their diction was peculiar to
Grundy alone. His sentences were rich with a riot of conjunctions, particles, and enclitics—"Very well now, with regard to
the Battle of Salamis, I may say that, with regard to it, very well."
Such sallies as this evoked a wild delight in some of his more
faithful disciples, who took them down; in the case of Pearce,
with tears of joy, whose blots can still be found on note-books a
quarter of a century old. Once in a while, the routine of a Grundy
lecture would be varied, picked out, by a purple passage. For
these the orator usually closed his eyes: "Dynasties falling . . .
Empires crashing . . . Assyria . . . Babylon . . . Persia . . . Greece
. . . Rome . . . and then there followed a period of intense *gloom*
. . . in fact . . . as a fact . . . I might almost say it was *dark*."

Those of us who used to read his books, especially *The Great
Persian War*, flattered their author by introducing into their own
essays parodies of the Grundeian style. It was Jack Lindsay,
afterwards Treasury Counsel, who found early practice at
drafting in such sentences as: "In the light of the absence of
evidence as to the nature of the character of the attitude taken
up by the Senate towards the question, one can only hazard, with
a reasonable degree of certainty, that it was one characteristic
of that august but comparatively unassailable body."

Dr Grundy was, and still is, one of the most celebrated of to-
pographers; and what he told us about his surveys in classical
lands combined with the invention of his hearers provided a
most attractive saga. It was known how he ran, in full armour,
over the course reputed to have been covered by the Athenian
hoplites in their charge at Marathon. Dr Grundy, on this evidence, decided that the Greek word used by the historian
Herodotus could not, as popularly supposed, mean "at the full
run" but, rather, "at a lively trot". Again, he, and as some aver-
red, his wife and two more relatives, floated across the Bay of
Sphacteria on pneumatic goat-skins, to prove that this form of
marine locomotion was possible, as reported by Thucydides, to
the Athenians during their escape from Pylos in the Peloponne-

sian War. Some added that the party were mistaken for a school
of porpoises; others, that they were fired upon by a Montene-
gran cruiser.

His interest in undergraduate sport was extensive and benevolent. He had played golf for Oxford against Cambridge in
1890 and 1891, but it was the Rugby game that most held his
affection. He loved to revive old games in which he had appeared
for Blackheath, when, as he said, that Club was in its infancy.
Especially popular to his listeners was a certain very violent
match between Blackheath and Bradford, played in Yorkshire.
"I," he would say, "was the lightest man on the field, at 12
stone 7 lbs. They tried the rough game on us. That was a mistake;
oh, yes, a very grave mistake. At half-time they had eleven men
left on the field; we had thirteen. The referee stopped the game
half way through the second half. (He pronounced the "a" in
"half" as in "hat".) We were leading. Most of their fellows had
to be taken home in cabs; four-wheelers, I mean."

He was a regular spectator at College rugger cup-ties. I recall
his presence on the Lincoln College ground. Before the match
started, he walked up and down the touch-line, in a green shirt
and grey spats, soliloquizing on past triumphs of the Black-
heathens; then, turning to Pearce, who had been taking a little
kicking practice, he said: "Do you know, Mr Purse, I believe
that, if I were to try a drop-kick now, I should drop-kick my leg
half off." Mr Purse agreed that something of this kind might
happen. Then, shading his eyes with his hand, Dr Grundy said:
"Mr Purse, do you see that row of trees over there on the horizon?" Pearce said he did not. "No," answered Dr Grundy, "for
the very good reason that I had them cut down for timber
during the War." No one but Grundy would have used this
method of drawing attention to his activities.

Seven or eight years after I had left Corpus, I was up in Oxford
for some cricket match, and, as our side was to bat that morning
and I was number ten or eleven on the list, I took time off to go
round to Corpus and listen, extra-murally, to a few minutes of a
Grundy lecture, whose hour I had noted in the current Faculty
list of lectures. It was Roman History, some aspects with regard
to the duties of the Praetors. I leant against the wall, close to an
open window, and drank in the cultural entertainment, recall-
ing the face of "Mr Purse", once purple with suppressed emo-

tion, and the tears of joy that had dropped on his note-book. How many University tutors have had the power to draw their old pupils back like magnetized iron, to the scenes and sounds of youthful learning?

A tall old man with broad-brimmed hat and a long, light step would sometimes stride into the College; Robert Bridges, greatest of Corpus graduates. He and President Case were old friends and arguers, and the President told us: "I submitted a poem of mine to the Laureate and he told me it wasn't poetry, but a pretty piece of versifying." Bridges read a Paper to us on "Free Verse", which he sliced into fine shreds. He was then in the grip of experiments with classical metre adapted to English poetry. He was almost alone in thinking them successful. But he did not allow them to grow from a hobby to an obsession. He was even then working on his *Testament of Beauty*.

At the end of his Paper on Free Verse, he quoted to us his lyric poem "Spirits":

> Angel spirits of sleep,
> White-robed with silver hair,
> In your meadows fair,
> Where the willows weep,
> And the sad moonbeam
> On the gliding stream
> Writes her scatter'd dream.

He explained to us the pattern of its prosody, and said: "In a few years' time, that will be a museum piece. Poetry, as we have known it, will soon be dead; and you will be able to say to us poets:

> Know ye how men say
> That ye haunt no more
> Isle and grassy shore
> With your moonlit play;
> That ye dance not here,
> White-robed spirits of sleep,
> All the summer night
> Threading dances light?"

X

MOSTLY CRICKET

I HAVE never regarded cricket as a branch of religion. I have met, and somehow survived, many of its blindest worshippers. I have staggered, pale and woozly, from the company of those who reject the two-eyed stance as Plymouth Brethren reject all forms of pleasure except money-making. I have never believed that cricket can hold Empires together, or that cricketers chosen to represent their country in distant parts should be told, year after year, that they are Ambassadors. If they are, I can think of some damned odd ones.

The air of holy pomp started from the main temple at Lord's, and it breathed over the Press like a miasma. "*Procul, O Procul Este, Profani!*" We are not as other men. Sometimes I look back at reports of games in which I took part, and I have thought: "And are these arid periphrases, these formal droolings, these desiccated shibboleths really supposed to represent what was done and how it was done? What has become of that earthy striving, that comic, tragic thing which was our match of cricket?"

University cricket is often written off as a rather advanced schoolboy affair; but the four matches in which I played for Oxford against Cambridge, between 1920 and 1923, produced eight England cricketers, of whom four, A. E. R. Gilligan, A. P. F. Chapman, D. R. Jardine, and G. O. Allen, captained England in Australia. The other four were G. E. C. Wood, J. C. W. MacBryan, G. T. S. Stevens, and C. S. Marriott. Besides these, J. L. Bryan, of Cambridge, was chosen as a member of Gilligan's team in Australia, but was never called on for a Test, and R. H. Bettington, of Oxford, while still an undergraduate, was little behind his fellow-Australian, Arthur Mailey, in skill as a leg-break bowler. Nor will false modesty or fear of "bad form, old chap" prevent me from saying that Clem Gibson and Norman Partridge from Cambridge, and myself, were all, at various times, good enough as bowlers to have played for England without being laughed at. Anyhow, I have seen several worse than us getting a few wickets in Anglo-Australian matches.

My brother Bobs, who had gone to work in a bank in Toronto, wrote to me in spring of 1920 saying, "I suppose you ought to get your cricket Blue," and I know I did so suppose. It came on a June evening, in a letter from Frank Gilligan, just as we gathered in the Corpus quad for dinner. Nothing compares with early triumphs. Young success kicks like a mule with a squib under its tail. The years come when friends are not so ready or able to share delight and grief.

Edward Pearce and I went to the pictures that night, in that house where the little manager used to stand at the back of the stalls with imitation diamond-studs in his shirt-front, waiting to restore order, which was almost nightly lost. During the rest of that term, and in the following winter, I liked to walk rather slowly along the High and imagine that other pedestrians were saying: "Look, that's Robertson-Glasgow, the cricket Blue." Alfred, Lord Tennyson, they tell us, also liked to be recognized in public. An innocent infatuation. A gift of divination would have diluted my vanity; but I was not yet to know that in four matches against Cambridge I would get only two wickets in 100 overs, for 243 runs. Nor did a batting average of 36 put things right. Few, except myself, cared whether I made runs or not, and, early in that summer of 1920, Frank Gilligan drew me aside in his grave and earnest manner and said: "I'm not going to let you make runs. You're not strong enough to bat and bowl." I was pained to think I looked quite so delicate. Besides, I had fancied myself as a batsman.

At the end of April came the Freshmen's match, if match be the word for that trial in which all hope to catch the judge's eye, and none cares which side wins. In their first innings, D. R. Jardine carried his bat for 60. This was the third season in which I had met Jardine. In each of the previous summers I had managed to take his wicket in the Charterhouse v. Winchester match. But in this first innings at Oxford, he made no shadow of a mistake. I had 5 wickets for 23 in 19 overs, mostly with in-swingers.

Douglas Jardine, at nineteen years, was the completest young batsman I have seen, both in method and temperament. It was said that while he was still a preparatory schoolboy, at Horris

Hill, he had politely but firmly corrected his master on a point of technique and supported his view by a quotation from C. B. Fry's *Batsmanship*. Tall and well-proportioned, he has ever been the perfect example of the orthodox English style. His off-driving, which in test matches against Australia he was apt to deny himself, was then free and strong, and the bowler who attacked his leg-stump was but wasting himself in vanity. But where Jardine excelled was in his back-stroke. It was professional, near to perfect.

I bowled Jardine for 18 in the second innings, which was abbreviated by the leg-breaks and googlies of R. H. Bettington. Reg. Bettington, tall, dark of complexion, and of immense power, had come to Oxford with his brother Jack from Paramatta, New South Wales. Both bowled spinners; Jack at a brisk medium to fast, Reg. at normal leg-breaker's pace. When Jack could pitch them, he was almost unplayable; but he was erratic. Both were free-driving batsmen. Both were tough Rugger forwards, but it was Reg. who got the Blue, playing against Cambridge in two years out of his four, largely on the strength of his left-footed place-kicking. Jack was the more finished golfer, Reg. the more terrific hitter. Here again it was Reg. who played against Cambridge. So Jack, who might so easily have played for Oxford at all three games, landed no Blue at all. He wore his disappointment invisibly. He fell gravely ill not long after returning as a civil engineer to Australia. Then he seemed to recover, but death won. He was as fine a fellow as you could want.

Reg. Bettington made the ball buzz like a top, and at the moment of delivery there was a sharp snapping sound. There was another and even sharper snapping sound when he asked for l.b.w. or a catch at the wicket. A Bettington appeal brought all Sydney to the Oxford Parks. Six feet and three inches in height, he took a longish run and bowled with a looping trajectory; not flat, like so many of his sort. I had a fine view of his bowling from short slip. His performance was brilliant that summer. Length, flight, spin, and persistence; he had them all; also a faster ball of vicious suddenness. Years later, when his skill at the leg-break had declined, I saw him bowl a fellow-spinner, Richard Tyldesley, with this fast one at Lord's. Poor Dick; he had disentangled the bat-handle from his ample circumference, and stood at the ready, blade in air; but, when he brought it down, the bails had flown.

Greville Stevens bowled leg-breaks and googlies nearly as well as Bettington, and was a distinctly more scientific batsman. Stevens arrived at Oxford with cricket honours already thick upon him. At University College School he had made 466 not out in a House-match. For Middlesex, he had taken 21 wickets at moderate cost in the 1919 County Championship. To crown all, he had played for the Gentlemen against Players at Lord's. As Lionel Hedges said to him: "Considering these set-backs, you're not a bad fellow!"

Greville had wit and a salty tongue, which some mistook for conceit. When he had walked out to the field for Oxford in his first match, he said to our captain, Gilligan: "And shall I field in the place that I've made famous?" That was backward point, where he was a fine catcher. "Yes," said Gilligan, "in the deep at both ends." Myself, I enjoyed his playful remarks; and I recall with delight Greville's comment on arriving in the dressing-room at Lord's for the Gentlemen v. Players in 1924; looking round at some of his fellow-cricketers, he said: "This match isn't what it used to be, and I'm rather tired of it." Not bad, for twenty-three years old.

Tall and fair, with a face that always made the schoolgirls ask for his autograph, he was yet not of athletic build. His run-up to the wicket was rather prancing and awkward, as if he were glad he hadn't to run any further, which, I think, he was; but he delivered the ball with a high arm, and, unlike so many of his kind, he never lost the potency of his leg-break. In the Freshmen's match, he failed as a batsman. I had him caught in his first innings. He had me bowled in my second. He took four wickets in each innings, twice defeating one H. P. Marshall, from Haileybury, who later was to become known to millions as Howard Marshall, broadcaster. On leaving Oxford, Greville Stevens soon deserted serious cricket for business, becoming a prosperous and astute stock-broker. But he played for England, and bowled C. G. Macartney in that memorable Oval match of 1926 when the tide at last turned against Australia, and Harold Larwood became famous, and Wilfred Rhodes ended his England cricket in clouds of glory.

From Tonbridge, with a name as batsman and cover-point,

came Lionel Hedges, bubbling with life and mimicry. Like Stevens, he had been early blooded, having scored 28 and 43 at Canterbury for Kent against Jack Gregory and the Australian Imperial Forces a few days after leaving school. Lionel was at Trinity, which fitted him like a glove. No pleasanter community is to be found in Oxford. Short and strong, he was the best hooker in the side, and at cover-point he was swift to cut off that square single which maddens a bowler. He favoured enormous collars to his cricket shirt and a knotted silk scarf. He was soon into his stride with 86 against Middlesex and 101 not out against Essex. But his nervous temperament was unsatisfied. "If they don't give me my Blue now," he said to me, "I'll make a string of noughts." He didn't. He played Rugby for the University, at stand-off half, on several occasions, but never against Cambridge. Lionel was full of parlour-tricks, including a ride up and down on a fictional hotel-lift. At the end of the first day's play of the Cambridge match in 1922, he bought a newsvendor's pitch and papers in Trafalgar Square and quickly sold out on "Oxford's deplorable plight". Later, he went as a master to Cheltenham, and played some fine innings for Gloucestershire. But he died cruelly early, in 1934, from a virulent form of influenza.

We lost the first match, against Warwickshire. It was cold and wet. I took a stinging catch from that craggy old warrior Charlesworth full on the breast-bone, whence it fell to the grass, at mid-off. I took no wickets, but a very long run-up to the crease. Stevens had 5 for 35 in the first innings, Bettington 5 for 48 in the second. Willie Quaife, smallest and correctest of great batsmen, batted a very long time for not so very many, and Jardine was bowled by F. S. G. Calthorpe for 0 in the first innings. A bleak start. But I was asked again for the next match, against Middlesex.

"Plum" Warner was in his last season of captaincy, which was soon to be crowned by that tremendous match at Lord's against Surrey, and the winning of the championship. Warner had taken the England team which beat Australia over there in 1911-12 and whose deeds I had rushed to read each morning at school. And here he was in the flesh, bald as an ostrich-egg under his Harlequin cap, slight, small-boned, pale of face, and with nothing but cricket in his conversation.

In my first innings I was bowled by the foxy J. W. Hearne, and
I still had the pride to be very annoyed about it. Then, near
the end of the first innings, I took my first wicket in first-class
cricket, Captain J. M. S. Love for o. I also had the towering
Jack Durston stumped trying some complicated form of attack.
After being led by 24 on the first innings, we ran up 349 for 8
declared. We won, by 139 runs; but that was nothing to me compared with bowling Hendren when he was well set at 50. It was
a snifter, though I say it, bending in very late from the off. I
walked on air, and would certainly have missed any catch that
had come in my way.

We followed this victory by beating Essex by 239 runs. The
match was doubly notable; first, because Douglas Jardine, in a
spell of seven overs and 3 balls took 6 for 6, including the mighty
P. Perrin, bowled for o. Douglas, with a pensive and halting run,
bowled what purported to be slow leg-breaks. Secondly, I
acquired a nickname which has stuck ever since. Charlie
McGahey and A. C. Russell had put on some 50 runs at the start
of their second innings when I bowled McGahey with a full-
pitcher which he later referred to as a yorker. In the bowels of
the pavilion, Johnny Douglas, the Essex captain, asked him how
he was out, and McGahey answered: "I was bowled by an old
—— I thought was dead two thousand years ago, called Robinson
Crusoe."

I came to know Johnny Douglas well, and I must have stuck
in his mind somewhat, because, when he invited me to stay in
his flat at Hampstead later in the summer, I left the bath-tap
running while having a drink, and an old lady from the flat
below came hustling up the stairs to say that her Persian carpet
was ruined and what about it. The incomparable John captained
England twelve times against Australia, and after winning four
victories to one in 1911-12 he lost all five in a row in 1920-21.
You knew, and could often hear, what he was thinking on the
field. It was battle, and nothing but, when he walked out, a
gladiator, from the wicket gate, thick black hair shining and
plastered down, rubbing the new ball on his strong forearm,
frowning at some imaginary flaw in its make-up; or else went
forth to bat, more grimly yet—for his batting was acquired and
his bowling was natural—with strong slow gait, feet outwards,
tugging his batting gloves on with his teeth, ready for a week,

for a lifetime of that fight which was his cricket, and damn the bowlers and blast the crowd. He won the World Amateur Middleweight Boxing Championship in a fight with "Snowy" Baker that has seldom been equalled. At the age of forty-eight, in 1930, he was drowned. He had gone below deck to save his father, and the ship, nearly severed by a collision, sank at about midnight in a few minutes.

On Wednesday, 2 June, 1920, I first met John Daniell, and next day he asked me to play a few matches for Somerset. This was an unorthodox request, as I had no qualification for Somerset, having been born in Edinburgh and living wherever the family, or parts of it, happened to be. Technically, I was qualified for Scotland, but the Scottish selectors have always been rather stuffy about Anglo-Scots, and I was never asked to play for the land of my birth. Not that it matters.

My connection with Somerset was our cousins, the Foxcroft family, of Hinton Charterhouse, of whom Charlie was Member of Parliament for Bath and a High Tory of the utmost spirit and pugnacity. But John Daniell reckoned that this would be good enough. At least I was in the position that no other County could claim me, even supposing they wanted my services. Herein was the mistake made by my friend Leonard Crawley. Being qualified for Durham, he went off to play for Worcestershire, and Durham objected. This little difference led, finally, to a quarrel between George, Lord Harris, Hon. Treasurer to M.C.C., and Lord Deerhurst, the High Panjandrum of Worcestershire. They met, it was reported, on the Pavilion steps at Lord's, and Lord Deerhurst swept off his grey top-hat and offered Lord Harris a short speech of congratulation on his alleged mismanagement of cricket. Stormy tea-cups long ago.

Back to the Oxford Parks. John Daniell had the idea that inswing bowling was muck and, going in first with John Cornish White, he proceeded to the proof of his point, swatting my bowling with scowling ferocity high to the leg-side. At length he hit one even harder than the rest, but rather lower, and Greville Stevens, defending his hopes of posterity, caught it at close square-leg. For us, Ronnie Holdsworth, a batsman of charm and power and a man of much absence of mind, scored 73. In the Somerset second innings Leonard Braund made 67 with his own inimitable and courtly grace, and I took 5 wickets for 20 runs. Needing only 116 to win, we were at first scattered by some grand fast-medium bowling on the part of Philip Foy, a civil engineer on leave from the Argentine. Stevens, with 30 not out, batted us to narrow victory. Soon, after losing to the Army with what amounted to only an "A" team, we started our tour, against Sussex at Brighton. There, I found time to visit the spot outside Sopers', where the elderly citizen had shouted "damn the boy" when Bobs pushed me on to his patent-leather toes; and I had a good stare at the cinema in West Street where we used to see the programme round twice, then stagger, half-blind, into the sunlight.

We beat Sussex by 8 runs. Throughout, it was the most even game I have ever played in; Oxford 231 and 214, Sussex 221 and 216. Maurice Tate was the man of the match. Batting at number three, he made 90 and 35, and in our two innings he took 11 wickets for 90 runs. He still bowled at a bare medium pace, and three more years were to pass before, at the age of twenty-eight, he became one of the greatest fast-medium bowlers of all time. He scored runs at high speed, hitting, firm-footed, anything a little over a length, and not minding much about the text-books. But in defence he had a very correct back-stroke.

Greville Stevens and I took all the Sussex wickets except one, and I was much elevated in spirit at bowling their opener, Ted Bowley, in both innings. The other wicket fell to Geoffrey Greig, of Westminster, son of the Bishop of Guildford. I recall his father coming for a Confirmation at my first school, and the excitement of the boys when they saw him adjusting the two pieces of his pastoral staff like a billiard-cue. A. F. Bickmore, from Clifton, scored 59 for us in the first innings. He was a tall and stylish batsman with great power of stroke, and a fine fielder at short-leg, who favoured a large sun-hat. Later in the season he made 104 not out for Kent against Essex. In our second innings, Bickmore's partner, C. H. L. Skeet, made 66. He was a pains-taking solid batsman and one of the greatest fielders I ever saw; swift of foot, and with a throw that would have satisfied Sydney. At the end of August he played for Middlesex in the famous match at Lord's, against Surrey, which decided the Championship, and with Harry Lee put up 208 for the first wicket in Middlesex's second innings. Skeet made 106, Lee 108.

From Brighton we went to the Oval, where Reg. Bettington took 13 wickets for 128 runs on a plumb pitch, having Jack Hobbs caught, when well set, at short-leg with a most erosive top-spinner. Skeet made a wonderful catch at cover-point to dismiss Frank Naumann, whose bowling had beaten Cambridge at Lord's the year before. In our first innings, I was top scorer with 48, at number ten. I was not promoted. We left them 313 to win. With the fourth ball of my first over, from the House of Commons end, I had Jack Hobbs caught at mid-off for o. I thought it was a bump-ball, and was staggered to see him walking out. It was my only wicket in the match, but I didn't mind that. I could live on my one wicket for weeks. H. D. G. Leveson Gower, emerging at the age of forty-seven to captain Surrey, made 54 in their first innings, and saved them in their second with a stubborn 17. He had little power of stroke, but a great heart for the battle. Harrison, a dour and silent cricketer, made 70 not out. F. Parris was one of the umpires in this match. He had a large and bristly moustache which was apt to catch the eye of Tom Webster, the cartoonist.

So we had beaten Middlesex, Essex, Sussex, and almost beaten Surrey. Our pride was squashed by M.C.C. at Lord's. J. W. Hearne and Aubrey Faulkner, two of the great all-rounders of cricket, diddled us out twice. Geoffrey Foster made 143 in the most perfect Fosterian manner, and in him Bettington for once met his master. Patsy Hendren scored 160; and, for the second time in our season, we had to call on Douglas Jardine as bowler. He did not fail. The Press told us we were not so good after all. We took little notice, and sallied forth to the delights of Eastbourne.

Here, each summer Leveson Gower opposed his team to Oxford and Cambridge; a final try-out. Most of the University cricketers were by now safe for Lord's and could indulge any hitherto repressed inclination towards social delights, but there were always a few who knew that this was their last chance to rise and shine on the field, and they, poor fellows, could be observed masking their anxiety with a sickly show of abandon, refusing a liqueur-brandy, or drawing the captain's attention to the fact that they were now going to bed.

"Shrimp" Leveson Gower knew how to handle these entertainments. He had an unrivalled touch with mayors and notables

whom he treated with wine and light conversation in his mar-
quee. He buzzed around like a benign little bee, introducing
people whom he had never seen before to others whom he would
never see again, and, when he felt like a change, he would excuse
himself abruptly with the remark: "Well, I must go and send
off a couple of wires now." Our headquarters was the Grand
Hotel, where Mr Gabb presided over the dining-room, like an
Archbishop of Canterbury undergoing a bout of head-waiting
for a bet. After dinner, in the lounge, the old ladies spread themselves to listen to the music, and it was here that Gerry Weigall,
while demonstrating a late cut with a light walking-stick,
knocked a Benedictine into some dowager's lap. We won the
cricket match through a titanic innings by Bettington, who
scored 101 not out in an hour and kept chipping pieces off the
wall at the sea end.

The match against Cambridge was a sorry farce. It began
with a brisk argument between the captains on the one side and
the M.C.C. Committee on the other about the desirable time
of starting. Rain continuing to pour down for two days, this
diversion soon lost its force. We started an indoor match of our
own in the Oxford dressing-room, and strong protests were sent
up from the Reading-room below. These were disregarded. On
the third day, after lunch, Jardine and Bickmore opened the
innings for Oxford on a wet and weary pitch. Bickmore batted
finely for 66, and C. S. Marriott bowled with wonderful accuracy
for Cambridge. Thursday was granted as an extra day, and the
most interesting sight in that morning's play was the effect of
the Cambridge Hawks Ball on the batting of Bettington. I
bowled Hubert Ashton with a slowish long-hop which just
reached the bottom of the stumps on the first bounce, and a
brisk 35 not out by A. E. R. Gilligan, supported by an eccentric
3 not out by the last batsman, Marriott, brought the Cambridge
total to 161 for 9; 32 runs behind ours.

So the argument on supremacy was never settled, and continued to be debated off the field for many months. I still think
we should have won. Be that as it may, they were two of the best
sides that have represented Oxford and Cambridge, and, as I
have remarked earlier, but have no shame for repeating, several
cricketers from the two teams later played for England.

I played a walking-on part in my first match for Somerset,

against Hampshire at Taunton, bowling third change with a mottled ball against that monumental left-hander, Philip Mead. In the second innings he made 176 not out. The Hampshire captain, L. H. (now Lord) Tennyson, and his valet-wicketkeeper, Walter Livesey, had three o's between them in four innings, the proportion being two to the master and one to the man. Tennyson was caught off Jack White each time. Each year he swore that he would hit Jack for six at Taunton, but the ground is just that little bigger than it looks, and down she used to come into the deep-fielder's hands.

Tennyson missed the poetry of his Laureate grandfather but inherited the constitution and the plain private speech. No stronger or bolder player of the forward stroke was seen in his day. He received the fast bowlers as the oak receives the storm; and, when he fell to them, he went down with no grace or compliancy, but with a sounding, defiant crash. In the next summer, 1921, he fixed his name for ever among storied cricketers, showing his fading companions how to face Gregory and McDonald and, one-handed, smacking them for 63 and 36 in the third Test at Leeds. In all ways of cricket and the world he was and is the perfect English Gascon, a gourmet of the whole feast of life which, for him, has been post-dated by a century and a half. He was cut out for the Regency. Lionel should have been the ancestor; Alfred the descendant.

And so to the return match with Hampshire, at Bournemouth, which was under the dyarchy of bath-chairs and Dan Godfrey. I spent the evening before it exploring with Jack MacBryan. I wonder how many of those who chance to see his name in cricket scores remember what a great player Jack MacB. was? In 1920, he struggled to a Blue at Cambridge. Four years later, he played as opening batsman for England against South Africa, being chosen from a field of openers that included Jack Hobbs, Herbert Sutcliffe, George Gunn, Jack (A.C.) Russell, Andrew Sandham, and Charles Hallows, all of them rightaway professional topsawyers. MacBryan had been a Prisoner of War with the Germans during much of the Kaiser's war, and had been awarded a spell of solitary confinement for using a soi-disant pudding as a Rugger ball.

That evening, Jack was in one of those moods of *en-tout-cas* preparedness in which a man tends to laugh at the morrow and criticize other people's hats. Soon after leaving the hotel, we were nearly run over by a car which, Jack remarked, was probably in the pay of the Hampshire Committee. At the next corner, the same thing happened. Jack MacB. shouted one of those terms calculated to cause all but the more experienced London taxi-drivers to draw up within a few lengths. There followed an altercation with the charioteer, whose fondness for alcohol was now manifest. Jack drew off his coat, but there the matter rested. As the driver receded, taking what revenge he could out of his gears, Jack turned to me and said: "Good. Now I'll make a hundred." And he did.

So did John Daniell; a solid, wearing-down innings, at which he excelled. Sometimes he had fits of thinking he was Jessop, and would be comfortably caught at long-leg. And when he holed out, he was apt to ask why "that ruddy captain can't keep his fielders where he put 'em."

We won that match; and I took 5 Hampshire wickets in their first innings, using the inswerve; and John Daniell told me that no batsman worth a sausage ever got out to inswervers, overlooking, in his disciplinary zeal, his own fate at Oxford two months earlier. Young bowler, don't be put off by the wisdom of the elders! Whichever way you bowl, they'll tell you of a better way. You and you alone will know whether you've bowled like a king or a cow. And, in cricket, the bowlers are the Lords and the batsmen are the Commoners; and you'll find that, as in politics, it's not the Lords who get the Press.

The great Len Braund was then in his last season but one for Somerset. It was twenty years since he had been the greatest all-round cricketer in the world, classic batsman, a destroyer with his leg-breaks, and a slip-fielder who could pick 'em off his toes while discussing the Derby with the wicketkeeper. He was, and is, the wisest judge of cricket I know. He could tell you, as no other, just what to try, against whom, and when. By 1920 he had stopped bowling, except a casual spinner between the fall of wickets, and, for batting, he preferred high noon to the shades of evening. At slip, he was catching the snorters. The easy ones he was apt to leave for the grass.

Now he has passed the three-score-and-ten, but his heart is still seventeen; and he treats his artificial legs as interesting interlopers. He told me how, as he lay in hospital soon after an amputation, he had what he referred to as a natural call, but found the ward temporarily nurse-less. "So," he said, "I got up, got there, and got back. But, as I was doing the last hop or so, the nurse came in, and said: 'Mr Braund, what on earth do you think you're trying to do?' And I couldn't help thinking of the time Mr Daniell said the same thing to me when I floored one in the slips. Only he didn't say 'on earth'."

H. C. McDonell, who bowled slowish tempters, was in that Hampshire side. He fielded to his own bowling like a red-hot jack-in-the-box, in the attitude of a man trying to catch butter-flies in both hands at once. He broke his finger catching-and-bowling Frank Woolley in the first County match I ever saw, at Canterbury, when C. B. Fry made a hundred in each innings and wore a huge white sun-hat. How easy it is to play the House-that-Jack-Built with the cricket generations. It was Fry's vote, though he did not know it or so intend it, which removed W. G. Grace from the England captaincy and team in 1899. And W. G. Grace was being shown a cricket bat by his mother at Thornbury while the Duke of Wellington was still alive; though what the Duke has to do with cricket I'm bothered if I know.

So, the match was over and we'd won. And our stock bowler, Ernest Robson, drank a pint of beer, curled his moustache, lit his pipe, and made as if to offer me a remark; but as usual found himself unequal to it, and walked thoughtfully from the ground.

And I, being nineteen, rushed away for an evening paper to see what they said about my bowling. They said that the Hampshire batsmen had failed unaccountably against an attack that presented no obvious difficulty.

Unaccountably? No obvious difficulty? Nuts.

There followed a defeat at Lord's by Middlesex, who were on that great spurt to the Championship under "Plum" Warner. And so to the Weston-super-Mare Festival. Of all County grounds, Clarence Park, Weston-super-Mare, is about the smallest and the most intimate. It was the home pitch of Jim Bridges, Somerset bowler, and there in club matches, he liked to come out strong as a batsman. "If only they *knew*," he used to tell me, "that you and I, Glasgie, are as good batsmen as any in the Somerset side . . . except, possibly, Dan Lyon and Jack

MacBryan." But this knowledge was somehow kept from our captain, who used to say: "Well, you two clowns can toss for who goes in ten or eleven." Jim never would toss, but took number ten with an air of injury and neglect. After all, the year before, he'd made 99 not out against Essex on his native sward; mostly by huge high balloons.

The Weston ground in August was a thing of marquees where the right stuff could be found, and deck chairs and wooden chairs, under which the spade and bucket could be parked for an hour or two. In those days the pitch was sportive, having sea sand close under the grass, and in the three matches of 1920 only once was a total of 200 reached in 11 completed innings. A short walk away from the ground were the golf-links, where Secretary Bob Riddell held sway. Bob was a left-hand golfer of much skill, and as a host he had no equal. He could produce you golf shoes from nowhere, and a complete change of clothing in rain-storms. There, peace was to be found in the evening, balm for any failure on the cricket field; and in the lounge, Doctor MacBryan, Jack's father, would be sitting, benevolent and conversational, in a drain-pipe collar that kept stiff up to his ears. Something odd always happened at Weston-super-Mare. It was there, in a hotel, that P. G. H. Fender, the Surrey captain, complained to the manager that there wasn't enough room in the bedrooms to swing a cat, and the manager told Percy Fender that he didn't know they'd come down to Weston merely for the cat-swinging.

We lost to Leicestershire in the first match of the Festival. It was a bad batting match, especially for the older gentlemen, our Ernest Robson and their J. H. King, ninety-five years between them, making only 1 run in their 4 innings. King made up for it by doing the hat-trick in our second innings, the third wicket of the feat being also his hundredth of the season. He was surrounded by congratulations; and his face was illuminated by triumph, as I walked to the crease, a possible fourth in hand. But I corrected his exuberance by hitting my first ball out of the ground and over the pavilion at mid-wicket. I added one more, then was feebly caught and bowled by Ewart Astill. In the Leicestershire second innings I took 5 for 33, and caught G. B. F. Rudd, 71, in the deep field with a sound like a bag bursting.

John King of Leicestershire, left-hand bat and bowler, went on playing for the County till he was fifty-four years old. In 1904, brought into the Players' side at Lord's as a substitute for J. T. Tyldesley, he scored a century in each innings. In his latter years he was a slowish mover between the wickets, and once, being run out at Leicester by many yards while facing the right way for the pavilion, he was told by umpire Reeves to "keep on running, John, while your legs are loose". John was very angry about this.

We lost the next match, against Essex, for whom there was playing an enormous man, P. Toone. He was a tremendous thrower, but wild, and once threw the ball from the deep field clean over the wicketkeeper's head against the far screen. He seemed well pleased with this feat. I made 15 not out, out of 99, and 22 out of 160. Hot going, I thought; and in the next match, against Derbyshire, I was promoted to number eight, much to the disgust of Jim Bridges. But as I scored 21, he couldn't say much. We beat Derbyshire by 10 wickets, Jack White, the greatest slow left-hand bowler Somerset ever had, taking 12 for 79. John Daniell scored 102 in the first innings, and was very severe on the off-spinner, Arthur Morton, sweeping him again and again to the leg boundary and reaching his 50 in less than half an hour.

Arthur Morton was a sturdy all-rounder, and later became a first-class umpire. When standing umpire some years after this, he called several no-balls against a certain West Indies fast bowler. The excitable victim, resenting these attentions, revenged himself by running towards the wicket, knocking Morton flat on his face, and shouting: "Was THAT a no-ball, then?" Apologies were made; Morton straightened his teeth and scraped the grass from his eyebrows, and the game proceeded.

So ended the season 1920. I finished with 55 wickets at 20·90 each, and John Daniell asked me to play again next year, adding the request, "and for heaven's sake, don't bring that bloody straw-hat."

Almost nothing, except the sunshine, went right with Oxford cricket in 1921. Technically, this was hard to explain. Of the 1920 team, we had lost only three, F. W. Gilligan, F. A. Waldock, and C. H. L. Skeet. But neither Bettington nor Stevens bowled as skilfully as they had done the summer before, and, as to me, I

took on a transitional shape in which I was increasing speed and
casting away the habit of the inswing. Probably, I ought to have
stayed in the nets and had it all out on my own. Our captain,
V. R. Price, was an erratic, occasionally a brilliant, fast bowler,
but, somehow, we were never a whole cricket side; just a collection of individuals playing cricket. Against such a side as Cambridge in 1921, this was just asking for defeat. And we had it.
They won by an innings and 24 runs.

That Cambridge team was just about the best University
eleven that went to Lord's in my memory. They batted thus, in
brackets being the runs scored in the only innings that they
found necessary: J. L. Bryan (62), C. A. Fiddian-Green (17),
G. Ashton (12), H. Ashton (118), A. P. F. Chapman (45),
C. T. Ashton (48), M. D. Lyon (9), A. G. Doggart (45), C. H.
Gibson (43 not out), R. G. Evans (0 not out), C. S. Marriott did
not bat.

Gilbert Ashton was captain. Their opening bowlers were
Clem Gibson, of England quality, and R. G. Evans, very accu-
rate and capable of both swerves. To follow, they had "Father"
Marriott, one of the finest slow bowlers who ever played in the
'Varsity match, and Graham Doggart, a sturdy stock bowler who
could nip them in awkwardly from the off.

In batting, they had that rare and enviable mixture of the
sound and the brilliant. Jack Bryan was sound, and also left-
handed. His partner, Charles Fiddian-Green, was the very
mirror of orthodoxy, and, further, an all-round games-player of
unusual ability, reaching the first-class at cricket, rugby, golf,
and hockey. Sartorially, he was the Beau Brummell of the side.
The three Ashtons between them provided all the known strokes
of the right-hander. Percy Chapman, on his own, already ap-
proached Frank Woolley in all but sheer grace. M. D. Lyon,
powerful and aggressive, was soon to become the stay of Somerset; and when these had made their runs, there was Doggart,
who was good enough to bat at number three in most 'Varsity
teams. To crown all, they won the toss.

In fielding, they were the one team in England that year who
could compare with W. W. Armstrong's Australians. At short-
leg, Hubert Ashton had no superior. At cover-point, there was
Percy Chapman. Some years later, Chapman set a new standard
in the gulley; but that was when his legs were heavier and his

frame set. At cover, in lithe and pliable youth, he was a nonpareil. Nothing stoppable seemed to escape his huge hands and telescopic reach; being left-handed, he could pounce on those balls that swerve away from cover towards third-man, and, still stooping, he would flick them back over the bails.

As a batsman, Chapman was something different from the other very good ones who were—just very good. His great reach, keenness of eye, and exceptional strength of wrist and forearm made him a murderous opponent. In later years, even while he was still captain of England, he had curtailed his full swing of the bat. He learnt cunning and what to leave alone. But, in his Cambridge days he used no cunning, no more than Cœur de Lion would have used it when knocking off some Saracen's head, and he left nothing alone. It was plain, when you bowled to him, that he believed himself able to score off anything, felt himself to be master of the whole armoury of the bowler's attack. And, when you put one past him, he didn't retract from that view or attitude, but thought "my mistake", not "your good ball". On and just outside the off stump he had those delayed strokes that defy description, half cut and half drive, and it didn't matter how good was the length of the ball. He never had the defence of Frank Woolley; very few have had that; but he was a stronger man, far, and you noticed it when fielding at cover-point. Chapman and records somehow don't pair together, but he is the only man who has brought off the "treble" at Lord's, of a century in the University match, for Gentlemen v. Players, and for England v. Australia.

They dropped him from the England captaincy soon after that century against Australia; and the Australians could hardly be persuaded of their wonderful luck. As a captain, he was the best I have known. He had the flair. He could encourage by a gesture or a look, and he had the whole confidence of the whole side. The critics talk of Archie MacLaren, and Noble, and W. G. Grace as leaders. But results can talk as well; and Chapman captained England in six consecutive victories against Australia. And that's another record. But he had so much that defeats words and the pen; gaiety, freedom, hope, enjoyment. In him was gathered all that makes cricket worth playing.

In the 'Varsity match, Hubert Ashton batted beautifully for his 118, and Douglas Jardine, having Chapman caught and bowling Doggart, surprised both friend and foe. For Oxford, Ward and Hedges made some runs in each innings, Holdsworth some lovely strokes in the first. As in 1920, A. F. Bickmore batted with distinction, and it was sad that his 57 should have been ended by a long-hop. I thought I bowled well, and had Chapman missed at wicket before he had scored, but the wickets wouldn't fall, and Geoffrey Lowndes rebuked me for gesticulating when they nearly did.

Meanwhile, the Australians, with J. M. Gregory and E. A. McDonald as their spearhead of attack, were knocking the dust out of English cricket. Their captain, Warwick W. Armstrong, was now in his forty-third year and weighed at least seventeen stone. He was the nearest thing to W. G. Grace that Australia had produced, both in bulk and ability. He somewhat resembled the Old Man in his method of bowling, rolling the ball from leg for as long as you pleased, with a sort of comfortable assiduity and strainless guile. As a batsman, he had become rather slow of foot, but he still drove with great power, and could stick at need.

As a captain, Armstrong was reckoned among the astutest of tacticians; but it must be admitted that, in 1921, he was not called upon to exercise any exceptional ingenuity, for what Gregory and McDonald left, Arthur Mailey mopped up. Armstrong was not a man of many words, but the few that he uttered were apt to be noticed. He crossed ideas with the M.C.C. at the very start of the tour, demanding a change in the programme to allow the Australians a day's rest before each Test match. This reasonable request caused an uneasy stir in the sanctuary.

The truth was, English cricket was in sore and crusty mood, like an old gentleman who has received a caning. There was another disagreement, humorous enough, if humour were appreciated in the high places of cricket. Armstrong asked that drinks should be served in the dressing-room at Lord's. F. E. (later Sir Francis) Lacey, the Secretary of M.C.C., said that the bar downstairs was the only and proper place for liquid refreshment. But Armstrong carried his point. These pin-pricks made sore relations, and, when Gregory and McDonald began to make free with the rather timorous remains of England batting, there were not wanting those who said there was something unfair in the bowling. They objected to their old men being knocked about. In result, Armstrong passed as something of an ogre in cricket that summer, and the climax was reached in the Fifth Test, at the Oval, when Armstrong, fielding in front of the Pavilion, trapped a wind-swept newspaper under his large boot, and read it. He said that the Racing news was more interesting than the cricket provided.

Farmer Jack Gregory was tall, strong, raw-boned, and like one of his native Kangaroos. He bounded up to the wicket in a whirlwind of arms and legs. He was a genial fellow, and enjoyed his cricket like a boy. He batted left-hand, and, free from style or responsibility, attacked with long reach and pendulum, not going out so much for sixes as for strokes that hummed low over the off-side fieldsmen's heads. Undoubtedly he frightened many batsmen from the wicket, but for what is a fast bowler if not for that? I never saw anything unfair in his bowling, and he followed the precept of Sam Woods: "If the batsman gets above himself, put one past his whiskers now and then."

Ted McDonald, born in Tasmania, was an artist among fast-bowlers, uncoiling his action with rhythm and controlled power. He was a handsome fellow, with strong and clear-cut features, but saturnine and mahogany-grim; like Carver Doone, he meant to frighten the young men with a look. He had not played in the Australian Imperial Forces team of two years earlier, and his performance against J. W. H. T. Douglas's England team in Australia during 1920-21 was but moderate. But, over here in 1921, he showed himself worthy to be compared with the great ones of the past. He had the wicked, thigh-grinding break-back, and the whipping out-swerve. In later years, he used the slow off-break to much effect.

McDonald came back to play in County cricket, for Lancashire, and his magnificence helped to carry his County three times to the Championship. Perhaps he would have done well to remain in his own Australia, for, over here, he found those who were only too ready to play up to his swashbuckling and devil-may-care nature. He loved to be thought the "tough baby", and he fell into ways of life that somehow foreshadowed tragedy; which came in 1937, when he was killed in a motor accident. I like to remember him as he was at his zenith, for nothing in games is so superb or rare as the great fast bowler in action.

Arthur Mailey tossed me up three voluptuous half-volleys,

off which I took 12 runs, then had me stumped a long way from the front-door. Arthur was a great bowler, with a teasing flight and acute power of spin. He was witty, quiet and easy-natured, and the seriousness required for Test cricket didn't rise naturally in him. He loved casual matches, where he could appear in old sand-shoes and give away please-yourself runs to some local mayor or notable.

I believe his early days had been something of a struggle; anyhow, he had a fondness for dead-end kids, and would sign their autograph-books with running questions about their private lives and ideas, and draw them comic and simian pictures of himself, with button nose and wide space between it and the mouth. I never saw Arthur bustled or bothered. If he got no wickets or plenty, why, there was another innings or match coming along. If he missed a train, well, someone could find a time-table with another one in it. He had a soft and quizzical way of speech. Of all the Australians I have known, he had the surest understanding of the English outlook and temperament, and the keenest awareness of Australian foibles.

There will often be argument as to whether Mailey or Grimmett was the greater bowler. Grimmett, with his persistent length and lower flight, was the more economical. Mailey, liked, and was blessed with, more runs to play with. He would seem to have been collared, then suddenly win with an unplayable leg-break. Of the two, both cricketers of genius, Mailey was the more likely to defeat the great batsman who was well set. Grimmett caused Mailey deep and quiet delight; and Mailey used to relate how Grimmett, a New Zealander, came to him soon after his, Grimmett's, entry into Australian cricket and asked questions about their gyratory art. Mailey told him all he knew. Years later, when Grimmett had won fame, there was some banquet or reunion at which both were present. Grimmett, probably elated by unaccustomed good cheer, for he was a man of abstinence, came up to Mailey and said in that voice like a ventriloquist speaking through a watering-can: "Arthur, you told me wrong about the Bowzie." Rather as if Virgil had been accused by Horace of giving misleading information on the number of feet in the Hexameter!

H. L. "Horseshoe" Collins opened his innings against us with the silent and avuncular Ernie Mayne. Mayne had played over

here in the Triangular Tests of 1912, but he took no active part
in the 1921 series. Indeed, he only played about 20 innings
during the tour. He was a sound batsman, but an indifferent and
rather uninterested fielder. A few years later, at the age of forty,
he and Ponsford shared in an opening partnership of 456 for
Victoria against Queensland, at Melbourne, which still stands
as an Australian record for the first wicket. At Oxford, I thought
I saw Warwick Armstrong look at Mayne once or twice as if
wondering why Ernie hadn't stayed at home in Australia.

Herbie Collins, of New South Wales, famous also as poker-
player and race-goer, was a slight but tough man with a free
wrist and a beady eye. He would have made a fortune on the old
silent films. He was just right for a Stetson hat and woolly door-
mats for the legs, and he would have been no more than a cat's
wink slower than Tom Mix on the draw. As a batsman, he was a
deflector, in a style followed, more gracefully, by Alan Kippax.
At Manchester, in the Fourth Test, when others fell to Parkin
and Parker, he dug in for nearly five hours and scored 40. He was
quite a good left-hand bowler: a fact scarcely evident from his
2 wickets for 269 during the tour.

Charlie Macartney scored 77, then played on to his wicket,
trying to late-cut a length ball from Greville Stevens. His
innings was an hour or so of brilliant net-practice. His batting
suggested a racket-player who makes winners from any position.
Length could not curb him, and his defence was lost and included in attack. A month later, he scored that wonderful 345
in three hours and threequarters against Nottinghamshire at
Trent Bridge. He was missed in the slips when 9, but gave no
further chance; an astonishing performance. No Australian
batsman since him, not even Bradman at his best, has ap-
proached Macartney for insolence of attack. He made slaves of
bowlers.

In the Australian innings, I took the wickets of Taylor,
Andrews, Mailey, and Oldfield for 74 runs, and some words of
praise from Armstrong that reached my ears made me immoder-
ately pleased. The rest of the season put that right; but his three-
year prophecy concerning me was not far from coming true.

The match was drawn. After the Australians had led by 14
on the first innings, we answered with 174 for the loss of Bickmore. Jardine followed 35 in the first innings with 96 not out in

the second. But the selectors were mistrustful of novelty, and they gave no place in any Test to Hubert Ashton, Chapman, or Jardine. Ashton, who averaged over 60 for several innings against the Australians, never had another chance, and remains as a memento of official timidity.

John Daniell, remembering my qualification and, perhaps, forgetting my straw hat, asked me to play for Somerset soon after the University match. I opened with a sparkling o, b. Tate, at Hastings, where Gilbert Jessop used to knock chips off the Congregational Church and where the distant cliff forms so helpful a pavilion for those who have spent all their money on telescopes. I took three not very grandiose wickets, and travelled on to play Essex at Southend.

I have a weakness for Southend, and in later years, when reporting cricket for the *Morning Post*, I never failed to impress on my employers the importance and brilliance of its Cricket Festival. In August, the homely smell of mankind in the streets was set off by the abundance of whelks, cockles, and stick-jaw rock. Rides were to be had on the miniature railway to the end of the pier and in mechanical boats on the lake below the Palace Hotel. Nowhere else have I found such invigorating air; and morning brought no sense of lassitude or remorse to the nocturnal reveller.

The cricket ground was adorned at one end by a lake, on which prophetic ducks floated, and quacked as nervous batsmen made their way to the crease. Festooned around were private tents, whose occupants said and drank what they liked. One of them belonged to the Mayor, another to the Yachting Club. In both of these the hospitality was warm, and from the latter marine telescopes were sometimes directed on to the cricket.

The Somerset v. Essex match at Southend, played towards the end of July 1921, stands out in my memory for its interest and humour. The pitch, like Jezebel, was fast and unaccountable. Soon afterwards, the whole playing surface was re-laid, and a new pavilion was erected on the other side of the ground, in front of the ornamental lake. The original pavilion was small and, like the pitch, rather crude. We won the toss, and, after some severe concentration by A. E. S. Rippon (35), some lusty blows by Tom Lowry (28), and some fluent drives by Peter Randall Johnson (38), we collected 163; not good; but not disastrous, on a surface that was already fierce and might soon become wicked.

The Essex innings, apart from a sparkling hour of Claude Ashton (48), centred round the performance of F. Loveday, one of their opening batsmen. This obstacular artist was taking the place of A. C. Russell, who was making 101 in the fourth Test match, at Manchester, against Australia. Loveday, a thin and resolute man, wore a cap with a large B on its front. I have a fancy, almost a certainty, that, after he had batted for some three hours, John Daniell asked him if he would like to tell us what the letter stood for. Truly, it might have stood for Batsman, as a more determined innings can seldom have been played. Jim Bridges and I, without being fast, often made the ball rise awkwardly from a length. Loveday was of the firm-footed type, and he sometimes became a sort of human kettledrum. But on he batted, nor resting, nor hasting, uncomplaining if not wholly unbowed. John Daniell was very restless throughout, and once, between overs, he hissed in my ear: "Glasgy, can't you get this ruddy contortionist out?" To add to John's annoyance, a plague of catch-dropping started in the slips. I was hauled out to mid-on, and John, scowling darkly, retired to the deep, where he dismissed H. M. Morris with a grand one-handed catch. Soon afterwards I bowled the everlasting and heroic Loveday, and our captain smiled again. Loveday had made 81 in 3 hours and 30 minutes and Essex headed us by 83 runs.

On such a pitch, this seemed more than half-way to victory. But our batsmen thought otherwise. Daniell, going in first with Rippon, hit strongly. At 10, he was caught over the boundary by Henry Franklin, and recalled after discussion. He added another 32. Meanwhile, Rippon dug in. Though a stylist in execution of the strokes, he loved to make an affair of the act of batting; he did much bat-twirling, in the Jack Hobbs manner, and resorted to Swedish exercises between the overs, and, to the disgust of the bowler, even between balls. He also rubbed his left hand on his behind, which grew ever darker as a result. Lowry and S. G. U. Considine having failed, Rippon was joined by Peter Johnson, an aristocrat among batsmen. Peter, using his height to stand well over the rising ball, batted as only he could, since the days of Lionel Palairet. He made 81 in less than an hour and a half. Tom Young, another stroke-player, joined in with 69 not out. Rippon reached 52 after 3 hours and 20 minutes of strife and bat-twirling, Bridges collected 18 by this way and that, and Essex were left with 222 to win.

From the first over, the ball flew. J. G. Dixon, a carefree cricketer, soon went, and Jack Freeman joined Loveday. Freeman, a very small man like his younger brother, A. P. of Kent, had made 30 in the first innings before being bowled by that accomplished amateur tenor, Monty Hambling. Freeman was a sound and experienced little batsman. He played a few strokes, then I bowled him one which rose sharp from a length, and, unhappily, cut his face badly. This accident cost Essex two wickets, for Loveday, exclaiming, "I don't like that," went in for a drink, and, soon after his return, he left his bat outside the off-stump to one from Bridges. Poor Freeman bravely tried again, but was almost immediately bowled by Tom Young. Then I had Hubert Ashton l.b.w., and we were on the right road. It was blocked by Peter Perrin.

Perrin, who was now in his forty-sixth year, batted superbly. A little slow on the foot, he stopped many balls on legs and body, but he showed why he had earned the name of one of the greatest players of faster bowling. The others came and went, but Perrin was unbeaten, if not unhurt, for 62. So we won a remarkable match by 65 runs.

Let us here turn aside and consider one of the great figures in English cricket, farmer John Cornish White. His father, in a comfortable silence that was presumed to represent approval, used to watch him trundling away his slow left-handers at Taunton. Jack inherited his father's tranquillity. I never saw him excited, though sometimes he would go a little redder when an important catch was missed off his bowling, and he would mutter: "The trouble about that cock is that he's fast asleep." Most cricketers were "cocks" to Jack, and he would say of some new batsman who had not troubled the scorer: "I didn't think *that* cock would last long, Glasgy; he had one of those fancy caps on."

Jack came from Stogumber when he first played for Somerset in 1909, at the age of sixteen. His beginnings were negligible. He took 1 wicket for 90 runs in three innings. Next year, he did little better, and for the next three summers, Somerset, oscillating around bankruptcy and the bottom of the Championship, did without him. But in 1914 he returned to head their bowling averages with 93 wickets. In 1919 he began that run of uninterrupted success which placed him among the few unquestioned great. In 1921, against Worcestershire at Worcester, he took all 10 wickets in an innings.

He differed from other famous slow left-handers in that he relied very little on spin. Varied flight, guile, persistence, liveliness from the pitch, these were his secrets. He also had the gift of making the ball bounce unusually high for a slow bowler, and he took many wickets by causing the batsmen to play the ball too high on the bat to silly-point, where John Daniell awaited the prey. Many times I stood to White at short slip, and I never saw a bowler who so harassed and teased the batsmen. He would peg down the most aggressive, till by sheer desperation they were driven to their doom. Frank Woolley, being left-handed, was usually White's master; but the most accomplished right-handers, such as Hobbs, Hendren, and Hammond, did not attack him. He bowled, and they played. Hendren used to say that no bowler made him so tired.

White was turned thirty-seven when he first went to Australia, and his fair hair was greying at the temples. Few could have prophesied that he was going out to his triumph. From the first, the Australian batsmen could not decide whether to play him back or forward. Young Archie Jackson, that beautiful player who was to die four years later at the age of twenty-three, solved the problem; but for the most part the batsmen were driven into the crease. The climax came in the fourth Test, at Adelaide, when, in stifling heat, White bowled 124 overs for 13 wickets and 256 runs, an historic feat of combined endurance and skill. England won by 12 runs. White had to leave the field to change his shirt twice during one afternoon, and, at the same time, to take in a draught of the right stuff. Hendren tells how, when the last Australian batsman, Don Blackie, came in to face White, he, that guileful Patsy, standing close to the wicket, said: "My word; I wouldn't be in *your* shoes for all the money in the world." "I shall never forget," said Hendren, "the look of pitiable horror that came over Blackie's face when I said this." Bravely Blackie defended for a few balls, then was caught by Larwood at deep mid-wicket.

White was a grand fielder to his own bowling, and a good

slip-fielder to anyone else's. He was less effective farther from
the wicket, as he could throw but little. As a batsman, he had
begun, and looked like finishing, close above the extras; but,
by industry and imitation, he made himself into a counting
player. He used his pads more than most, and I have a fancy that
the umpires whose decisions Jack, as a bowler, accepted with
such equanimity gave him the benefits of many doubts. I never
saw him throw his wicket away. He had the husbandman's dislike of waste. Apart from cricket, he was no games-player, but
he was a cunning cardsman, and one of the best poker-players
in Somerset.

He migrated from Stogumber to Combe Florey. No other
County knows so well how to name its places. I used to drive
with Guy Earle on summer evenings after the cricket from
Taunton to Minehead, through Bishop's Lydeard, Combe
Florey, and Crowcombe. Guy was a mighty hitter, the highest
and farthest of his day, with arms like a grown man's thigh. At
Bristol, in 1923, he hit 111 off Gloucestershire in the August bank
holiday match, scoring his first 76 in half an hour and lifting
Charles Parker four times clean over the track that encircled the
ground.

But it was the Kent bowlers who most suited his designs,
and "Tich" Freeman most of all. "Tich" would arrive at Taunton on his way to his annual 200 wickets and Guy would hit him
over the river or into the timber-yard. The supposed variety of
the leg-break and googly lost all relevance. Guy put his left leg
down the pitch and clapped the ball an awful blow. He regarded
all bowlers as so much sawdust and any success on their part as a
personal insult. Returning to the pavilion after being caught at
third-man while trying a six to square-leg, he would cast down
his bat with a resounding boom and say: "I'll wring his . . . little
neck." Within three minutes the thunder-cloud had almost
passed, returning in little puffs when Guy would say, as he gazed
at the cricket: "I can't think how anyone ever gets out to that
bandy-legged . . ."

At Watts House, near Bishop's Lydeard, Sir Denis Boles used
to entertain the Somerset cricketers. It was here, on his private
cricket-ground, that I was guilty of a social solecism at the tender
age of eighteen. Jack White, who was my captain, had put me
on to bowl and asked me whether the fielders were to my liking.

Casting around my eye, I saw the host standing by the sight-screen in conversation with Burgess, his butler. Without hesitation, I shouted, "Up a bit, Boles!" The abruptness and titular inaccuracy of this request caused Jack MacBryan to sit down on the grass and laugh. Years afterwards, when I was setting a field, he turned from mid-on and whispered, "Up a bit, Boles." Burgess was a very solemn humorist, and, when the head of the family was looking the other way, he used to pretend to trip with a tray full of glasses.

The church at Bishop's Lydeard used to be attended by one of the loudest singers I have ever heard. He was said to be a butcher who had removed himself, or been removed, from the choir after some dispute about his required share in an anthem. His revenge was to try to drown the choir from the front pew. Having considerable power of lung, I was put up as a rival, and I at least succeeded in making him turn round and stare at me with rubicund and surly amazement.

If you wanted to know Taunton, you walked round it with Sam Woods on a summer morning before the match. Sam was Somerset's godfather. He was a lover of life and of nearly all things living. On those walks, he would take you into the back-parlours of little shops and inquire after the youngest son's measles, and whether it had been decided to put Tom into the cornchandling trade. "Much better let him be a farmer, Missis," Sam would say, "and marry a fat wife who can look after his money. For *he* won't, no more than I could, my dear."

Everyone loved Sam, for the whole world's manliness and generosity seemed to have gathered into his heart. He lived at the George Inn, Mr E. J. Lock, and when not there, might be found at the Club. I believe he decided to do some looking after of me, because he thought I needed it, and also because I opened the bowling sometimes, though not as Sam had opened, continued, and closed it, with speed and invincible hope.

I wish I had seen him in the prime of his bowling, but I only saw him trundling a few down, in waistcoat and watch-chain, at the Oxford nets, when he was fifty-two. He had tremendous shoulders, but was lame in walk owing to rheumatism in the hip. This he attributed to a fall off a camel in Egypt. "I was in charge of a bunch of those sods," he said, "when they stampeded and made for a cactus forest; so off I rolled, and fell a bit wrong."

C. B. Fry told me that Sam, when a young man, was the finest build of an athlete stripped that he ever saw.

Sam came over from Australia to Brighton College when he was fourteen. He was one of a family of thirteen, at Manley Beach, near Sydney. "At least I *think* we were thirteen," he would say. For Cambridge against Oxford, he took 36 wickets in four matches, at nine each, and, while still an undergraduate, he played in three Test matches against England for Australia. At rugger he played forward for England, and was a terror in the loose, for he weighed nearly fifteen stone and could run the hundred yards in under eleven seconds. He had neither the wish nor the aptitude for any settled profession. In early youth, he tried a little banking, but was so often absent at cricket when he should have been shovelling sovereigns that he, and his employers, both felt that he should try something else.

As a batsman, he was an attacker, and only G. L. Jessop excited more anticipation in the crowd. Many a time he pulled Somerset out of the ditch; especially at the Oval, when he would walk out, chin first, to tame the fury of Richardson and Lockwood. In technique, he always advised against deflections to leg. "You're not Ranji," he would say, "so aim at mid-on's nut, and you'll find the ball will go to the square-leg boundary." I was with him at the Oval when he met little Bobby Abel, who had gone nearly blind. Abel touched Sam on the arm, smiled, and said: "Oh, Mr Woods, the times you've nearly knocked my head off out in the middle," and Sam said: "Ah, Bobby, but the times you carved me off your whiskers to the boundary."

Sam would hear nothing against W. G. Grace, and loved to tell of the Old Man's hundredth century, 288, for Gloucestershire against Somerset in 1895. W.G. scored at 50 an hour, and gave no chance. "I had him plumb Leg Before," Sam said, "when he'd made only three or four, and that was the only time I got one past him. I bowled him a shooter when he was in the nineties, and he didn't stop it; he hit it for four to square-leg." My great-uncle A. P. Wickham was keeping wicket behind Grace, and he told me that W.G. only let five balls pass his bat throughout his innings.

After that match Gloucestershire supporters gave Grace a complimentary dinner. "He drank something of everything," Sam said, "before and during dinner, and afterwards he sent for the whisky. You couldn't make the Old Man drunk. His nut was too large. About midnight, some of us thought we might start for home; but the Old Man said to me: 'Shock'ead, get two others, and we'll play rubbers of whist till two in the morning.' So we did."

Sam had his learning from nature, not from books; but a strong memory and a vivid power of corroborative illustration made him a talker who never lacked for an audience. He was convivial; too convivial, some thought; but I could never see that it mattered. Drinking was just part of his life, and it made no difference to his kindness and his humour. He made the younger ones among us stick to beer and early hours—"Whisky and one o'clock in the morning won't suit, you, my dear."

Sam will never be forgotten in Somerset, and they still talk of him as if he were just round the next corner. Not long ago, I met an elderly lady on a railway journey near Taunton. Within five minutes our talked reached Sam. "Ah," she said, "I last met him at a dance when I was eighteen. I had been told that I was not to dance with Sam. But I did."

1922 was the worst cricket season I ever had. During the Oxford term I was dropped from the side. I came in again on tour, at Leicester, and Douglas Jardine, acting as captain, and having a sense of the situation, said: "Now then, my boy, either end you like." I took 6 for 40 in their first innings. In the end, Jardine and H. O. Hopkins had to stand down through injuries, and I played against Cambridge after all. I bowled 43 overs to a humdrum length and took 0 for 97. Much ado about nothing.

One incident of rich humour relieved the dismal scene. It was against Surrey at the Oval. Tom Raikes and I were batting, at numbers ten and nine respectively. Tom was a Freshman from Winchester, a robust and clever bowler, with a be-damned-to-it attitude towards life. It began by my playing a ball to the deep-field at the Pavilion end. We ran our one comfortably, and, when Tom asked if there was another, I said "yes," and we started for the second. Strange things then happened. As we were about to cross over, Tom suddenly turned round and scuttled back to his wicket. I followed him; but thinking this crease overcrowded, I set out for the other (at the Pavilion end). Not to be outdone, Tom did the same. I beat him to it by a head.

Meanwhile, the fielders, driven temporarily insane by these goings-on, were having a private game of rounders. At length the ball reached Strudwick, the wicketkeeper, who took off the bails. It was one thing to remove the bails, another to know who was out. We had occupied both ends two or three times each. The umpires, Bill Reeves and Frank Chester, stood impotent with laughter and doubt. But Tom solved the problem by striding away to the pavilion. "Over" was then called, and, as I prepared to receive the next ball, Bill Hitch, the Surrey fast bowler, said hoarsely at short-leg: "You know who was out *really*, don't you?" But I didn't. Nor did he.

The Varsity match was like 1921, only more so. Cambridge, with brilliant Hubert Ashton as captain, had lost two fine bowlers, Marriott and Gibson, but they had an admirable attack in G. O. Allen from Eton, P. A. Wright from Welling-borough, and F. B. R. ("Tishy") Browne, from Eastbourne College. Allen had not yet reached his full pace nor acquired that temperament which can disregard set-backs, but he came fast from the pitch and had a vicious break-back, with Hubert Ashton hovering at short-leg. Browne, tall and strong, had an awkward delivery, almost off the wrong foot, but he was a grand bowler of fast-medium pace, who was lost all too early to the first-class game. Wright was of the old-fashioned sort, medium in pace, with a beautifully easy action and tireless accuracy. A formidable trio.

It had rained in torrents just before the match, but cleared in time for Cambridge to take innings on a slow and soggy pitch. For us, only one bowler touched his true form, Tom Raikes. We could not part Charles Fiddian-Green and Willie Hill-Wood before lunch. They were not exciting; indeed one Oxford sup-porter rudely described Hill-Wood's batting before lunch as being like a monkey trying to climb an impossibly slippery pole. But their policy was right. At lunch the total was sixty, and no one out.

Soon after the interval, Raikes bowled Fiddian-Green with one of the vastest off-breaks I've ever seen. It pitched nearly off the mown surface. Graham Doggart and Hill-Wood then added 118 quite briskly, till Doggart was bowled by Raikes with a full-pitch. Raikes said he'd tried everything else first. Hill-Wood was caught for 81, made in four hours and three-quarters.

Shelmerdine was soon caught at slip off Bettington, but Hubert Ashton and Percy Chapman stayed together till the close of play, when their score was 271 for 4.

On the second morning, Ashton and Chapman batted beautifully. By ten minutes past one the Cambridge score had reached 403 for 4. In a shocking light, Chapman went to his century with a drive off me which Hedges, at cover-point, only heard. Then came the rain, and Ashton, though needing only 10 runs for his second consecutive century against Oxford, declared his innings.

Our innings was opened by Bettington, a temporarily converted hitter, and Frank Barnard, a Freshman from Charterhouse, with a beautiful wrist and style. With little hope of anything better than a draw, they stayed together for an hour, but, by tea-time, they, Holdsworth, and Beverley Lyon had all gone for only 63. Hedges and Stevens then stayed together till the end of the second day, putting on 71. Stevens, the captain, had spent the term in rescue work at number six, and ended with an average of 48. At Lord's he was still suffering from the effects of jaundice.

Early on the third morning Hubert Ashton made a glorious catch at short-leg to dismiss Hedges, and the innings closed for 222. The follow-on was catastrophic. Allen and Wright certainly bowled very well, but our batsmen helped them with some eccentric strokes. As I sat in the Oxford balcony and read our score of 17 for 7 wickets, I could only laugh. Stevens again batted heroically, and I helped him to take the total into the sixties. Tom Raikes added a few lusty whacks, and we staggered to 81. Oxford cricket had hit the bottom of the barometer.

After the 'Varsity match, I played in only two games of first-class rank, both at Cardiff, against Glamorgan. One was for an Oxford and Cambridge team collected by "Shrimp" Leveson Gower. In this, our gallant captain, aged forty-eight, scored 61 not out at number ten, and I assisted him in a last wicket stand of over 70. He played the slow left-hand leg spinners of Frank Ryan in masterly style, holding the bat loose on the forward stroke, so that "any snick", as he said, "is more likely to go along the ground." He was a very downy batsman. I took 7 for 79 in this match. John Morrison kept wicket. His athletic deeds at soccer, cricket, and golf were current tradition when I was a small boy at Charterhouse. He was the inventor of the water-proof golf skirt as worn by himself, and of a unique implement for sucking up golf balls without stooping. A great character, John Morrison, and for years one of the shrewdest foursome players in the game.

My other match was for Somerset. On this occasion, I had lost my cricket-bag, which had a habit of catching me up just too late. It was a skimpy thing, known in the family as "the éclair". "Essentially a bowler's bag", as Douglas Jardine once remarked with a meditative air. For all its tenuousness, it yet contained my only pair of cricket boots. I was unable to borrow any on the Cardiff ground, so went out to field in black walking-shoes. This performance so shook John Daniell that he refrained from putting me on to open the bowling with Jim Bridges. Jim scratched his head, and smiled dubiously at my foot-wear. I was put on first change, and, in my first over, had J. R. Tait, who candidly admitted a likeness to Charlie Chaplin, caught at short-leg. But John remained unconverted, and took me off soon afterwards. Sidney Rippon won the match for us with a superb century. In bidding me goodbye for the season, Daniell said: "First it's a straw-hat, and now you come and bowl in a pair of bloody dancing-pumps." Happy days.

Halfway through the Christmas term of 1922 I was ordered a rest by the doctors. I was sleeping badly and when I began to despise the pleasures of the table, I knew things were out of joint. No name was given to the ailment, which was, in fact, a con-siderable nervous breakdown. I received several up-and-down physical examinations, and a great many wise nods and "well—well—wells." What I needed was bed for six weeks.

This chapter being concerned with cricket, not neurology, I will rest content with the remark that only those who have suffered it know the hell of nervous illness. Twice again was I to be similarly afflicted. This much of good has emerged from it all; first, that I have learnt to regard physical ailments with the contempt that nine-tenths of them deserve; and secondly, that I know the unutterable delight of health found after a long and seemingly hopeless search.

Cut off from work, I went to Jersey, where, after a few weeks, I revived, took to playing badminton, and fancied myself to be in love with the leading lady player. There was also golf at La

Moye, with its sand-dunes and sea breezes and friendly club-house. Here I met a man with the only perfectly purple nose I have ever seen. Perhaps he had taken Beachcomber's advice—"How to cure a red nose—drink till it's purple."

I came back to Oxford for my last summer term with two objects immediately in view, to make myself necessary to the cricket team and, on almost no work at all, to squeeze through the Final School of Literae Humaniores or "Greats". So I rose at six each morning for Plato and Aristotle and unintelligible books on Appearance, Reality, and the Absolute. My whole being revolted against philosophy and its abhorred terminology. I am still sometimes visited by a noxious dream in which I am about to take the "Greats" Exam; knowing that I know sweet Fanny Adams, and worried at my ignorance. I squeezed through —just.

In cricket, I knew from the start that I had "found something". Instead of just toiling away to a mechanical length, I could make the ball, and sometimes the batsman, hop. This was better than any First in "Greats", thought I. Further, Oxford were once more a team. This was largely the work of Reg. Bettington, the captain. We believed in him. He recaptured his own great skill as a bowler of leg-breaks and googlies, taking 61 wickets for Oxford at 16 each. Also, Greville Stevens returned to something like his old form. Between us, we three accounted for 159 of the 227 wickets that fell. With Tom Raikes as stock bowler, and E. P. Hewetson of Shrewsbury as a shock-troop, our attack was as good as that of most of the first-class Counties.

In batting, we were strengthened by the return of Douglas Jardine and H. O. Hopkins. Hopkins, from Adelaide, South Australia, was a sprightly old gentleman in his twenty-eighth year, a quick-footed and neat player with a calm temperament, a pleasant wit, and a leaning towards comic songs in the Frank Crumit manner. Later, he played for Worcestershire with considerable success. He was also an expert at lacrosse.

The stylist of the side was Claude Hilary Taylor, a Freshman from Westminster. He had been coached by that classic batsman, D. J. Knight, and resembled him strongly in method and gesture. He began with 45 against Lancashire, and followed up with 114 against Middlesex, 98 against the Army, and 115 against Sussex at Brighton.

In a very different way, C. H. (John) Knott was equally effective. Coming, like his elder brother, F. H., from Tonbridge, he had failed to strike form in 1921. In 1922 he won his Blue, but, like nearly everyone else, failed against Cambridge. In 1923, he really began. Knott, becoming a schoolmaster at Tonbridge, never played throughout a season for Kent. Had he done so, he might have reached the England side; for he was very good against all types of bowling, and could hit furiously or defend stubbornly. Further, he was a great fieldsman. Five years after he left Oxford he played a wonderful innings of 261 not out, at Eastbourne, for the Harlequins against a representative team of the West Indies, hitting 5 sixes and 29 fours, and seriously disturbing the old ladies and gentlemen at their croquet. In method, he used the short back-lift, like W. M. Woodfull and Greville Stevens, but his strength of hand and forearm enabled him to hit tremendously hard with no obvious effort. In temperament, he was solid and shrewd.

For entertainment, the batsman of the 1923 side was Beverley H. Lyon, younger brother of M. D. Lyon of Cambridge. He was an adept in all those wristy strokes that "may or may not," and would surprise the most complacently successful bowler with a high pull to the boundary. In fielding, as in batting, he was fearless and rapid, excelling in the slips, at silly-point, and short-leg. His bowling, when required, was slow, twisty, experimental. In 1922, he had elated his brother, who was keeping wicket for Cambridge, by making a pair of noughts at Lord's. Next year, after playing a brilliant innings of 91 against M.C.C. he made only 14 against Cambridge, but brought off two remarkable catches at short-leg. In later years, he won fame as a daring and original captain of Gloucestershire. He warred against dullness and drawn matches, and in his crusade was always seeking ways of defeating convention and tradition. He was a constant butt of the older critics, but he was among the first to see that County Cricket might die from dullness and from the rivalry of sports where results were quicker.

Sometimes he made the mistake of pursuing speed merely for its own sake, but Gloucestershire cricket flourished under Bev. Lyon. No doubt he was lucky in having in his side the greatest English cricketer of his day, Walter Hammond, but he knew how to exploit such a possession. He made people talk about Gloucestershire and come to see them play. Nor was he only a master of tactics. He had humour, human understanding, and persuasion. He could handle that temperamental genius, Charles Parker. He knew to a fine exactitude what he could and could not expect from his players, and he clothed a profession and a routine in the finery of rollicking adventure.

Our wicket-keeper at Oxford, as in 1922, was the sturdy Mark Patten, from Winchester, "Mark Pizzy" as his horse-racing friends called him. No day was too long for him. He was pink of face and very tough. A blow on the head served only to sharpen his skill. He was also a strong and determined batsman, who had seen too much bowling from one side of the stumps to wear much respect for it on the other. He and his fellow Wykehamist, Tom Raikes, shared in some lusty partnerships, and were sometimes known to their intimates as Falstaff and Sir Toby Belch.

After a defeat by Lancashire, we beat Hampshire by 3 wickets. Lionel Tennyson made 74 in their first innings of 258, and was plainly delighted at the feat. I had 4 wickets for 58. We answered with 346, nearly everyone making runs; then Bettington and Stevens shot out Hampshire for 173. Kennedy and Newman bowled beautifully in our second innings, but Stevens' steadiness carried us through.

The Kent match was played in icy weather, and it was no joke fielding to Frank Woolley. He made 107 in their second innings. In the first, I took 6 for 82, sometimes making the ball fly from a pitch that was hard with a top-dressing of rain. Wally Hardinge, an England player against slow and medium bowling, showed an inclination to retire towards square-leg, and soon snicked one off me to Bettington in the slips. George Collins, a useful left-hand bat and right-hand bowler, and an expert at crown-and-anchor, made 47, and the left-handed Ronnie Bryan made 68 not out in his own delightful manner. Business kept him from all but a little County cricket. I can think of no other family that has produced three such left-handers as J. L., R. T., and G. J. Bryan. Of the three, R. T. was the most graceful. At number eight, one W. Ashdown was bowled by me for 0. Later, he scored many runs off me batting at number one. He was a stylist, with the full old-fashioned off-side strokes, and a useful bowler, with a late nip from leg.

For this match, Tom Hayward lent me his huge-collared

sweater. Tom was our trainer-coach. Good easy man, Tom was not cut out for work. In the nets, he bowled off-breaks from sixteen or seventeen yards. His verbal instruction was limited to three comments: "How's that?" "Hit 'em 'ard," and "Oh, what a shot, sir!" The last was reserved for the many occasions when his pupil swept one into the longer and wetter grass, just to see Tom amble after the ball. When pressed to take an innings, he would smile and put the question by. Only once did we persuade him into pads, and then, for about five minutes, he showed enough to remind us of his greatness. His brother Dan was in charge of the rival pavilion at Fenners, Cambridge. Tom fancied himself somewhat as a masseur and kept himself very busy with bandages and liniments when the team went on tour. But he was best of all as a spectator, with his face balanced like a luminous walrus over the wall by the dressing-room steps.

I met Tom once or twice in his retirement at Cambridge. Retirement was, perhaps, not quite the word, as he was supposed to be taking some part in the conducting of the family business. But business was not his line. Over a glass of beer, we went over to the Oxford scene, and I reminded him of how Lionel Hedges used to pull his leg. "Ah," said Tom, "that was all right." He implied that his present life was all wrong. About a year before the Hitler War I asked for him again, and brother Dan said Tom had taken to staying in bed for breakfast. He died in July, 1939. I wonder what he would have made of that second war. I suppose he would have curled his moustache and said "Ah."

We lost to Middlesex, after leading them by 101 runs on the first innings, Jack Durston taking 8 for 27 in our second. This was set right by an innings victory over Gloucestershire, whose opening pair were Dipper and the twenty-year old Walter Hammond. I bowled "Dip" for 3 with what Tom Lowry would have called a "lallapaloozer", and Bettington had Hammond l.b.w. for 22. In the second innings we ran him out for 15. Already he had signs of greatness about him, but was still impetuous and slap-dash. The innings of the match was 73 by Greville Stevens, played on a wet wicket.

Absent from the match against the Army, which we unexpectedly lost, I was going through the farce of the "Greats"

examination. I wore horn-rimmed spectacles, to induce a sensation of wisdom, but it was no good. I think the Logic paper was
the worst. It was "harder than Bezique". The only relief was a
gigantic negro who kept retiring to the lavatory, surely not in
the hope of reading secreted and relevant information.

Between the end of the term and the 'Varsity match, we beat
somewhat emasculated teams of Sussex, at Brighton, and
Surrey, at the Oval, and lost to M.C.C. at Lord's, and H. D. G.
Leveson Gower's team, at Eastbourne; the former by habit,
the latter through high living. But we returned to Lord's with
buoyant confidence that we should lay Cambridge low. We
had much to wipe off the slate.

Our optimism was justified, and we brought off the record
win of an innings and 227 runs. A thunderstorm broke in the
very early morning after our innings of 422, and Cambridge
batted twice during the second (and last) day of the match on a
pitch that was at first sodden, then progressively "sticky". This
storm has often been used to explain the Cambridge defeat; in
truth, it did but increase the margin of a victory which we would
have won over them on any pitch in nine matches out of ten.
We had, in Bettington and Stevens, spin bowling of the first
class. Cambridge had no spin bowling at all, nor the sort of
batsmen likely to cope with ours. Further, we were the more
experienced team. Six of their batsmen came from Eton or
Harrow, two schools that have seldom produced batsmen strong
in the art of back-play. Style and enterprise they had in plenty,
and, in Tom Lowry, of New Zealand, a rugged and dangerous
player who had scored 1,000 runs for Cambridge during the
term. But a pointer to the standard of their batting was the presence at number three of G. O. Allen who, in those days, was a
sound enough player, but no more. Besides, he was their chief
bowler.

Here, Cambridge suffered an irremediable blow. Allen,
opening the attack from the Pavilion end, bowled a few overs in
his best style, then broke down with a recurring injury to his
back. He went off for treatment, but not all the Colleges of
Surgeons and Physicians can suddenly conquer Nature, and,
though he returned to the field, he had to be written off as a
counting part of the attack. At the other end, P. A. Wright
toiled on with skill and courage, but, as the runs ticked up, the

absence of all danger in their change bowling was naked to see.

Greville Stevens, opening the innings with Claude Taylor, was caught at short-leg off a rather negligent stroke. Jardine joined Taylor and soon showed the he was not meaning to allow himself any entertainment on the off side. Far otherwise did Taylor bat. He was "all elegance, fit to bat before the Queen in her parlour". Off-drives and leg-glides brought him many boundaries. Claude Ashton, the Cambridge captain, was blamed for not blocking these strokes. But it is easy to be wise from the grand-stand. In the nineties, Taylor gave his first chance, a return catch to the bowler. At 109 he popped one into the hands of short-leg. Never before had a Freshman made a century in his first innings of the 'Varsity match.

Beverley Lyon began as if he meant to score a hundred in an hour, but was soon l.b.w. Hopkins and Knott batted easily enough. At 266 for 6, I joined Knott. I was using a most displeasing bat, like an alloy of teak and tin, and here, at last, was a chance of batting, instead of just filling up the space above the extras. In the intervals of exchanging rude remarks with Tom Lowry, who stood under an appalling homburg hat at short-leg, I moved along to 12. At that point, John Knott was bowled and E. P. Hewetson appeared.

Hewetson's method of batting was simple. Holding his bat very firmly at the very top of the handle, he thrust his left leg towards the pitch of every ball not obviously a long-hop, and swung the bat like a son of Anak. The short ball on the wicket or to the off, he prodded coaxingly towards third man. He was tall, florid, and of great strength, and he feared neither man nor demon. Soon after he came in, Ashton put on Ronnie Aird to bowl at the Pavilion end. Now Aird was, and is, an admirable batsman, but his bowling was the answer to the blacksmith's prayer, straight, pitched up, slowish, and innocent of bias. So Hewetson began with two high curving fours over mid-off and a colossal six on to the lawn-tennis court which then lay to the left of the pavilion. Soon, he smashed his bat, and another was sent out. In 25 minutes he scored 57, and strode away with a face like steaming strawberries. I borrowed his bat. During Hewetson's innings my score rose from 12 to 14, and I was once barracked for failing to let my partner have the bowling. Joined by the jovial Raikes, I decided on haste, and cracked several balls over cover-point's head. At 53 I skied a dolly to mid-off. The innings closed for 422.

During the following night the heat was terrific. At five o'clock in the morning came the long-threatened storm. As the rain swished down, I thought gratefully of Bettington and Stevens, and so to sleep. Stevens, bowling off-spinners, did most of the work in the Cambridge first innings, only Ashton (15) reaching double figures. In the second, Leonard Crawley was promoted to number one. Bettington, blacker than ever in the heat and toil, told me to "pitch 'em up wide on the off, and I'll skirt about down by the Tavern". Crawley made a few glorious strokes, then skied one high to Bettington who, having caught it, said: "That's enough for you," and began his last spell, at the Nursery end. By now the pitch was biting fiercely. Allen, Ashton, and Tomlinson each resisted for a time. But Bettington was not to be denied. He took 8 for 66, 5 clean bowled, and walked rapidly towards the pavilion, snapping his fingers, as if asking for a few more batsmen. He had waited four years for this.

So, my four years of bowling against Cambridge produced 2 wickets, Hubert Ashton and Leonard Crawley. In all matches for Oxford, I took 146 wickets at 21 each, and made 518 runs with an average of 15. In this period, I caught, and missed, my share of slip catches; and talked millions of words.

A week later, I joined the Somerset team against Kent at Maidstone. Three of our best cricketers, J. C. White, M. D. Lyon, and T. C. Lowry, were playing for the Gentlemen against the Players at Lord's, where Lyon made a brilliant 120, Greville Stevens 122. George Louden, the Essex amateur, after having Jack Hobbs l.b.w. for 6, took 5 for 49 in 26·3 overs. Very tall, and with a lovely high action, Louden was a bowler of England quality, but, owing to business, he could play rarely in County cricket.

To return to Maidstone. We lost a good match by 73 runs. I had 6 wickets, including Hardinge twice for the second time that summer. This started me on a run in which I took 39 wickets in 4 matches at just under 14 runs each. Our defeat by Kent was followed by two victories over Sussex. At Eastbourne, we won by 10 wickets. I had 14 for 106. At Taunton, set to make 268 in the fourth innings, we won by 6 wickets, Lowry hammering Tate, Gilligan, and George Cox for 77, and MacBryan making a masterly 116 not out. Here I had 8 wickets for 138 runs. Going to Bristol for the bank-holiday match, we beat Gloucestershire by an innings and 70 runs. M. D. Lyon and Earle both scored a century, and that once-famous spectator, Joe Bottle, roared his impartial advice to both teams. I took 11 for 157. So, with six matches left, I needed only 10 wickets for the hundred.

Three matches at Weston-super-Mare yielded only eight, though I have always reckoned that the ball which bowled George Challenor, of the West Indies, was worth five wickets— a shooter that also cut in from the leg. Then, at Portsmouth, after getting rid of Kennedy, I had Jack Newman caught at slip, and the thing was done. I have made a good fuss about this performance, but I knew that 1923 would be my last and only chance. Never again was I able to play through a full season, or near it. I also knew that it was my last chance of reaching a Test Trial match. I didn't, though I watched the chief selector of that year, "Shrimp" Leveson Gower, picking his teams for England v. The Rest in the Royal Hotel, Weston-super-Mare. I had earned the right to hope, but no more. Jack MacBryan went up and played for the Rest, and made 80, the highest score in the match.

At the end of that season, I went up to Blackpool and played in a Festival match for Jack Sharp's team against Lionel Tennyson's. Financially, the Festival was a flop, and was played almost in camera. It needed a far richer house to counterbalance the free lunches that the friends of the Committee gave themselves. But the fun was unquenchable. At the start of their innings, the umpires announced that they had been instructed to be "very generous about l.b.w. decisions". This was cheerful news in face of a batting order that started with Russell, Sandham, Ted Bowley, P. Mead, and H. L. Dales. George Gunn, sidling up from mid-on, said to one of the umpires: "and, I suppose, if any one's bowled (rhyming with 'scowled') it's just a nusty accident?"

In 1924 Somerset beat Middlesex at Lord's by 37 runs. In their first innings of 128, I had 9 for 38. On the strength of this I was chosen for the Gentlemen v. Players at Lord's. So were White, Lyon, and MacBryan from Somerset. There were a few places still left for the England team that was to sail under A. E. R. Gilligan for Australia, and hope flickered faintly

around my fancy. The Players won the toss. Johnny Douglas
(Pavilion end) and I opened the bowling to Jack Hobbs and
Herbert Sutcliffe. The pitch was very lively. Hobbs was clean
beaten by Douglas three times in the first over, and, in answer to
Douglas's whirling execrations, said: "Well bowled, Colonel,
well bowled". My first ball hit Sutcliffe in the midriff. But they
batted themselves out of the trough, and Hobbs went on to one
of his incomparable hundreds. Sutcliffe, when 20, was caught
off me and his splice by Douglas at backward point. Later, I
had J. W. Hearne caught low in the slips by Greville Stevens for
61 and caught and bowled Maurice Tate, for 50, as I stood nearly
on his huge feet. "Why," he said afterwards, "you came down
the pitch like Abraham." They made 514, Roy Kilner contributing a very hearty 113. He died four years later, and Yorkshire
lost a grand all-rounder, a very true and gay sportsman.

Our batting broke down twice. In our first innings, Johnny
Douglas, at number six, was batting away tooth, gloves, and
nail, against Tate and Warwickshire's fast bowler, Harry
Howell, in an awkward light. I joined him at number eleven.
The light grew worse, and Bill Reeves, as he stood umpire at
square-leg, and watched some bouncers pass my nose, said in a
loud, hoarse whisper, "Do you want to be killed?" I said I didn't.
"Well then," he hissed, "why don't you appeal against the light?"
So I did; and in we all went. Johnny Douglas was amazed.
"Well," he said, as we walked in, "if that doesn't beat the bloody
band; an appeal against the light by a number . . . eleven! Why,
I was just getting my eye in."

I played again for Gentlemen v. Players at Scarborough, and
listened to that famous gourmet and hitter and criminologist,
C. I. Thornton, discoursing on Madame Fahmy and mutton-
fat; and I bowled out Sutcliffe in a sea-mist.

But I had shot one bolt for ever across cricket's door. Till now,
I had been a practising cricketer. Afterwards, I was but an
intervener.

XI

MOSTLY MORE CRICKET

I WENT back, as a master, to my first school, at Hindhead, and Mr Cyril Morgan-Brown pushed his nose reflectively with forefinger and said he wasn't sure what the right salary was, but he would look it up. I was just going back to what was always my second, and often my first, home.

It was the easiest, but the only, course, if some sort of a living was to be made. Had I known what I afterwards knew, I would somehow have rested for a year or two. I was still aware that something was far wrong in my health. For several hours in each day and for many weeks in each winter, I felt like warmed-up death.

The outdoor part of the schoolmaster's life was agreeable to a temperament that had no wish to grow up or to conform. So I doubled the years of man's minority, and stretched bachelordom to the limit of the elastic. I found time to "stand and stare", to play much more cricket and golf, and to live among people whom I liked and understood. Such things are not measurable. I also began to read. For fifteen years I had been tied to the literature of Greece and Rome. Now, I explored Dickens, Thackeray, Swift, Trollope, Jane Austen, Lewis Carroll, the Brontë Sisters—and, as fast as he could write, Edgar Wallace. Even medium-brows dismiss all Wallace's books as pot-boilers. They can't have read *Educated Evans*, or *The Four Just Men*. It depended on whether Wallace wanted a few thousand pounds in four days or four months. He had rare humour, and those who know say that his police details are right. Sometimes, in his haste, he allotted to the same character two different christian names in one chapter. Such charming inconsistencies shock the mole-mind of the pedant; but what are they, compared to his unequalled flair for drowning reason in excitement? He never committed the fatal mistake of mere ingenuity. He was seldom interested in the long-delayed solution. He meant to make our flesh creep, and it crept. His throne is still empty.

Meanwhile, brother Bobs was finishing at Edinburgh University, where he was a Military candidate sitting also for an Arts Degree. He had aimed to go up from Radley to New College, Oxford; but the 1914 War knocked that idea sideways. Demobilized from the Scots Guards, he had a short spell on circuit with tribunals set up by the Ministry of Pensions. He took notes, and was sometimes roped in as a chucker-out, when disappointed applicants threatened violence. The trouble then, as since, lay in the question of whether a disability had been caused, or only aggravated, by War Service. The government were over-ready to claim the benefit of a doubt. This stinginess was in scandalous contrast with the departmental extravagance of the Lloyd George régime. The war-dodgers grew gross on their contracts. The King of Commerce bought his peerage, while those who had suffered to save him were told that they were too old to be taken on as office-boys.

Visiting Edinburgh from Oxford, I found that a fresher wind of life blew on their University. They had more chances to sink or swim, fewer people to care which they did. There was one student in Ramsay Lodge, which stood high on the hill overlooking Princes Street, who was making the University his everlasting rest. Officially, he was studying for a medical career, but he had the means to defer the profession indefinitely. From time to time, he satisfied appearances by sitting an examination, his principal training for which was to lie in a bath with the hot tap gently running, his heel in the waste-hole, a can of beer on the soaptray, and a novel in his hand. Breakfast at Ramsay Lodge was commonly taken in a dressing-gown and served by a lady known as "Catherine of Russia", who smoked cigarettes through the night and lived through the day in a perpetual passion, bouncing plates till the soup flew right and left.

As a relief from learning, the men of Ramsay worked a gigantic catapult which was fitted into a window-frame, concealed from unwanted gaze by a convenient tree. With this engine they controlled the steep road from Princes Street. The effective range was several hundred yards. Oranges were the ammunition and the favourite target was any gathering of serious citizens in top-hats. On any threat of police inquiries the artillery was dismantled and hidden.

At the end of all this, Bobs took his degree and was commissioned to the Royal Scots. He has kept much of his Scottish patriotism, and at Rugger Internationals he backs Scotland, while I shout, unashamed, for England. My father could never understand an English bias, and used to count with pride the years since he had last been to London. In the last twenty-five years of his life, he rented a series of houses in Scotland. Some of them were intended only as residences of passage; others inspired vain hope of permanency. There was Barwhinnock, near Twynholm; Biggar Park, where a lady chauffeuse knocked down one of the posts of the front-gate, and pleaded a migraine as the cause of the lapse. Then, for a year after the war, we settled at Harvieston, near the bleak village of Gorebridge, ten miles from Edinburgh. It was here that a white-haired and dignified parlour-maid arrived for the Christmas season, and on her first evening laid out on the dinner-table every piece of silver and glass in the house. When asked why, she replied that such had been the custom for dinner in the family of her last noble Lord. Suspicion became certainty when she brought down a bunch of forks and spoons on the head of a visitor who had foolishly poked her nose into the pantry. She picked the right visitor.

It was at Harvieston that we found an old trunk of clothes which had belonged to my father in the late Victorian days and which we took, piece by piece, into Edinburgh and converted into money for the Cinema. A smashing frock-coat I kept, and for some years used it as an outer covering when going to dances.

In those days, Edinburgh society was like a mountain that grows ever colder towards the summit, where, dead from the kneecaps upwards, teetered the frozen few who spoke to God on Sundays and to a finely sifted residuum of mortals on one afternoon in the week.

Among the principal snow-women was Lady ———, Scottish wife of a foreign Consul in Edinburgh. She held receptions, where nothing below an Honourable received her smile, which resembled that first crack of the ice so dreaded by skaters. Some one persuaded her to give a dance, and invitations reached the less obviously brutal members of the military. Among them was young M——, a second-lieutenant in a very ancient regiment, who had drifted into the Service through sheer instability of purpose. He, and two particular pals, rightly decided that total abstinence was no preparation for the consular ball-room; but, by one of those mistimings so frequent in youth, they began the treatment too early. Arrived at the front door, they penetrated, by supreme will-power and luck, straight to the cloak-room. There, the two particular pals parted, one to irrecoverable seclusion in the closet, the other to a soporific and horizontal position in a large roller-towel. Second-Lieutenant M——, after one glance of envy at the roller-towel, decided that the honour of the Regiment now reposed in him alone. He ascended. Entering the ball-room, like Dr Brydon emerging from the Khyber Pass, he found, to his horror, that he was not merely alone, but also last. Flight was impossible. He had to cause himself to be announced. There, between him and his awful hostess, stretched an eternity of polished parquet, as once stretched those last hundred yards of the Olympic marathon before the glazing eyes of the luckless Dorando. But that Italian baker at least wore shorts and running shoes, whereas our victim was trussed in tight trews and tighter shoes. He was also impeded by a sword. On he floated, with mincing gait, watched by a now silent and, in parts, silently wagering company. He was almost there, when the sword and Bacchus won. His legs crossed, and he measured his circumference. The last barriers of courtesy were broken, and from his recumbent posture he shouted, "Damn and blast these bloody Mansion House dance-floors!"

The Scottish residential sequence was broken by a few descents upon Southsea, though my father's visits to that bracing resort of retired mariners were spasmodic and reluctant. Once committed to this environment, he would ruminate for a day or two, "regretting the warm mansion" whence the fork of fate had goaded him, and reading the *Scotsman* a day late; then, as a compromise with necessity, he would walk purposefully to the sea-front and examine the Isle of Wight through a telescope, commenting on the nature of the terrain and the possible deficiencies of its inhabitants. Next, the ships of peace and war; their tonnage, draught, class, origin, destination; everything that the telescope would take came up for scrutiny, for technical comment or humorous surmise.

He despised and disliked the sources of amusement and occupation that are open to the Southern Englishman. Piers and picture-houses, shopping, morning coffee, circulating libraries, tram-rides, golf. Most of all, he loathed gossip as something fit only for quite useless women and effeminate men. He was that which cartoonists cannot mock nor Tammany bosses understand, an intellectual and athletic Tory democrat. By sheer natural courtesy, he could appear, at a tea-party or some other unavoidable occasion, to be interested in the talk of those lives outside his own temple of mysteries. Above all social nuisances, he hated the specious young men who talk books and know "people". Their choicest epigrams he received with a succession of irritated "oomphs". He was a man of inexhaustible but unshowy kindness; totally just; with wit in plenty, whose full warmth was kept for a few over an evening fire. But, for him, when old friends went, they were never replaced. He saw the world that he loved and understood falling away around him. He cursed the substitutes of modernity, and was lonely in the crowd.

At Southsea, we were swindled by a retired Marine, who wore a white jacket and managed the kitchen and was very pleasant to everybody, including himself. So another Scottish venture was decided upon. This time it was Forres, which I had previously known only through Macbeth's famous inquiry. It is a beautiful district, as many will know; famous for its production of that political problem, Ramsay MacDonald, who was backed through life by the Forres biscuit magnate, Sir Alexander Grant. Sir Alexander had a fine private cricket ground, where he often entertained visiting international teams. Here, in 1926, I watched H. L. Collins's Australian eleven in the process of dispelling, at the expense of Scotland's bowlers, the melancholy induced by losing the "Ashes" to Percy Chapman's team at the Oval.

At the Episcopal Church, the clergyman preached the shortest sermons on record. They began with the sentence, "This week I just want to leave a little thought with you," and they ended with that "little thought". Whether this brevity was ascribable to lack of material or to an intimate knowledge of the local bus service, I never knew. But, as he descended from the pulpit, I used to smile inwardly when I thought of the tens of thousands of Scotsmen sitting, all over the country, under the reverberating extemporizations of hundreds of ministers.

It was at Forres that my father, for the only recorded time in his life, was trapped by a drawing-room tea-party on an away ground. How he was deceived, I do not know. But he found himself to be the only man in a room full of women, where smoking was either forbidden or forgotten. He solved the difficulty by locking himself into the lavatory and smoking three cigarettes on end.

Next year, my father and mother moved to Moffat. The great Scottish pilgrimage was over. They now contented themselves with purely local gyrations. There for a time, we will leave them; my mother, a little exhausted, but happy with her books, or writing her famous 20-page letters; my father, in the smoking-room, with the *Scotsman*, the *Morning Post*, *Truth*, and the *Autocar*, still in the late hours of the night pin-pointing the map of Scotland for the next migration, which never came off.

Schoolmastering. "One day telleth another, and one night certifieth another"; or, as Mr H. F. Ellis sometimes asked in *Punch*, "Assistant masters, are they insane?" Some of them decidedly. Mr K, for instance. A boy came to me one day and said, "Please, sir, Mr K told us this morning that, if we didn't get our equations right, we would never go to the heavenly mansions, and he pointed upstairs, sir, to the Green dormitory. Funny idea of heaven, hasn't he, sir?" Mr K took a violent dislike to all the other members of the staff. One way in which he worked it off was to award a very low rate of marks when examining the boys of another master. I. S. found that his star pupil had been given 12 out of 100 in the end-term Algebra paper. He multiplied the marks by seven, and everyone smiled again; except Mr K, who learnt of this stratagem, and left the school in a huff before the prize-giving.

The school flourished from year to year on common sense, humour, and a robust old-fashioned religion for which no substitute has been found by the cleverest reformers. The school's secrets were good-will, a right balance between work and games, and the minimum of supervision during free hours. A school in which the boys are always being "invigilated" is a bad place for boys and masters alike.

The village cricket club played its matches on a pitch which had a fair enough appearance, but was, in fact, little more than a whited sepulchre. Our opening bowlers were Mr Messenger, the village policeman, and Mr Percy Burrage, painter and decorator. The policeman, at slow-medium pace, was yet the more artistic attacker of the two. He had some subtlety of flight and a persuasive way with different umpires. Like Yorkshire's Wilfred Rhodes, when he hit the batsman's leg and knew it was not quite out, he would do much peering down the pitch and taking of angles, as if unwilling to let the umpire commit himself to a false decision. Then, when the moment came, he would turn round and say: "But how's *that?*" When the umpire failed to accept the bait, Mr Messenger would shake his head sadly, as at a sick child refusing a cream bun.

But Mr Burrage used no arts. He bowled round the wicket, at a very brisk and threatening pace, with lowish arm, and he grunted at delivery. He was short and stiff-built, with short, stiff, grey hair. He didn't care about angles and flights, blasting his way at the stumps, and appealing without apology or doubt when the ball hit the batsman on any part soever. When decisions were good, for him, he allowed himself a bleak smile. When otherwise, he cursed, loud and openly, and, retiring to a fielding position of his own invention, a sort of deep fourth slip, continued to rumble away like a frustrated volcano. Rest his soul; he was a proper enemy at cricket, and, in his season, a very prominent poacher.

We will leave the boys to their Latin Grammar and Algebra, and wander forth again to some County cricket. 1925. My own bowling was in a sorry muddle that summer. I was trying for speed; a stupid ambition, because what I gained in pace through the air I lost in nip from the grass, and I was always pitching them just too short. I persisted, obstinately, in spite of wise advice from Nigel Haig, of Middlesex, who bluntly told me that I hadn't the bottom for a fast bowler. My only success was for Somerset against Sussex, at leafy Horsham, and here the pitch was so fast and uncertain that my natural pace of fast-medium was enough.

Our own first innings amounted to 199, of which Tom Young made 86, Jack White 41. Maurice Tate took 5 wickets. Young was a free and beautiful stroke-player, to whom batting averages meant little. He enjoyed starting an innings with a four over cover-point's head, and, especially against Yorkshire, with another four past the slips. "That'll make the ——s chatter," he used to say. Jack batted stubbornly, as usual, with more wisdom than grace.

In the first over of their innings, I bowled Ted Bowley for o. Wicketkeeper "Tich" Cornford, opening the innings as if he'd never heard of places 10 and 11, batted very soundly. Two or three times a ball from me bounced over his head from a length, and the crowd barracked in defence of the little man. "Tich" was much amused, and said to me, "The trouble is, Mr Glasgow, they forget I'm not very far above the ground." I had him l.b.w. for 30, and soon half Sussex had gone for under 100. But we were held up by that admirable all-rounder, Bert Wensley, and the cunning George Cox senior, then in his fifty-third year. When these were parted, Maurice Tate whacked around like a genial policeman. So, for a shorter space, did the lusty Colonel A. C. Watson; and they led us by 14.

Eight of us reached double figures in the second innings. Tom Young added 48 to his 86, and that miracle of vigilance, C. C. C. Case stuck for 19. Guy Earle shook the trees of Horsham with a brisk 31, and George Hunt, chewing impassively at number ten, made 28 not out. Bowley brought our own little battle all square by having me l.b.w. for o. So Sussex needed 217 to win; the ideal match. They lost 4 wickets for less than 30, and though A. J. Holmes batted gallantly for 40, and George Cox was unbeaten for 23, they never quite looked like doing it, and we won by 76. There's nothing like a victory to think over as you tootle home on a motor-bicycle through an evening in June.

Two months later, at Taunton, I was an assistant in the final round of a famous record-hunt, when Jack Hobbs equalled and beat the number of centuries, 126, made by the immortal Doctor Grace. Records can be very dull affairs, especially if achieved by arrangement. But they have their great moments, and this was one of them.

Hobbs was now forty-two years old, but, whatever he may have lost in the matter of brilliance, he was at the very zenith of technical proficiency. In this summer of 1925 he scored 3,024 runs averaging 70·32, more than 11 units ahead of Pat Hendren. Age had respected the moderation and discipline of his life. He was still the trained athlete, broader of hip and thigh than when Tom Hayward first took him from their native Cambridge to open the innings for Surrey, but swift of foot and thought, balanced, enduring, and infinitely wise in knowledge gained from triumph over every kind of bowling on every variety of pitch. They often tell us, with wonder, and a certain finality of tone, how W. G. Grace would go for days without purposely letting a ball pass his bat at the crease. Well, that was W. G. To Hobbs belonged a judgement in leaving an awkward ball alone that I have never seen equalled. The late outswinger, with which you might cause the best County batsmen to give a catch to wicket-keeper or slips, Hobbs would allow to pass within inches of his off stump. There was a serene certainty in the process that was only his.

On Monday, 20 July 1925, Hobbs completed his 125th century with 105 against Kent at Blackheath, he and Sandham putting on 199 for the first wicket. Here the newspapers took up the matter, and their cricket correspondents gathered for the kill. For a month they were kept waiting. At Brighton, Tate had Hobbs l.b.w. for 1, and Surrey won in a single innings. In the return match against Kent, at the Oval, he was caught at wicket for 22. At Gloucester, he scored 52 and 38, and the headlines said, "Hobbs Fails Again". Back at the Oval, he went very strong up to 54 against Nottingham. In the second innings, he was again caught at wicket, for 1, off a young newcomer called Harold Larwood. Then the weather broke up. Fate, jealous for the great Doctor, seemed to say, "Thus far, and no farther." So, on 15 August, Surrey came down to us at Taunton, with Hobbs, a little doubtful, but still pursuing.

It was a Saturday; and the rubicund face of Mr Secretary Davey smiled to its limit as he saw the crowds roll in, but turned a little paler as he watched the motion-picture experts, with their impedimenta, climb on to the tin roof of the old pavilion. Most of the West Country, and several segments of London S.E., seemed to be present; clergymen, schoolboys, cockneys, farmers, Jack White's father on his favourite bench, and the still excited but visibly tiring cohort from Fleet Street. Even the ladies, without whom all cricket matches grow dull, forbore to discuss husbands and the contents of shop-windows, and joined in the single question—"Will he do it?"

Not at once, anyhow; for the toss had been won by Somerset; but not by the captain, John Daniell, who had severely strained his leg in making 174 not out and 108 in one match against Essex some weeks earlier. How many cricketers, I wonder, have made a century in each innings at the age of forty-six?

In the first innings, we batted very much as if the world were waiting for something better. Tom Young scored 58 in his own gay and resigned fashion; Peter Johnson followed with 30 in the classical manner, Reggie Ingle with a perky 22, and Jim Bridges with 25 in the old Weston-super-Mare style. All out for 167. We had brushed ourselves aside for the occasion.

At about four o'clock, Hobbs, with Sandham, walked out, to the whirr of cameras and the applause of his well-wishers, namely, the whole crowd. The bowlers were Jim Bridges, Quantocks end, and myself. In the very first over, from Jim, there were cheers and groans and those hybrid sounds that are begotten by excitement out of shock. Hobbs had been caught at cover-point, off a no-ball. Then, when he was but 7, I bowled him one that he cocked up, not hard, just wide of mid-on, who had anticipated, but in the wrong direction. And here it should be said that, from start to finish of the match, everyone concerned went flat out to have Hobbs's wicket. There was no arranging. Such a cricketer did not invite the indignity of help. A few overs later, I thought I had him l.b.w. The umpire did not; and that was that. Thereafter, till the close of play that evening, he gave no chance. But Old Man Record sat heavily upon him. The timing was often imperfect; each stroke to the length ball was a considered effort. He was batting, as Arthur Mailey would say, from memory. He was saved by perfection of style. At half-past six, he was 91 not out.

Apart from the bowlers, three men helped him to beat W. G. Grace's record. One was that most artistic Surrey batsman, D. J. Knight. He joined Hobbs on that afternoon, when Sandham had been caught off Bridges for 13, and, not for the first time, Knight was batting in a way that might have induced a stranger to ask which of the two was Hobbs. Knight had scored 34, when Hobbs called him for a very sharp run indeed. Knight said "No," but, seeing that Hobbs had gone too far to recover his ground, he darted past him, just past, and was run out; a courteous sacrifice.

It must have been a long week-end for Hobbs. Even at Sunday afternoon tea he was nailed by the motion-picture photo-

graphers. On Monday morning, the crowd poured in again, and
Somerset committee-men beamed affably alike on friends,
enemies, and total strangers. Jim Bridges had the first over at
Hobbs, whose partner, worthily, was Douglas R. Jardine. Hobbs
scored three singles, and so was 94 when I took up the attack.
How I longed to unloose something supremely and eternally unplayable, an inswinger, say, pitching on the leg stump and
sending the middle flying. Never the time and the place and the
"snifter" all together! I bowled four running that were very
straight and proper. He played back to each one, and I chose to
believe that he was nearly late to the fourth. Then, Lord bless
me, I bowled a no-ball. Whack went she, to the square-leg
boundary. From the sixth and last ball he scored a single: 99.
Then, with a single to leg off Bridges, he was there. At last the
cheering died away, and, at the end of the over, all on the field
shook him by the hand. Percy Fender, the Surrey captain,
carried out a glass. Hobbs ever since has maintained that it
contained only ginger-ale. Be that as it may, he raised the glass,
and, in the handsome words of a chronicler, "bowed to the crowd
before partaking of the refreshment". Within a few minutes, he
was caught at the wicket for 101.

And now for Hobbs's second and indirect helper, who made
possible the innings by which Dr Grace's record was surpassed.
This was MacBryan, who played one of his finest centuries for
Somerset, 109 in two hours and a quarter, with 16 fours. Young,
71, helped him to hoist the hundred for the first wicket. Hunt,
at number 8, smacked up 59, and Bridges weighed in with 26
at number 10, before, as he said, allowing for some spin from
Fender that never occurred. So we reached 374, and Surrey
were set to make 183 to win. Hobbs's second century in the match
was a beauty. His cares dropped from him, as the poet has it,
like the needles shaken from out the gusty pine. The same balls
which, in his first innings, he had pushed severely to cover-point
he now cracked to the boundary with serene abandon.

And with him was his third helper, that great junior partner,
Andrew Sandham, who played the needful part with intelligence and unselfishness. So Surrey won, and Hobbs beat the Old
Man's record, and the crowd went happily home, and Sam Woods
told us that it was all very fine and very nicely done, but that there
was only one Champion for him, and his name was W. G. Grace.

Next summer, in the middle of June, I was released from the academy for the Somerset match against Surrey, at the Oval. It was to rise to a rollicking, crazy finish. When Surrey came in to bat, a strong sun was working on a soft pitch, and there was the prospect of a royal battle between Hobbs and Jack White. Soon it was on, art stretching art to the utmost limit. Hobbs and Sandham, whose share was 19 runs, coaxed the score along to 75, when White forced Sandham back on to his stumps. Then he had Jeacocke and Baldwin caught by the hard-glaring Daniell at silly-point, and Jardine stumped. Next came Percy Fender. This was his sort of hour. But, before he could raise steam, White had him caught at wicket, for 0. Hobbs, now 70, fell at last, in the same way, and Jim Bridges sent back Peach and Strudwick. Surrey all out 136, and wicketkeeper Mervyn Hill smiling his way, like a sunset, to the pavilion. Mervyn, son of Vernon Hill, Somerset's left-handed hitter of the generation before, was properly framed for his job, strong as a Suffolk Punch, easy of temperament, an artist at working, sleeping, and eating; and when he stooped, he had something behind worth stooping with. A bastion of a man, and a gay good wicketkeeper.

Our own first innings was what the kinder critics call "undistinguished"; in other words, a blooming procession. Jack MacBryan relieved, or punctuated, it with 38. Our chief troubler was Alan Peach. He used a late inswing, and came briskly from the pitch, but he was primarily a fast-wicket bowler. So much the better his performance on that day and surface. Alan was the utility man of the Surrey side. He could, and later in this match did, hit with most muscular freedom. His meadow style had been raised, not spoilt, by sophistication. He was a fine fielder anywhere, notably at extra cover-point, with a very strong and accurate throw. In aspect and outlook, he had a round and ruddy health.

By the time Surrey batted a second time, the pitch had grown fast and true. Hobbs again. Not wholly forgetting Sandham. In his last three innings against us, Hobbs had scored 101, 101 not out, and 70. This time, he scored 5; then I had him l.b.w., bowling from the House of Commons end. As in Oxford against Surrey, six years before, I had no other wicket in the match; and, once more, I didn't bother about that. For some minutes, I trod privately, and several yards from the earth. Sandham corrected this lapse with 54; others scored with moderate comfort, Peach with immoderate haste. Guy Earle was called from his vast defences at mid-off to bowl. Though unsound as to a knee-joint, he could still, with a few steps, generate a very peppery speed, and he was as hot for the kill as in his youth at Harrow and Sandhurst. He had Sandham l.b.w. and knocked off two other victims; but Surrey were winning now. Percy Fender ran up 39 with that india-rubber wrist of his. Fender's batting was unequalled for a certain astute abandon, a disciplined recklessness. Most noisome to the bowler, and exhilarating to the crowd, was his high and far square-cutting. He could defend. Sometimes, the facts of the match, or perhaps some grave and ironical admonitions from Douglas Jardine between the overs, would persuade Fender to "try a little abstinence"; but just stopping up an end was not his line. It made him look like a wading-bird without any water.

So we needed 402 to win, and we began all wrong. John Daniell and M. D. Lyon were out very soon, and Tom Young was bowled just as he was growing warm. MacBryan added 51 to his 38 of the first innings. Quality stuff. Guy Earle was smacking about lustily when the imperturbable Shepherd bowled him with a ball that was neither better nor worse than the others. Jack White, George Hunt, in and out they went. Jim Bridges, remarking, according to wont, that the sun was shining and the bowling "not as good as yours and mine, Glasgy," proved his point to the limit of 23. Mervyn Hill, stout left-hander, was cursed with no emotions beyond defiance, but he was at once caught and bowled by that lazy-looking leg-breaker Stan Fenley, and so strung himself a pair of noughts and returned to arrange more hospitable processes than batting. On the morrow, Somerset were receiving Middlesex at Bath, and some of the side were already moving Bath-ward when it fell to number eleven, me, to join Peter Randall Johnson, whose score stood at 38, made in the old and classic style.

He, though none, least of all his partner, had a right to suspect it, was on the way to his last century in County cricket. He was in his forty-sixth year, but still youthful in figure. Randall Johnson was something to see at the wicket; tall, with aquiline good looks, graceful of movement, favouring the forward strokes. Not that he lacked skill in back-play. He was a sufficient master of that art. But driving was his glory. Like Lionel Palairet before him, he "leant on them" and they went. There was a courtesy in his cricket which exquisitely rebuked all that was merely effective and coarsely utilitarian. It was the difference between a minuet of old Versailles and a strict-time one-step in a dancing competition at Manchester.

The rain, as I write, is flogging the window; the wind howls like demons baulked of a sinner's soul, and the trees bow to it in their naked mock-humility; the Minister of Food is taking a whacking from the Country; "The sedge is withered from the lake, and no birds sing"; there is no elastic in our braces. But the sun, and the excitement, and the serious striving figures of that afternoon at the Oval come back, not in the exactitude of re-presentment, nor anything like it, but in that kaleidoscope which is the memory's motion-picture house.

It is only twenty years ago; in eternity, nothing; in swift mortal span, little more than a sleep and a waking. But, since then, many friends have gone, during would-be peace and senseless inevitable war; gone, too, a few enemies, if such we are silly enough to call those around us who love a different way from ours. Besides, it was only a game, nor even of its kind a game that mattered much to any except a few cricketers and cricket-watchers, a few unsmiling statisticians, a few reporters, who cursed cricket for missing their trains for them and damned first slip for standing too wide to catch that very late, that almost posthumous cut. Yes, yes; but it was *us*; with one wicket to fall and 217 runs to make; and we saw no reason, on earth, above it, or below, why we shouldn't make them.

Peter Johnson, with silk handkerchief knotted round his neck, smiled as I came to the wicket; in welcome, I chose to think, not just in tolerant amusement. That would be like him. He neither said nor implied "leave this to me". But I left it to him, when I could. He increased his driving, especially off Alan Peach, and favoured the skimmers that bisect mid-off and bowler, and make the umpire mind his corns. 200 went up. Soon, I joined the fun; and I knew where we stood when Percy Fender deserted leg-breaks for his faster experiments and medium all-sorts. I hooked him into the road behind the crowd. The ball bounced high into view and then into the precincts of a once famous hostelry.

And now we had the crowd with us; which is the solace and reward of last-wicketers. 250 up. 300. Cheers from the ring, with advice, exhortation; gestures of delight, and surprise, from the "lucky people" in the Somerset balcony; in the middle, some stirring around of already well-stirred fielders; Peach still very high-spirited; Fender less so; wicketkeeper Strudwick communicating sympathetic benevolence without abating hostile vigilance. 100 to win. Easy. Johnson to his hundred, and what a beauty. Under 80 to win. A cake-walk. Johnson, even more terrific; Glasgow wondering whether the Test match selectors are anywhere around.

Then Fender called on Jardine to bowl; whether by tactical design or, as I prefer to believe, because the glazing eye fell upon none other both fit and willing to bowl, I cannot, and Fender would not, say. Let not ambition mock the useful, if somewhat intermittent, toil of bowler Jardine. Let not envy deride the obscure destiny, or question the obscurer intentions, of his deliveries. In his Oxford days, we have seen him inspired to unhook such as P. Perrin and Jack Russell from the perches of the mighty. But it is not for his own bowling that this Spartan cricketer and great leader will be remembered, except by me. Yet, at that fatal instant, it was not Jardine, but the telegraph-board, that ruined me. It showed my score, 49. The once pale ghost of victory was almost a body; alive, tangible, possessed. Some sudden madness seized me; so pardonable, if the Fates of cricket knew how to pardon; with one eye on my score and the other on the presumed perimeter of the ball, I chopped, avid but casual—and there was the ball in Strudwick's hands, and Jardine smiling, and Randall Johnson alone in his glory.

XII

CORNER OF FLEET STREET

IT is doubtful whether more nonsense is written about the
Press or by it. On the whole, the Abouts have it. Journalism
has been disguised in two popular masks which may be
called, for convenience, Philip Gibbs and Hard-Boiled Harry.

Philip Gibbs's *The Street of Adventure* is a pleasant enough novel
in the genteel and emasculate manner, and it is already acquir-
ing the faded charm of a period piece. Part of it, you may recall,
describes how a few young gentlemen, seeking a livelihood by
the pen, are looked after by a kind and competent lady. Prettily
done. But it exudes a mild perspiration of snobbery rather than
the rank sweat of reality. The young and as yet unhailed
geniuses go forth with virgin thoughts and note-books, with
glossy new fountain-pens, and come home to tell mother all
about it over a cup of tea and an egg, whose very frying suggests
a gentlemanly Bohemianism; and mother, who has Christian
patience, listens, then counters with eager sympathy and advice,
then sends them with her blessing to bed, as they do look so
burnt out with well-bred ardour and so exhausted by semi-
colons and metaphors. But why "The Street of Adventure"? All
streets are exciting; Watling Street, the Appian Way, Totten-
ham Court Road, Lombard Street, if you are Becky Sharp; the
local High Street, if you have a cork leg and a bottle of Red
Biddy inside you. The only adventures I have had in Fleet Street
are buying a bottle of Eau de Cologne for five shillings in the
twilight from a gentleman with a porous nose and a confidential
voice, and nearly being cut down by a taxi when making for
the Men's Lavatory in Ludgate Circus, which anyhow was closed
for repairs.

Hard-Boiled Harry is a modern Romance. He lives in motion-
pictures and detective stories. In the latter, he helps the detective after early snubs, eats little and sleeps less, and, if the sleuth
falls down on his footwork in the last chapter, marries the heroine.
On the pictures he is more urgently needed, because the blind

detective's Alsatian dog is apt to commit some error in deduction or be chloroformed by an unfrocked doctor. Hard-Boiled Harry risks dismissal by neglecting all other assignments in favour of murder. The Flower Show—First Prize for Medium Trumpets, Miss Gilling-Anstruther—has to get along without him. He sits on the desk of the Editor (who has no jacket but six telephones), smokes sideways and wears his hat on the back of his hair-parting. He's always right, and the Editor, in other respects an ignorant bum, knows this. The film-going public, that is, the public, enjoys Hard-Boiled Harry, and what the public enjoys it also comes to believe. Oddly enough, the journalist himself, though not strictly to be ranked as part of the public, may also come to believe that he is Hard-Boiled Harry in person.

So he goes into training for the part. If he is not by nature tough, he overcomes the deficiency by art and practice, speaking in clipped and commanding tones. He affects to have no spare time except for drinking. He has long conversations, of spurious intimacy, with Floozy Flo, the fat barmaid. He learns how to drop off fast-moving motor-buses while giving the clippy a naughty wink. Fearing the laughter or surprise of his peers, he pours the cynic's cold water on his own little fire of idealism. He speaks with jocular contempt of the Old School Tie, Oxford and Cambridge; but, if he allows himself time for a wife and a son, he will probably aim to send the boy to public school and the university. He professes to regard the House of Commons as a bundle of bribed half-wits and careerists. Yet, if he saw a Member of Parliament strolling into the saloon, he would desert any one short of his own editor for the chance of an introduction. Also, he's a sentimentalist. And, the higher up the ladder, the more sentimental; till you reach the Manager of the newspaper himself, whose tenderness is such that he would order the largest wreath in the country to adorn the mortal remains of the chap whom he sacked because of five shillings the wrong way in expenses. Hard-Boiled Harry is neither better nor worse than the rest of us. But he wastes his vitality in a futile hoax. He's an ass in a spotted lion's skin.

Also to be found on the Silly Side of the Street is the creature known as Scoop. A Scoop, from the point of view of the Scooper, is a piece of news or information which the other newspapers have missed, overlooked, or thrown into the wastepaper basket. For instance, if St Paul's Cathedral were burnt to the ground during the small hours of the morning, and the conflagration happened to escape the notice of all save the junior reporter of the "Daily Whistle", who was proceeding homewards after six games of snooker at the Club, then it is possible that the "Daily Whistle" alone, in its Late London Edition, would report the incident and so have a Scoop. But, if the fire also reached the eye or ear of some vigilant representative of the "Daily Saxophone", then no Scoop.

It is not difficult, therefore, to infer that the Scoop Real, as distinct from the Scoop Supposed, is in these days virtually unknown. Press Bureaux, Scotland Yard, and Ministries of Information see to that. And, if they should chance to slip up, there is the Radio, which enables the 7 o'clock a.m. listener to anticipate the spice which the editor of his newspaper has considerately imposed on the daily cake.

Years ago, before Science got us down, the Scoop must have been quite a jolly affair. The King Stanislas of Ruritania dies, after a fifty-year reign devoid of excitement except an occasional change of mistress or variation in the design of military helmets. Resident in the Royal capital are Colonel Jenkins, a correspondent of *The Times*, and Commander Funnel, ditto for the *Morning Post*. There are no telegrams or telephone. Railways are unknown, steam-ships still in a laughable infancy. Letters to England, when collected, take two years. So the Colonel and the Commander get together over a few bottles of the best Hockburgheimer. The Colonel, dismissing the wine-drops from his moustache with an old-fashioned sweep of the hand, says: "Funnel, I suppose you have heard that His Majesty King Stanislas died the day before yesterday while reviewing his cavalry in the Palace Yard?" The Commander, breaking a silence of forty-eight hours, replies: "Jenkins, I have. Silly fool would review in the afternoon heat without his hat on." The Colonel, disregarding the backhander at the Army, pours out a half-pint, then passes the bottle. After a short interval of swallowing, the Colonel says: "I shall take the news by land; horseback, diligence, and so on." "And I," says the Commander, "shall take it by river and sea; Danube, Black Sea, Bosphorus, Aegean, Straits of Messina, Gibraltar. And I bet I get there first." "How much?" says the Colonel. "A champagne dinner at

Brookes'," says the Commander; and off they go. The Colonel
is mistakenly arrested in Budapest on a charge of fraudulent
impersonation and incitement to rebellion, and, when he comes
out, finds he has missed the last drosky for six months. The Commander, meeting contrary winds off Cape Spartivento and losing his compass and half a spinnaker, is driven steadily backwards to Sevastopol. Disgusted, he returns to Ruritania via
Odessa and the Carpathians. Both are recalled to London,
which they reach in time to read of King Stanislas's life, reign,
and death, in *Chambers' Encyclopaedia*.

To return to Fleet Street. It has always surprised me that
the Kings of newspapers, who must rank among the shrewdest
salesmen in the world, do not seem to notice that 9,999 out of
every 10,000 readers don't care a sausage for a Scoop, for the
good reason that they wouldn't know a Scoop if they saw it.
Anyhow, the man who reads the *News Chronicle*, say, is not going
to chuck it over for the *Daily Mail*, say, because the *Daily Mail*
reports the Rationing of Pepper and the Return to Constitu-
tional Monarchy in Spain, while the *News Chronicle* reports
neither. The reader is far more likely to say, "To hell with pepper
—and Spain," and pass on to the Racing, Soccer, or Cricket;
or, in the case of a lady, to the latest photograph of a Princess
dancing with a Guards Officer.

The truth is, our daily newspapers have been forced into a
state of flux and dither between their ancient desire to educate
the public and their increasing need to entertain it. No Editor,
even if four out of his eight pages exhibit little else but potted
pictorial sex, is wholly free from the idea that he must teach his
readers what they ought to think. He knows, and they know, that
they don't *want* to think. They've had enough thought on
whether Chelsea can beat Arsenal and on how to heat a room
without a fire. But he sticks to it, does the Editor. He slips in an
occasional leading article on Bessarabia or Calories; that's for
education and the look of the thing. Then, surrendering his
brain to the need for public entertainment, he hits on that perfect mixture of instruction and amusement, the General Knowledge Paper. With all the skill but none of the labour of an
itinerant vendor of quack medicines, he imposes on his readers
a taste for general information. The reader enjoys this. He is
stimulated by emulation, and, discovering that Paracelsus is a

poem and not a Derby winner, fancies himself to be half way to a professorship.

The Editor of a daily newspaper is a clever fellow, and I raise to him what passes for a hat. But there is one thing that he cannot do, even if he were willing; namely, to produce a newspaper that bears any true relation to what is happening in the world. As to matters of fact, in time of peace he is restrained by the policy of the proprietors, in time of war he is restrained by Security and the policy of the proprietors. As to matters of opinion, in war or peace he is restrained by the policy of the proprietors and by libel laws which are as monstrous as the dinosaur and no less out of date. "There's nothing in the newspaper" is an old and popular lament, but it's true. How could it be otherwise when newspapers, subjected to every artifice of restriction and suppression, must rest discontent with distorted opinions on castrated facts? What a joke! What a tragedy! Ought we to laugh or weep when, at the celebration of the 50th or 100th birthday of some newspaper, the proprietor of a rival newspaper rises, and with all the solemnity and sincerity that he can summon, makes a speech on the Freedom of the Press. Freedom of Wormwood Scrubs.

It was in March, 1933, that I had a message from Tom Hodder, sports editor of the *Morning Post*, asking if I could go next day to Prince's, Sandwich, to report the singles in the golf match between Oxford and Cambridge. Major C. K. Hutchison, he said, who was writing on the foursomes that very day, had decided to retire from the scene. My first sensation was one of delight. I could have a free view of an exciting event on links that I had long wanted to see. Then doubt stepped in. Why was Hutchison, the regular Golf Correspondent and a player of distinction, receding from his duties? Was golf-reporting so severe a pastime that it might suddenly strike down even the expert? Had he been sacked? If so, what chance had I of survival? But did it matter if I was sacked? Not much. I should at least have had a nice day by the sea-side. So, without inquiring into the matter of pecuniary remuneration, I said, "Yes," then got and took my leave.

Rushing fools have more fun than refraining angels. Had I been less ignorant and Tom Hodder less desperate, I would have stayed at Hindhead to inflict Increasing Genitive Plurals of the Third Declension on the ears of reluctant students, and Tom would have received an intelligible report from the Press Agency in time for the second edition instead of an imaginative parody at eleven o'clock p.m. The extenuating reasons, should you be wondering, of my selection for this task was that the *Morning Post*, some time earlier, had printed a report I sent them on a match of golf played at Hindhead between James Braid and Alexander Herd, during which Herd, the senior in years, had remarked, "The old man seems to be holing the long ones to-day." It had also printed two pieces of verse, "The One-Way Boy" and "The Critic", which I contributed to P. F. (now Sir Pelham) Warner's magazine the *Cricketer*.

Princes, Sandwich, was all, more than all, my fancy had painted. The sun shone, a light breeze blew, and the Club kept an excellent table. A paradise but for two points: I knew as much about reporting as about the Dong with the luminous Nose; and Cambridge was beating Oxford nearly all along the line. Time has effaced the significance, but not the memory, of those two tragedies. As to the golf, one match on the day, and ever since in memory, pushed all the others aside, the match between P. H. F. White of Cambridge and C. Middleton of Oxford. Both came from Charterhouse, and so did I. I wanted to see them in action, and, for once, my own desire and the requirements of the public coincided in happy marriage.

Middleton was an athlete, tall and strong; a man of long silences punctuated by a shrewd and sometimes Rabelaisian wit, which showed that the silence hadn't been wasted. He played soccer for Oxford, and came near also to a Cricket Blue. White, though a less accomplished all-rounder, was known to be a tough and rapidly improving golfer who, playing from a handicap of five, had already beaten several players of distinction in this tournament and that. He, too, was no chatter-box. From the very start, they played golf worthy of any Amateur Championship final. Calmly, vastly, with almost no mistake, they matched shot for shot. At the end of the first eighteen, Middleton, with a score of 72, was 2 up. After lunch, White holed the first nine holes in 33 strokes, and Middleton, out in 36, allowed himself the single comment: "Look here; you're supposed to do the long holes in four, not three." White still had his lead of one on the eighteenth tee. Something or somebody was due to burst, and at last human nature had a say. Neither played the last hole quite as intended, and White was left with a little putt, say two feet, to halve the hole and win. It was a slithery, tricky little beast; he allowed just too much for the slope from the right, and one of the greatest matches of golf ever played between undergraduates ended all square and with justice done.

There was little else to please an Oxford heart, except a brave, if eccentric, finish by Oxford's J. S. O. Haslewood against W. E. Carr. These two came all square to the eighteenth tee in their second round. Carr hit a good drive, then cut a spoon shot into the not very malignant bunker on the right of the green. Haslewood was short from the tee and short with his second. Then, wearying of shortness, he struck a mashie shot with such venom that the ball seemed to disappear into the Club-house. It was found, if I remember, on a path skirting a little flower-bed by the Club-house wall, just playable by a golfer both pliable and optimistic. But Haslewood also had to deal with an object of strange architecture that might have been either a bird-bath or a portable sundial. At last the way was cleared, and he played the stroke, a forcing winner of some forty yards, up the bank and on to the green. Carr chipped out on to the green in three and putted up stone dead. Haslewood, mustering his last reserves, holed his four-yarder, and the match was halved.

Nearly everywhere else, it was Cambridge. In the top single K. T. Thompson, a fine iron player from Scotland, beat E. H. Moss of Oxford. "Jimmy" Moss was a first-rate but unlucky games-player. Twice in the Oxford v. Cambridge golf match he ran into players who "went a little mad", as they say, and he was one of the very best batsmen who failed to get a Cricket Blue; stylish and strong in attack, and sounder in defence than many a more famous Malvernian. On tour with the Oxford Harlequins he would bat with a skill and grace that made us wonder how he had eluded his full due. He was a master at Radley when the Hitler war came. After a short spell in the Army, he transferred to the Royal Air Force, became a Bomber Pilot, won the Distinguished Flying Cross, and was lost in an attack on Germany. He will be remembered as a character of purest gold.

During this match at Sandwich, I first met Henry Longhurst, a scratch golfer and a then recent captain of Cambridge, soon to become well known for his golf writing in the *Evening Standard* and the *Sunday Times*, to say nothing of some straight thinking and talking in one of the weekly illustrateds. Longhurst is as individual as a bright green pillar-box. He is not to be impressed by tradition because it is old or by novelty because it is new. He is not shackled by inhibition or bothered by custom. He is an unswerving disciple of realism. Others may dress up or water down their report to suit a known policy of the proprietors or a supposed interest of the readers. Not Henry. When you've read him, you've had it.

Like all golf writers, he would not seek to be compared with Bernard Darwin, who for many years has delighted thousands that scarce know the difference between Mr Snodgrass and a stymie; but Longhurst is the true complement to Darwin. No writer before Longhurst has so accurately expressed the outlook of the professional. Darwin could be great on the great professional, on his hero J. H. Taylor, or James Braid, Harry Vardon, or Walter Hagen. But Longhurst casts a wider net, and throws back no fish just because it's small. He is a humorous, but understanding, student of Mr Everyplayer, the 18-handicap fanatic who can't carry the rough from the Tiger Tee and tells the green committee so; of caddies, who to so many golfers are just porters in cloth caps and give advice that their employers are either unable or unwilling to follow; of lady golfers, who may not be quite so skilful as they would have their public believe. He invites and enjoys controversy; with an individual, or, as on one memorably comic occasion, with a Town Council, whose collective hackles he raised by writing in a public organ that the only exciting event in their town was the daily passage through it of a train carrying fish. For some years, Longhurst was something of a lone hand in his profession; and so it was natural that he should have become the friend, explainer, and champion of the once solitary Henry Cotton; natural, too, perhaps, that he should have appreciated and been appreciated by his boss, that tempestuous peer, Lord Beaverbrook, who is said to value the man that does not fear to wag back at him. Not long before the war, Longhurst published a book called *It Was Good While It Lasted*. Within a few years he had ceased to drive an Army Lorry and became a Conservative M.P. In the election of 1945 he lost his seat. "It was good while it lasted," shouted the successful electors at the announcement of the poll. I have a notion that he will soon be a legislator again, and for a good many years.

It was now Larwood time in Australia, and half the world seemed to be talking Body-Line. Books are still published on the supposed rights and wrongs of the Cricket Sensation Number One. It was the climax, and funeral, of one of the fastest and most accurate bowlers that cricket has ever known. Fourteen years have passed since Larwood scattered the Australians. The prime object of the system was to reduce the scoring of the miraculous Bradman to the normal, and the object was achieved. That admirable Australian cricket writer, Ray Robinson, has described the scene at Melbourne when, a fortnight before that first Test in 1932, Jardine first commanded the full salvo from his new weapon: "Poor Don! He had suddenly discovered that the game of cricket, which had been such fun, could be made harsh and bitter, when, about an hour before he came in that afternoon, he saw one of Larwood's bumpers strike Woodfull a sickening blow over the heart . . . When Larwood came on, with the new field-setting he had used against Woodfull (one slip, five leg fielders), Bradman lashed at the bumpers, if they were straight; when they bounded at him he skipped back or tumbled out of harm's way outside the off stump, reminding one of the hare that can look backward for danger while fleeing. Gusts of mirth came from those in the crowd who imagined Don was putting on a jitterbug turn to entertain them, or to make the English bowlers look cheap." It was the crash of their idol that enraged the Australians, and upon the instrument of his ruin they poured their boiling rage. I wish that Jardine had never put his new system into action. Victory at such a price was not worth it. At the same time, what would Larwood's treatment have been if the mighty Bradman had mastered him? Would he have been hooted in the streets, insulted publicly and privately, spat at and jeered? There is only one answer to that. Those matches, supposedly a Test of skill between teams of eleven, were in essence a single combat.

From those stormy days a comic little story has survived. Melbourne Inman, the English billiards player, was touring Australia. Attendance at his matches was thin. So one day, he said to an Australian billiards-fan: "Why don't people come to

watch us? After all, you know, I *was* champion of Great
Britain, more than once." "What do you expect," replied the
Australian, "if you come over here in Larwood time?" "—
me," said Inman, "you don't expect me to come over here in
lilac time, do you?"

One day in that April of 1933, Howell Gwynne, Editor of
the *Morning Post*, sent for me and asked me which of the two
games I would rather report for him, golf or cricket. I picked
cricket. He told me that Warner was giving up the job of cricket
correspondent. "Plum" was just finishing a not unexacting spell
of joint managership to Jardine's team in Australia, a task that
had proved too great a strain for even the well-known Warnerian
gift of diplomacy. I believe that "Plum" had had some misunder-
standing with the *Morning Post* about ways and means. It was
not for me to inquire. Here was a chance; hardly golden; 9
guineas a week, not free of Income Tax; but a chance; and I
took it.

I don't know where Gwynne would rank among Editors. I
imagine that he was shrewd, and I know that he was kind. He
happened to be fond of cricket, and, each summer, he used to
take a cricket team down to Dunmow, Essex, where he had a
very pleasant house. We lunched in the garden, through which
ran a trout stream, then played against a side called Dunmow
and District. It was the devil of a large District, too, and many
were the good cricketers who chanced to be in the neighbourhood each year for this match. Gwynne, too, cocked a selectional
eye, and in the last year of *The Morning Post*, the paper was
assisted by Alan Fairfax, the Australian Test cricketer, who made
a glorious century, starting with a cracking hook for six which
passed between the horns of an unwitting cow in the meadow
beyond mid-wicket. Fairfax was one of the finest figures of a
cricketer I have ever seen; tall and debonair, with both grace
and power in his batting. He was also a very good bowler, with
a high action and much speed from the pitch. One of the
finest all-rounders produced by Australia between the two wars.

Heroic figures come back to me from those matches; Peter
Lawless keeping wicket, and taking the risers on his echoing,
chest; A. S. Roncoroni, the vast England Rugby forward,
chanting strange ditties in the local pub, and carrying two pint
glasses in the fingers of one hand. Myself, in a waving glossy

black beard, grown perforce during an affliction of the skin; Tom
Greig, the librarian, whose younger son was our gay scorer,
whose forefinger drilled into your chest like a woodpecker's
beak to emphasize the obscurer ideas of his conversation. Tom
knows London as intimately as ever Sam Weller knew it; a Scot,
but a cockney by adoption. Jimmy Greig, his father, was the art
critic of the *Morning Post* for years beyond counting. He, too,
haunted cricket; a sharp but kindly wit, with rich memories of a
bygone Fleet Street. The two Greigs introduced me into the
Savage Club, where, in the dear dusty Adam house that overlooked the Thames, there talked and drank the few last who
had time, in a rushing world, to be "characters" and live at
magnificent random.

So I became a Cricket Correspondent, and my name, all of it,
appeared in large blue letters on the posters. I had always
laughed when playing cricket, except when the slip fielders
showed signs of lumbago, and I saw no reason to stop laughing
when I wrote about it. I knew nearly all the cricketers about
whom I was to write, many of them intimately; and in writing,
I fancied myself to be among them on the field, listening to the
comments and quips and complaints which are the unreported
life of cricket.

I have a poor memory for whole matches. But one match
comes back pretty clearly from that year of 1933, the Test between England and the West Indies at Old Trafford, Manchester. It was the last time D. R. Jardine played for England. For
the West Indies, Constantine and Martindale bowled a passable
imitation of Body-Line. Hammond was cut over the eye, and ran
off the field to have his face plastered, then ran back. But the fury
of attack fell upon Jardine. He met it like a rock in a storm.
Again and again he played the head-high risers down to his
toes, stone dead, or bowed under them when he must. When he
was 127 he cut Martindale into Constantine's hands, low in the
gulley. He stood waiting for the umpire's decision; then turned
to the pavilion, which rose and received him with the most
thunderous cheers I have ever heard on a cricket field.

That winter, I came to know more closely the strange and
delightful community which was the *Morning Post*. My job was
nominally that of a sports sub-editor, preparing other people's
writings for the printer. I avoided it whenever possible, and my

kindly boss, Tom Hodder, realizing, as I did also, that I was the worst sub-editor in Fleet Street, gave me outside assignments whenever he could. Thus, I haunted third-rate games of Association football, where Directors soothed me with whisky and technical information; I contrived to be present at 'Varsity golf matches against clubs of the London district, when the mighty Peter Lawless, our official correspondent, was needed elsewhere: I attended lunches of eminent sportsmen who wished for publicity in return for hospitality; I found myself at table tennis tournaments, where the players wore hair-nets and retrieved tremendous drives from the front row of spectators; and I even reached the Crystal Palace to describe the badminton match between the experts from Oxford and Cambridge. Here, my flippancy led me into rhyming indiscretion. The heating arrangements at the Crystal Palace were negligible. I compared our discomfort unfavourably to

> the days
> When Jack would take his Alice
> For a sixpenny trip on a paddle-ship,
> Or a spree to the Crystal Palace,

and declared that the best view of the Crystal Palace could be obtained from the twelfth green of the Purley Downs Golf Course. A correspondence followed, angry on one side, apologetic on the other; and Mr A. Podmore, doyen of sporting writers, took me severely to task for my behaviour, saying; "You know, the Admirals and Generals are furious about it." He did not disclose which of the senior officers had expressed discontent.

"Poddy" was a character. He lived and worked in Anderton's Hotel, Fleet Street, now removed for something far less interesting. His line was Public School sport, for which he was the sole reliable agency. "Poddy" sat in Anderton's, planning like Professor Moriarty, while his faithful aide, "Babs" Manfield, collected the evidence which "Poddy" then prepared with a view to publication. I had known him for twenty years, from the days when he used to appear at Charterhouse cricket matches in straw-hat with Old Haileyburian band and a white tie. He also arranged, for the benefit of us boys, a yearly and much loved cricket week at Mitcham, whence the great Tom Richardson had once walked with his cricket-bag, 15 miles to the Oval.

"Poddy" followed the careers of his "babies" with interest and encouragement. Nothing mattered much to him except Public School rugby and cricket. All else was dross and innovation. Anything that went wrong in the world was to be attributed to lack of the P.S. spirit.

But now, in the middle 1930's, the demand for his information was on the wane. His weekly, or even bi-weekly, two columns in the *Morning Post* were dwindling to a column or half a column. "Poddy", boiling away in his chair round the corner to the left in Anderton's lounge, must have known the change in the public taste and the increased pressure of sport that was not Public School, but he rejected the knowledge, and cursed. To me fell the task of appeasement when Tom Hodder had failed to include Podmore in his entirety. "Go and see the old man," Tom would say, "and tell him how things stand." And off I'd go, and drink a pint with him—his chair was close to the bell-push—and try by every artifice to persuade him that my visit was merely social. It never succeeded. He just waited for me to stop, and then started in. Tom Hodder never knew what I came in for. The *Morning Post* was taken for an up-and-down ride. "Dishonest" and "impolitic" were Poddy's mildest adjectives. Sometimes Manfield, faithful and rather exhausted, would enter during these monologues, and hover around with expressions of deprecating and despairing agreement. Then we'd all have another beer, at the expense of the *Morning Post*, and the audience would end. Poor, dear, angry old "Poddy"! Many were the stories of his benevolent but choleric nature. The best came from H. J. "Bertie" Henley, later of the *Daily Mail* and once a colleague of "Poddy's" on the *Sportsman*. Bertie had come home on seven days' leave from the Kaiser's war. "Poddy" met him in Fleet Street and took him into a pub. The old man's patriotism swelled up and he ordered four double whiskies, which were placed on the counter. Conversation turned on the War, and "Poddy" referred to the Germans as "those murdering swine". Whereat Bertie said: "Oh, I don't know, some of them aren't too bad." "What!" cried "Poddy"; "what did you say? Not too bad?" And, with one sweeping gesture, he swallowed all four whiskies, and stumped into the street. R.I.P. The world suitable for Poddies has gone for ever.

Edward Russell, our Managing Editor, had warned me

that journalists were cut off from social life. He was right. I lived in Chalk Farm, in a rather tumble-down little house, jointly managed by my old friend Winnie Morgan-Brown, and the Wheeler Robinsons. Bernard Wheeler Robinson, one of the ablest men in England, combined science with music. The house was for ever resounding with orchestral performances, Bernard being conductor of the London (Amateur) Orchestra; and, when the interior was silent, Haverstock Hill outside rang with itinerant instrumentalists. The most faithful and skilled was a cornet-player who rendered "Believe me, if all those endearing young charms." On Sunday mornings, the Chalk Farm Salvation Army silver band, the local champions, cheered the lie-a-bed with brisk and ecclesiastical marches. Also, the neighbourhood abounded in hideous and immoral cats. I once knew a monogamous cat.

The *Morning Post*, earliest founded of the London daily newspapers, was over a hundred-and-sixty years old. It is hard to appreciate that newspapers, like those who write them, are mortal. Hints of dissolution sometimes floated around. But I thrust away these black prophecies, and thought up new epigrams like any foolish undergraduate. Yet we were indeed the last retainers of a journal to which Charles Lamb had contributed jokes at 6d. a go. We were Outward Bound. So, I sit once more in that sub-editorial room, any Sunday afternoon in winter.

On my right, Tom Hodder, our chief, is saying, "I'm afraid not," into the telephone, with polite and weary patience. Tom always sounds weary, but he misses nothing, except when his mind strays away to some Utopian sports page, and his eye settles, not without anxiety, on Peter Lawless who, with yesterday's notes billowing around him, is already 300 words beyond what Tom knows he can give him on Richmond v. Blackheath. Behind his genial-glinting spectacles and ruddy countenance Peter is manufacturing endless metaphors from the tramp of forwards and the swerve of three-quarters. Across, at the other table, Mr Harmer, the chief sub-editor, looks up and, from impassive face, delivers a wink, then calls for an office-boy. "Fetch me some pins, boy." "How many, sir?" "Oh, about a hundred-and-fifty."

On my left sits Ernest Ward, who started in journalism in the 'Eighties, and wrote, always with enthusiasm and flowery delight, on every game that uses a ball. Rugger and cricket were his loves. Ernest was supposed to teach me the intricacies of headlines and varied prints. He had a weakness for the print spelt Bourgeois and pronounced Be-joyce, but the "M.P." didn't use it, and he regretted it, and recalled its frequent use when he was on *The Times*. "Once a *Times* man, always a *Times* man." But I learnt little from him of all that, and would lead him on to talk, "in a soft undercurrent of sound", on heroes of the past—Grace, Ranji, Stoddart, MacLaren, Arthur Shrewsbury, Poulton-Palmer, Gabe, Teddy Morgan. Ernest was all for the amateur, and he was perplexed and enraged by the commercial and sensational trend of sport. He was an irreclaimable Tory, and, for him, Tennis meant only the indoor court game of Henry the Eighth, Peter Latham, and Edgar Baerlein. The other game was pat-ball. Swimming, in his last days, was coming into popular favour and practice, and Tom Hodder decided to "splash it". Often, Ernest had to deal with this monstrous novelty, and he would sit looking at the "copy" on how to use the Back-Stroke as if at some repulsive insect, and murmur, not so softly, about "bloody bathing-machines and bloody bath attendants". He was of an age when all work should have been behind him, but he had ever been as generous with money as with trope and simile.

On the other side of the desk, guarding his private drawer of india-rubbers, pencil-sharpeners, and sporting compendia, sat Martin, known to our readers as the "Bellman". He prepared the racing intelligence for the printer and selected the supposed winners. Like most prophets, he was saturnine of aspect. He had a gift of trembling at the eyebrows when speaking. He was precise and meticulous, like an expert crochet-worker, as befitted one whose duty it was to arrange race-horses with a proper regard for their names and speeds. Duty was the word, for he evinced no pleasure or excitement in his work, and, even if he gave six winners, he entered the office as if fresh from a funeral. Unlike most of us, he used to read the paper from end to end, and drew grim satisfaction from gathering examples of faulty grammar or erratic syntax. At the news department he directed a special suspicion and contempt. He would have been a socialist if he hadn't been, unknown to himself, a Conservative. His professed politics were liberal, but he disliked the *News Chronicle*. It was hard to find what Martin admired. I did find it at length;

David Lloyd George. He was the hero. I had slated LL.G. with doggerel verse one day in the "M.P." It was soon after LL.G. had torn up Sir Douglas Haig in print, and I expressed contempt for one who "tramples on the unresisting dead". Martin was furious, and, over our evening tea and kipper, with trembling eyebrows, he explained my crime. But for all his angers and sarcasm and fault-finding, Martin could not conceal the benevolence beneath.

There were mysteries in that room not easy to solve. One of these sat aloof, at a private desk. He was of heavy and hippopotamine aspect, with thick spectacles and a furrowed brow. When the Sporting Desk exceeded in any way with sudden laugh or curse, he would slowly turn round, pivoting not only his head but his whole body, and fix us with the look of a Presbyterian beadle who suspected card-playing during the sermon. He came first of anyone to the office in the afternoon, and left reluctantly. It turned out that he was a Glaswegian who alone understood the workings of the wool market. He was also, I found, a soccer fan, and he gave me a history of the Glasgow Rangers from their inception and the reasons for the alleged superiority of Scottish footballers over English. He scolded me for my English sympathies. Poor Mr T. He knew, I fancy, that the *Morning Post* was his last and only occupation and hope. He confided to me reasons for its imminent disappearance, and, when the crash came, he did not long survive it.

Peter Lawless, seventeen stone and a heart to match, was Number Two Rugger correspondent. Number One was Teddy Wakelam, famous for his broadcasts of Internationals, which he conducted with a humour, a speed of thought, and an exuberance of phrase never since equalled. Peter was also our Golf Correspondent Number One, under the pen-name "Vagrant". Aptly was he named; for he scoured the links with stupendous ubiquity, at one moment erect like a Colossus on a sand-hill, the next, jutting the top 12 inches of his 76 over the crowd by the putting-green. He bulged with notes on the play, a perambulating encyclopaedia. His motto was "I shall be there". Like the relay system of the ancient Persian Kings, nothing stopped him; not hail, nor winds, nor flood. He loved to tell how, carrying an involuntary hod of snow on his hat, he went out to the furthest point of the course, took four pages of notes on the shivering golfers, and returned to the club-house to find that play had been cancelled.

A mighty man, Peter Lawless, amateur heavy-weight boxer; oarsman who had rowed in the Grand at Henley; rugger forward for Richmond and for England in a Victory International; vast and gentle; hearty and sensitive; expansive and reserved. In a cynical profession he was a mostly unsuspected and utterly incurable romantic. When Edward the Eighth abdicated, he lifted a pint "to the King across the Water". Before coming into Fleet Street, he had been engaged in the family wine business. The ways of that friendly and easy-going life survived in him. There was a magnificent irrationalism in his arrangements. Always with Peter things would come right, and their temporary wrongness was beneath a fellow's notice. Financial knots would conjure themselves undone. "How are you, Peter?" "Oh, fighting a rearguard action, you know; but the enemy, in their bloody little bowler hats, faint and fail." Gargantua would have raised an eyebrow at Peter's eating and drinking. Steaks vanished like particles of dust; pint-pots were thimbles. Often he would come to the office on a Sunday in short black coat and city gent's trousers. Some might attribute this habit to Sabbatical deference. But I knew it was a sign of wassail; a designed gesture of respect to Bohemianism. Smiling, he would select the soundest chair in the office, and, like an illusionist, draw from pocket his endless memoranda. "Fetch me some K's," he once shouted to an astounded office-boy; "mine don't work to-day."

When Lord Camrose bought the *Morning Post*, the purchase included Peter, and he entered the orderly halls of the *Daily Telegraph* like a rush of air. The Hitler war came, and he was sent as correspondent to France, where as a boy he had won the Military Cross. His messages kept the Censor on his toes. When France fell, he retired, on Intelligence work, to Oxford. His office was in Pembroke College; in Oriel he entertained; and it was there that we shared sixteen slices of spam in our last meal together. D-Day came, and Peter, now fifty-five, was out in France again. His messages rose to the full height of the demand. Driving through Paris on its day of liberation, he wrote— "Every mother wants her child to be kissed, and the latest addition has just been firmly placed on my typewriter." On to the Rhine. Calculating, but quite fearless, he crossed the Re-

magen Bridge, to do his work. He was hit, and mortally wounded.
He had stuck to his old motto: "I shall be there." As an American
officer said: "They don't come much better than that guy."

Our News Editor on the "M.P." was Mervyn Ellis, an able
and mercurial Welshman who, though interested in sport, and
therefore a potential danger to any cricket correspondent, soon
recognized in me one who could not distinguish a Scoop from
a fire-iron. He therefore sent me out to describe The Lord Mayor's
Show, which I did, easily, from the billiard-room windows of
The Baynard Castle in Queen Victoria Street. My only other
assignment from the News Room was to describe the funeral
cortege of George the Fifth as it proceeded down Park Lane towards Paddington. This I watched in a small mirror mounted
on a walking stick. The wind whistled through the bare trees.
The new King, Edward, looked haggard and anxious. I had a
deep and undefined feeling that some different and unsafer life
was beginning for every one.

Yet, allergic to Scoops as I was, I once came near to landing a
big fish for the paper. I was sitting one winter's evening in the
office, wondering whether Tom Hodder would notice my absence for half-an-hour, when an office-boy came up and confided
to me in sepulchral and adenoidal tones that a gentleman would
like to see me in the waiting-room, please. The visitor proved to
be a tall young man of mysterious manner and pale, flaccid face.
However, as he might be the Chairman's nephew or a valued
contributor on one of the less reputable pastimes, I suppressed
my desire to ask him to withdraw instantly. He told me that he
was on the staff of a certain Weekly Illustrated, as also was
Lady ——, the niece of a noble Duke. I found no reason to dis-
agree. "The point is," he said, gazing into his glass, for we had
now reached the saloon bar, "the point is that the Duke of——
has issued a writ for libel against our paper and his niece because
of an article of hers on the Duke, her uncle, which was published
recently." Words of Sherlock Holmes floated to my mind—"A
little indiscreet, no more." "And now," went on the flaccid young
man, "do the *Morning Post* want this Scoop?" I agreed to take
soundings. "I expect," he said, "you would like to see the writ?"
So, not averse from such an inspection, I said yes, I would like to
see it. I paid for the drinks, and we proceeded by taxi, though

bus would have served, to the offices of the certain Weekly Illustrated. Here, at a desk in an inner room, sat an unsatisfactory
man, munching an apple. The editor, it seemed. "This," said my
escort, "is Mr Robertson-Glasgow, from the *Morning Post*, and
he'd like to see that writ." At this information, the Editor became very angry, and asked the flaccid young man who the hell
had told him he could tell any one they could inspect the writ.
The f.y.m. retorted in kind; so I withdrew to a convenient window, and waited my turn. At length the Editor, with surly reluctance, like a schoolboy taking an open dictionary from beneath his desk, drew the writ, or a copy of the writ, from under
his blotter, and submitted it to my inspection; but warily, as if I
might make a snatch at it. "That seems all right," I said for
want of something better to say. "All right?" shouted the apple-
muncher; "I'll say so. It may cost us five thousand." Wearying of
high life, I took my leave, promising to give the f.y.m. a ring
about the result. Back at the "M.P." I was advised by Tom
Hodder to see Edward Russell. Russell was interested. A discussion between the high-ups followed. It was later reported that
the Editor and Russell wanted to print the story but that Robert
Hield, the Editor's deputy, advised to the contrary. Be that as
it may, caution prevailed. A pity, I thought. But, in the "M.P."
Dukes were Dukes to the very end. I shall never again be so near
to a Scoop.

Doubtless on the strength of this performance, I soon afterwards asked the Editor for a rise in salary. I was still being paid
the minimum. "And what," said the Editor, "is your present
salary?" I told him. "A great deal of money," he replied, "for
a young man." So, like a rejected vendor of vacuum-cleaners,
I withdrew.

XIII

PRESS BOX

CRICKET reporting used to be a solemn affair, and the Press Box, anyhow at Lord's, recalled the Silence Room of a Carnegie Library in Scotland. Small wonder, then, that the reports emanating from these precincts were as severe as a written judgement from Chancery. Humour was almost unknown, and cricket was conveyed to the reading public with a gentility which seemed to imply a rebuke to hastier and more vulgar pastimes.

The champions and exemplars of this method were the Pardons, of whom Sydney Pardon was the ablest and most illustrious. The Pardon Reporting Agency began, and still carries on, the business of serving to the newspapers reports of the principal cricket matches. The Agency achieves a remarkable standard of accuracy and impartiality. The firm have also for long been responsible for collecting and editing *Wisden's Almanack*, probably the most reliable sporting handbook in the country. Sydney Pardon was editor of *Wisden* for thirty-five seasons, from 1891 to 1925. His writings were distinguished by integrity and lucidity, and his opinion, though he himself had no practical experience of first-class cricket, was much sought by high authority. But the psychology, as we should now call it, of the cricketer was wholly unexplored. Off the field he had no relevant existence. A dry objectivity was achieved, and decorum, at all costs, was preserved. In the hands of a master, for such Sydney Pardon undoubtedly was, this method justified itself. But, when debased by clichés and rank "journalese" it had little to commend it but its lack of impropriety. There were a few rebels. Of these, Freddy (F. B.) Wilson was the wittiest and most notable. He had strong natural ability at ball games, playing cricket for Cambridge against Oxford in 1902-3-4 and being captain in his last year. He also excelled at tennis and rackets. He played with a sort of casual brilliance which was later to be reflected in his writings, where he invented technical terms of his own, and delightfully explored the limbo between fact and fancy.

The pendulum has swung full distance. Dullness is feared and avoided. So, unfortunately, is fact. The News Room has invaded Sport, and, on the occasion of Test matches, the cricket correspondent is often reinforced by a columnist or news-hawk, who, with furrowed brow, scours hotels and pavilions on his dark and dubious assignments. The technique of the game now ranks far below the "story", and you will often hear reporters, at the end of a full day's cricket, lamenting that "nothing has happened". No one has fallen dead while taking guard, or been arrested while placing the field.

In my own reports of cricket matches, I tried for naturalism. Flippancy was never far absent, because cricketers, especially bowlers, need flippancy to live and to avoid going a little queer. I was doomed, therefore, to affront those to whom cricket is a quasi-religion. As old Podmore would have said, "the Admirals and Generals won't stand it". Well, I cannot answer for the higher ranks, but some of the Colonels were very angry, and wrote complaining about "inane asides and abominations" and demanding the immediate return of Sir Pelham Warner and his articles.

In the Press Box, I have always been attracted to the unknown. Who, for instance, was that devotee, silent as the Sahara and methodical as the ant, who attended matches for the sole purpose of keeping the score? Was he the cricket editor of "Vital Statistics"? And to what mysterious end did sit, melancholy and on the back-most bench, a drooping red moustache on a mottled face and enormous ears? Some said that he was a telephonist, but I don't think so. That moustache would have entangled itself in the instrument. I think he had stepped from the pages of Lewis Carroll; he was the illustration for "the wild man went his weary way to a strange and lonely pump". Perhaps "Old Ebor" might have solved such problems; but he was never one to give knowledge away.

I am glad I overlapped "Old Ebor", whose legal name was Mr A. W. Pullin; an able critic of the old and tawny school. It was he who should have had a famous Scoop at Lord's. The Australians were here; 1926. On the first day of the second Test Australia had scored 338 for 8 wickets. Early on the Monday

morning it was discovered that someone had been careless about
a hose-pipe, which had over-watered a large area of grass, including a segment of the pitch. "Old Ebor", who rose early, was
first of the journalists on the scene, and he at once sent off a
Press telegram to his Yorkshire Evening paper, describing the
untoward incident; the Scoop Complete. Then he sat back in
comfortable silence. Some hours later, a messenger-boy came
into the Press Box and asked if a Mr Pullin or Bullin was present.
"Well," said the boy after introduction, "I was to tell you that
the telegraphist is very sorry but he can't read the writing in
your message early this morning, and would you very kindly do
it for him again?" It was then that "Old Ebor" broke silence.

H. J. (Bertie) Henley was the cricket correspondent of the
Daily Mail, and also a member of the Kitchen Committee of the
Surrey County Cricket Club at the Oval. Heavy, tall, even
Falstaffian of aspect, Bertie loved controversy. Somewhere, I
doubt not, he is still rapping his stick on the floor, and saying, "I
don't agree". He had strong powers of exposition and a strange
gift of being able to sketch with both hands at once. He said it was
something to do with the hemispheres of his brain. He did not
believe in watching all the cricket all the time. "The world is too
much with us," he would say, "and too many facts clog the
judgement." But he had a sixth sense for knowing what mattered,
whether he saw it or not. Bertie was a defender of defensive play
and of matches heroically saved, and he belaboured the Brighter
Cricket School. "All sixes and sevens", he called them. He wrote
his reports on paper that looked to be intended for less literary
purposes, and scattered his notes round and round the free spaces
on the score-card. When this was full, he would sometimes be
seen gazing in a predatory sort of way at the white stiff collar of a
colleague in front. He was never quite happy away from the
Oval, where he knew the very gasometers by name. Ernie Hayes
was his hero, and, when they met, the cricket could look after
itself. For matches in distant parts he travelled with a bag of very
small size and professional aspect. He loathed luxurious hotels,
preferring inns of unfashionable address but satisfactory cellar.
Bertie Henley cannot be replaced.

The Oval for H. J. Henley; for Major "Beau" Vincent of *The
Times*, Lord's. Not that there is anything pompous or conven-
tional about R.B.V. Far otherwise. He has a reverence, well con-

cealed, for tradition; a belief in oligarchy; but he is no respecter
of persons; nor of his dentures, which sometimes live in his overcoat pocket. He goes to Lord's in summer as he goes to Richmond Rugby ground in winter, to meet his friends. These are his
clubs, where he pursues leisure and his profession. Both are ad-
mirably done. His writing reflects the soul of cricket; its dignity
and humour; its old age and perpetual youth; and he has a
unique gift of transferring to print, without loss to either side, the
inconsequent wisdom of conversation.

He is an authority on the inner life of Rye, and can tell you,
better than books, about Henry James and E. F. Benson. His
father was a memorable and loved law to himself as Secretary of
the Rye Golf Club. Dacre Vincent had his own ideas, coincident
with most of his members, as to what visitors should play golf at
Rye, and he was not to be won over by important motor-cars and
expensive golf-bags. His best friends were not safe from criticism.
"You can always tell," he remarked one day, "when the Eton
masters have been here; the wash-basins are left full of dirty
water." To which the most famous of golfers among Eton masters,
stung beyond bearing, replied, "I would have you know, Vincent,
that, if seven people died, I should be a Viscount." I asked "Beau"
what was his father's answer to that. "Oh," said "Beau", "he
walked off into his office and addressed a few envelopes."

I know no stronger partisan than "Beau" for places and teams.
He is not wholly answerable when Cambridge, for whom he
played golf in the late Edwardian years, are pitted against Oxford. For many years too, he was unfavourable to Manchester as
a venue for Test matches. Restlessness would seize him soon after
the train left Euston, and he would prophesy a choice between
sunstroke and death by drowning. It was in that citadel of Free
Trade that we were ambling disjointedly one day when we saw
two newspaper-posters, placed side by side. One said, "Read
R. C. Robertson-Glasgow in the *Morning Post*"; the other, "Read
The Times and see what really happened".

The turf at Manchester's Old Trafford, unlike the neighbourhood, is a thing of beauty, and has broken the hearts and loosened
the tongues of many bowlers. The present groundsman, however, promised and, to some degree, performed a reformation.
But the Press Box was surely designed by Einstein, after a Re-
union Banquet of Mathematicians. From its rear-most seats, on

the right, only a castrated version of the match is visible. One umpire, one batsman, and three or four fielders, according to the length and flexibility of the critic's neck. Hardly a quorum. The front row gives a more total view. Here sat Neville Cardus, of the *Manchester Guardian*, slim, grey, contained; master of the rhapsodical style, cutting his sharp epigrams from the most amorphous material.

Like Bernard Darwin with golf, Cardus has made cricket-readers of many who would not walk across the road to see a stump fly or a ball driven against the sight-screen. Also like Darwin, he has the gift of fluency. "Page 48", he once said to me half way between the lunch and tea interval, "and I'll soon be off the Sports page and round to the Agony Column in front." But, amid his copiousness, he is eclectic. He scorns the common phrase, just as, in daily intercourse, he eludes the common man. I know a worthy fellow, a good cricketer, who, spotting Cardus in a crowd waiting for a train on the platform, went up to him and said, "Mr Cardus, I presume." This is not the right approach to Cardus. It did not succeed. On the great moments and the great cricketers, he has no equal. He is made for the mountain top, and he ranks among the English essayists.

Harry Carson, of the *Evening News*, was like a Bishop who had absentmindedly strayed into journalism. Tall, debonair, with white hair and ruddy complexion, he gave the Press Box a strong social uplift. Writing on cricket was one of his hobbies. He also dealt in Acrostics and Chess Problems. He was something of the same cut as Philip Trevor, C.B.E., formerly of the *Daily Telegraph*, an able and abundant writer, who once showed a startling contempt for the sensational at Manchester. This was in the match between Australia and South Africa during the Triangular Tournament of 1912. T. J. Matthews of Australia had done the "hat-trick" in the first South African innings. Near the close of play, with numbers 6, 7, and 8 of the second innings, he did it again. Trevor merely reported the second event as if it were some change of bowling. Neither Matthews' nor Trevor's feat is likely to be repeated. Harry Carson was a wise and witty talker, if a little hard to hear. Sometimes, too, the general sense was difficult to pick out of the volleys of "doncher knows" which punctuated his information. In comparison, his writing lacked ornament, possibly because he under-rated the scope and desires of his readers. A man of great charm and kindliness, he was the author of much silent charity. In 1936 he went to Australia to report the Test matches; but the work and heat and travelling were too much for his advancing years, and, to the sorrow of his friends, he was struck down by illness.

Bill Pollock, of the *Daily Express*, like Bertie Henley, had dropped into cricket reporting from dramatic criticism. Bill was a benevolent, witty, leisurely man. He disliked hurry, disputes, and over-rapid drinking. For nearly all of which reasons he was oddly cast for his journalistic part. By nature gentle and reflective, he was called upon constantly to be writing something telling and brief. So, incapable of being lurid or unkind, he turned to light comedy; experimenting in puns and such-like quirkeries. But he was not afraid to criticize, and he once offended Herbert Sutcliffe by referring to the great man's over-lordly fielding at the Oval. Some days later, Sutcliffe and Pollock met at the latter's club, the Savage, where members of the Yorkshire team have been frequent and welcome guests. An introduction was, as they say, effected. After some rather sticky preliminaries Pollock remarked, "I did not know that cricketers were as touchy as actors." To which Sutcliffe answered, "Believe me, Mr Pollock, infinitely more so."

Bill Pollock's last illness was difficult and painful. He took it, as he had taken a switch-back life, with a wry smile. I connect him most with Brighton, and Maurice Tate bending vastly at short-leg, and The Old Ship Hotel; just as I connect Frank Thorogood with an inn in Gravesend, where we danced some solemn steps, which, he said, were a saraband, to mechanical music. Frank wrote for the *News Chronicle*, keeping notes of the cricket in a sort of Chinese shorthand of his own, and tucking away quarter-smoked cigarettes for some benevolent but undisclosed purpose. Each year he produced a handbook on first-class cricket, presenting a copy with up-to-date alterations and an air of proprietary apology.

Of Australian correspondents, Arthur Mailey is the most familiar on English grounds. He appears, like a parachutist, from nowhere, picks up the latest about our cricket, renews friendships, and withdraws without demonstration.

There was a blighted atmosphere about English cricket in

summer 1934. The "Body-line" volcano had erupted, and, having been told not to do it again, had subsided into unintelligible mutterings. Nothing had been explained to the public. How, for instance, did Jardine stand with the oligarchy of control at Lord's? Was he to be vindicated as a hero, forgiven as a prodigal son, or cast away with gnashing and wailing? The England captain, then on tour with a Marylebone team in India, kindly solved one knot by announcing that he had no intention of playing in our forthcoming Tests against Australia. About the same time, a newspaper article appeared under Larwood's name in which he expressed the same decision as Jardine, only in more ample and rhetorical terms. Certain mandarins condemned the newspaper and Larwood for his outburst. But newspapers can hardly be blamed for interesting themselves and their readers in a matter of fervent public interest, nor Larwood for expressing himself in unequivocal terms after sustaining some five months of personal abuse.

In this imbroglio, the most hopeful sign was the presence of W. M. Woodfull as captain of the visiting Australian team. Bill Woodfull, in an office where character counts for even more than skill, stands as one of the greatest Test captains of all time. It is easy to be tactful for merely utilitarian reasons, but Woodfull's tact sprang from kindness and a true interest in others. As a slight instance, in 1930, on his first captaincy in England, when we were playing the Australians in the Folkestone Festival, he threw out a generous reference to a short spell of my bowling. I had taken no wicket and earned no praise. Cricketers remember little things like that. Not that Woodfull's name for benevolence depends from such insignificant hooks. He had the greatness to rise above quarrel and clamour. He could keep together pride and the personal touch. He rode the worst storm in the story of international cricket, and his stature grows with time.

We spent many hours of those 1934 Tests wondering under what new law or infringement of law Bradman and Ponsford might be removed from the wicket. Within the framework of Australian victory, these two champions were playing out a private match of their own. In bald arithmetic, Ponsford won by a short whisker, averaging 94·83 to Bradman's 94·75. It is the joy of the critics, when appraising a great player, to say why he is not quite to be compared with this or that hero of the past. When all else fails, they bring up the question of style. "Wonderful," they cry, "yes, very wonderful, but not so *beautiful* as so-and-so." So-and-so, in his day, of course had the same thing said about him. Thus, elusive perfection is chased ever back. Maybe Adam had an off-drive that made the Serpent weep for very delight.

Since the days when the other Sussex batsmen watched Ranji and C. B. Fry, I doubt if any cricket team has produced such a duet as Bradman and Ponsford; the lightning of Sydney and the thunder of Melbourne. In modern times, Hobbs and Sutcliffe, or Hobbs and Hammond, or Hammond and Woolley, or, we hope, Compton and Edrich, might stand technical comparison with the Australian pair, but there is no evidence that any one of these had envy for each other, whereas Bradman and Ponsford, we have seen, pursued the individual championship without comment or relaxation. At the wicket, Bradman saw what needed to be done sooner than the others, and did it with more precision. He may or may not have equalled Trumper, Ranji, Macartney, Hobbs, Woolley, in sheer artistry. Such things are arguable. He was not Jovian, like Doctor Grace. He had not the splendour, the mien, of Hammond, who came from the pavilion like the *Victory* sailing to destroy Napoleon. But Bradman went on. He had one eye, as it were, on the heavens and the other on the ledger-book. In the whole game, he was the greatest capitalist of skill. Poetry and murder lived in him together. He would slice the bowling to ribbons, then dance without pity on the corpse. It has been objected that Bradman was fallible on a damaged pitch. He was. This is like saying that a man may slip when walking on ice. But the critics condemn him on one act of rashness against Verity. Verity himself knew better, and told me how Bradman, for over after over at Sheffield in 1938, played his sharpest spinners on a sticky pitch in the middle of the bat.

Bradman's pads and gloves seemed incidental, just a concession to custom; but Ponsford always suggested the old advertisement for Michelin tyres. His pads would have made a summer cottage for little Willie Quaife, and his square and muscular frame further bulged with indefinable shock-absorbers. Ponsford was a wonderful driver; like the earlier Hammond, he played most of his scoring strokes off the front foot. His bat looked horribly broad, and it weighed only four ounces under 3 lb.

Against fast and rising bowling, he favoured the turn-about
method when he feared a catch to the short-legs, tympanizing
his ample back and buttocks. Against slow spin bowling he was
near to infallibility, and seemed to sight the bias from the start of
flight. His foot-work, for a heavyish man, was dainty and precise, and I recall a lesson he gave me, as I stood at short slip, on
the playing of "Tich" Freeman. Freeman was bowling beautifully, with accurate length, clever flight, and acute spin; but
Ponsford, with his crustacean sidle, kept playing the leg-breaks
firmly off the middle to the covers. You needed to be near Ponsford to understand his full art. You could catch Bradman's
mastery with half an eye, while guarding a pint of bitter from
predatory hands. The talk is always of Bradman, but I doubt if
the bowlers fancied themselves more against Ponsford. Either
end was a headache and a marvel.

There were also Woodfull himself, ripening for retirement, but
still a great stayer; Stanley McCabe, that gay genius who across
the years and the miles had caught the sense of great English
batsmen in times untrammelled and unperplexed; the classical
W. A. Brown; the busy and competent A. G. Chipperfield. And
all the bowling that mattered was done by the magician Grimmett and the unconquerable O'Reilly. Grimmett we thought
we knew; but it was one thing to know, another to answer. No
bowler of his kind has so accurately controlled the amount of spin
imparted; English batsmen used to say that his top-spinner was
born in hell.

Bill O'Reilly was new to England. At first, the critics were
happy to find much to blame. He was vast and awkward. They
searched about for metaphor and simile. There was mention of
camels and windmills, of carpenter's rules unfolding. He came up
to the wicket like a perambulating pump-handle. He ducked at
delivery. But, soon, we had to confess his greatness or go out of
business. O'Reilly was faster than is thought decent or practic-
able in leg-spin and googly bowlers. The size and strength of his
hand could make the spin live with the pace. His variety was
most difficult to detect. The post-mortem was monotonous and
inconclusive. Off the field, he was a friend; as a bowler, he showed
with all of him that batsmen are objects of loathing, forts to be
stormed, enemies to be confounded by violence or ruse, erosion
or subtlety. He wasted nothing. A ball let past by the batsmen

was not a ball at all. He would attack Hammond's leg stump by the over and the hour. At Nottingham, in that first Test of 1934, he took 11 for 129, and put Australia's hand firmly on the urn of Ashes. He took 28 wickets at less that 25 each in the Test series, and he and Grimmett together took 53 of the 71 England wickets that fell. But he stands clearest in my memory and admiration at the Oval in the Australian disaster of 1938. For many hours he was the whole Australian attack. Fleetwood-Smith twiddled himself away into vanity. The opening bowlers opened nothing but the scoring; but on and on O'Reilly went, with no help but hope and no prop but the indomitable heart.

In 1934, only Maurice Leyland wholly answered O'Reilly and Grimmett. Leyland scored three centuries in these Tests. His was a broad-bottomed administration, body and mind. For strength of character and purpose and arm he comes second to none in his generation of cricket. "Jannock" was not enough for him. True, he excelled at heavy rescue; but, he was never dour just because dourness was a native tradition, an inescapable inheritance. I fancy he found relief and fullest expression in his own left-arm bowling. Jauntily, with a kick-up of the heels, he experimented with oriental spins, and accepted their frequent success with an air of modest pleasure and candid surprise.

Leyland was never finer than in his 110 that summer at the Oval. Australia had topped 700. Half of the England side went for about 150. Leyland refused to understand reasons, and batted as if only three hours were left to win a victory depending on him alone.

Frank Woolley was brought out for that match. As a player of strokes in County games he was still incomparable; hero of Canterbury; on every ground that he visited, a perpetual expectation and a frequent fulfilment of delight. At forty-seven, he made ten centuries in the Championship. Numerically, he had played himself into the Test. But it didn't do. The years can be cajoled, but not mocked. Ames, while helping Leyland with the batting, was suddenly bent double by a strain; and there was Woolley, keeping wicket with merely formal grace. We were hoping that fate would allow him, now if ever, an innings with stuff in it to remember; little enough, perhaps, if set against the inexorable quantity of the Australian masters; not an oratorio, only a melody sweetly played in tune. But Woolley just swished and was gone. He waved the wand, and the magic didn't work.

"Beau" Vincent and I drove back to Fleet Street to write, somehow, a column each; for readers who would already know the horrid truth. We were silent; except for interjections.

XIV

CHARLES THE GREAT

AMONG those who conveyed information on this melancholy match to the enduring public was Commander C. B. Fry, R.N.R. In cricket, triumph and disaster will come again; but, in this world, Charles Fry will not. The ingredients for such a dish are lost.

I have never heard that C.B.F. was much of a golfer, and I believe him to be an uncertain mathematician; but he has fewer things that he cannot do than any other man I know; and, even when he cannot do them, he can talk about them with a fluency which descends, clear and free, from the wits and philosophers of ancient Athens. In his uniform of Captain, R.N.R., he looks like six admirals, and, probably to preserve symmetry of figure, carries his tobacco-pouch in his cap.

In company, not caring to dominate, he outshines, without effort or offence. He is an unrivalled host of a mixed society, inspiring its most divergent members with interest in each other and forgetfulness of worldly care. In his box at Lord's he will write an appreciation of some new Test batsman with his right hand, while his left hand is pouring out a drink for a late arrival, and, at the same time, a subsidiary brain, which he seems to keep in readiness alongside his primary intellect, is correcting a mistaken view on the poetry of Hilaire Belloc. He can never be said to be "amongst those present"; those present are around Fry. It was at Lord's, outside the pavilion, that I first met him. Rain had prevented the start of the match; but he was hard at work, standing. I ventured to ask him what attracted his pencil, and he said, "my dear fellow, I am writing about what ought to be happening if anything were happening at all. In short, the perfect critic."

Repton, and Oxford University in the 1890's, sound an easy ladder to life, but from the start Fry made his own way. He went to Oxford with top scholarship at Wadham and thirty shillings in his pocket. He remained at Oxford, its King, by the money he

made with his pen. He moved along the walks of privilege without the inherited means which ease and support that motion. He
showed, and shows, a contempt for tradition as an end in itself
and for those who believe that to be a gentleman should content
a gentleman's desire. The almost Sinaitic slate of good form pro-
vokes him to crack it across his knee.

Easy conquests in almost every activity of mind and body did
not depress him into a genteel modesty. He said and did what
came natural and uppermost, thus making silent but important enemies in influential snuggeries; enemies who, when they
could, excluded, when they couldn't, belittled him. Thus, though
for years he stood without rival in the combined theory and practice of batsmanship, Fry was never elected to the Committee of
the Marylebone Cricket Club, where birth and convention have
always ranked higher than originality and knowledge.

Soon after leaving Oxford, he enriched journalism and
affronted amateurism with a series of sketches of famous games-
players. There followed an engagement with a Manchester
newspaper, which ended when the young author, while enjoying
a fishing expedition in the Outer Hebrides, sent 1,200 words to
his employers at ordinary telegraphic rates. Soon, he was set up
as Editor of *C. B. Fry's Magazine*. He was also registering immor-
tality as an England batsman.

At the height of his athletic powers, he took over control of
the naval training-ship, *Mercury*. It was to become, and remain,
his life's work. It was a losing cause when Fry took it over.
He applied to it the vision of an idealist and the acumen of a
business man, and made use of every contact that fame had
brought him. The idea still prevailed that training-ships and re-
formatories were much the same thing. Fry persuaded *Punch* to
publish a cartoon in which a boy was asking the First Lord of the
Admiralty, Mr Winston Churchill, whether it was necessary for
a boy to be a thief in order to enter a training-ship. Games, clean-
liness of mind and body, something worth aiming at, corporate
spirit, all those the Commander gave them. He gives it still.
Lord Birkenhead, visiting the ship after the first European War,
said, "Well, Charles, this has been a backwater for you." But
which had climbed higher, the Captain-Superintendent or the
Chancellor and Secretary of State?

After the defeat of the Kaiser, Fry went out to Geneva as

financial adviser to "Ranji" in the League of Nations. In his fiftieth year, he was considered as cricket captain of England against the conquering Australian team of Warwick Armstrong, and made 59 and 37 against them for Hampshire. But he asked to be excused from consideration. During the next years, he stood for Parliament as a Liberal for the second and third time. He came near to carrying Oxford City; and when, for the sake of oratory, he hopped from the bonnet to the roof of his car, a spectator shouted, "Well, he hasn't forgotten how to jump." Then, for a space, illness laid him low.

In the middle 1930's, like a legend come to life, C. B. Fry returned; bang, with another jump, down into the arena of work, competition, argument; a Victorian as young as the latest aeroplane. Nothing like it, like him, was to be found elsewhere.

Nearly all his contemporaries of the Golden Age of cricket were gone, or in retirement on Committees. Fry seized his pen. He had wished to write what is known as "straight", but others were already employed to do that for his newspaper. So he turned columnist.

It was inevitable that he should have something to say with the Brains Trust. He struck in to that symposium, on Egyptology, philosophy, and rhythmic co-ordination in athletics, and had an agreeable quarrel on the air with the Secretary of the British Medical Association on the topic of the stomach. At seventy, he offered himself as a Bevin Boy for the coal-mines. At odd minutes, he writes Latin verses, and posts them to his friends for their opinion.

I was seeing him off, after lunch and conversation, on a journey to his old College of Wadham. I asked him what he meant to do on the way. "See if I can stop talking, my dear fellow," he answered; "but I shan't, you know."

XV

OVER THE BORDER

O N February 1st, 1937, very early in the morning, my father died at Moffat. When the telegram came, my first thought was that I hadn't written to him for some time, and each excuse that the mind presented was kicked by conscience to the devil. It was pneumonia, abrupt and virulent, storming a constitution which had been sapped, more severely than was known, by an illness of some years earlier. There was no "M and B" to help in the fight. At the crisis, the old doctor, his car suddenly immobilized, had run half-a-mile to our house with a camphor injection.

It was as if dawn had failed to succeed night; for I had never thought of my father in terms of death. He had always been *there*, not just thereabouts; a stay, unchanging and magnificently unchangeable. He was constant, within and from without; constant in a kindness at which one hint from the receiver was an unrepeatable mistake; constant in outlook and habit; not, as with so many, from any non-receptivity of the new, but because, after very accurate and thorough tests on the weighing-machine, he preferred the old. Over most politicians, professional and amateur, he had this advantage, that he knew his facts.

In memory's pictures, the clearest and, as it were, most representative shows him, in early August of 1914, walking to his car and the War, with a large tight hand-bag and hardly a goodbye, as if for some accustomed week-end visit. There was no affectation in his calm; it was a natural process of temperament. Service was his routine; part of his inheritance. My father died a landed gentleman without his land. Before Hitler had begun to paint Austrian houses under his own name, the lights in the country-houses were dimming one by one in the big financial blackout. The liberal, unadvertised, and responsible life on estates was dying under death-duties and taxation more radical than ever a David Lloyd George conceived, dying to the gibes of second-raters, to the laughter of fools whose sons may one day—

soon—feel what England has lost. Tradition knows how to die bravely; theories will not fill the empty chair.

Not long ago I heard one taxi-driver say to another, "There ain't the toffs about there used to be." He was an elderly man, of genial if corrugated aspect; so maybe he was thinking of the Edwardian cane-suckers and beauty-chasers, mural ornaments of the Long Bar, Filberts on life's dessert-plate. If so, he was thinking of a set—a sociological cross-section, if you prefer it—who, whatever their faults, had an "air" about them. There is no "air" about urban England to-day; just a miasma of obstinate mediocrity. Also, these "Johnnies" did not squeal. When trouble or poverty struck them, they fought it out on their own; they did not run blubbering to that over-worked nurse, the State. When War came, they went to it, early; with no more than an even chance of coming back. They did not sit down and argue about whose fault the war was, then sit back and tell other people to "go to it", then, when danger was past, turn round and bite the hand that rescued them from death and from death-in-life. No; the bell rang, and the butterflies turned into men.

Maybe, again, the old cabby *was* thinking of the country gentlemen. Before they are dispossessed of all their land, by taxation or by robbery disguised under Act of Parliament, it were well to remember that, beyond those qualities which are shared by real people of every opinion and status, the country gentlemen contributed to the State the ever rarer gifts of leadership and responsibility. They were willing to hold the baby, without payment or desire for thanks. They could command because they had been used to obey. Without losing personality, they worked for the common good. They exemplified, with a very low rate of failure, that high philosophy of life, individualism with service. Most of them feared God, and all of them honoured the King.

It was the last time I saw Moffat in peace-time. Cars tooted round corners, and disgorged candidates for a whacking lunch at Mr Fingland's Buccleuch Arms. You could walk into Miller's and buy half-a-dozen shirts. The knick-knack shop was not yet ashamed to hang price-labels on its knicks and knacks. Golfers set out, unharassed, for the links on the hill; and that brigand Jamie, who turned caddie when it was worth it, fixed them with selective gaze. Antonio still sold ice-creams and Sunday newspapers. Soon, he would be interned; in spite of protests, sufficient to have made a couple of Cantos of Dante, that he and his family had traded in Scotland for forty years and that he was only Italian by a long-forgotten compulsion of birth.

I missed old Mr H—. Moffat will miss him; and, for all I know, he will be missing Moffat; for he loved the very cockles of the heart of the place. He had come there first in the early 1880's, as a young and adventurous music-master. Moffat had no railway-station then, and he carried his bag from Beattock to the Buccleuch, where, for one shilling and sixpence, he was served with a breakfast of porridge, bloaters, fried eggs and bacon, toast, butter, marmalade, and coffee with a nip of something to keep away the cold. He was good at nips, was Mr H., and, with the years, they lent a luminous distinction to his nose.

But he was good at many other things. He was good at loving life and the people in it and at not caring much what it or they made of him. He was good at fishing for trout by moonlight, and, in the matter of their ownership, he did not always inquire who came a bad second to their Creator. He was good at photography, and sometimes he would invite me into his abode and regale me with the likenesses of many generations of scholars and athletes from the school to which, almost immemorially, he had been attached as organist and instructor in the pianoforte. Local citizens had also submitted, often unknowingly, to his art, and he delighted to snap Provosts and other big-wigs in attitudes and circumstances unbefitting the dignity of their office. One particular photograph in this collection used to puzzle him. It showed a gentleman of late middle age, with over-generous side-whiskers and a Derby hat worn at the correct angle, seated in an iron garden-chair and endowed with a face in which irretrievable melancholy and unutterable stupidity disputed for possession. "No," Mr H. used to say, after some minutes of scrutiny, "it is a case of lost identity; but I *do* remember that it was considered a very fair likeness at the time."

Mr H. was also good at crossing the High Street, in his own way, which was, to take no notice whatsoever of vehicles. He was born in days when life ran gaily as the sparkling Thames and traffic nearly as slowly as a glacier, and he was not disposed to have his reactions sharpened by modernity. He survived by easy foot-work and that auxiliary branch of Providence which cares for rudderless ships. Perhaps it was the knowledge of this im-

munity, combined with his musical training, which disposed him
to whistle while he walked. In times of elevation and especial
sympathy with the cosmic sphere, he would exchange whistling
for outright song. He was not choosey as to melody, and, as he
flipped along, he would rip out anything from "Swanee River"
to a complicated Prelude and Fugue from J. S. Bach. In his
schoolmastering years and duties he used to be sent, at the end of
the holidays, to accompany young students on the train-journey
from Glasgow, and he would sing, strongly but with an agreeable
variety, till the train reached Beattock. One of that audience,
now an impending grandfather, has told me that it was only many
years later that he realized that Mr H.'s performance was attri-
butable at least as much to his luncheon as to his kindly desire to
obliterate a youthful regret for home.

I peered into the coffee-parlour, where the Moffat ladies were
wont to discuss the crimes of the weather and the world, the latest
styles and novels and babies, and, distance just permitting, each
other. Then, an amble down the southward road; past the
garage to which Mrs Somebody had transferred her custom and
her car because Mr Something-Else at another garage had
spoken rudely about her magneto; past the enormous Kirk,
which tickled memory back to the professional basso who had
there sung his recitatives from *The Messiah* like Walt Disney's
Noah, magnificent, barybromic, solemn, then gone off to a
"swarry" at the hotel and sung "Phil the Fluter's Ball" to complicated dancing-steps of his own invention—people, like things,
are not always what they seem; past the municipal putting-
green, where citizens and their ladies putt municipally, and the
little municipal boat-lake, where the swans might abate their
pride if they knew they were dependent on the rate-payers; and
so to Mount Charles, the house which was being made ready for
the family move in the spring; family no longer.

Nearly nine years later, when the official Wars were over,
military under-pants were hanging out of the windows of Mount
Charles, and the garden was a desolation. Oh yes, Mr Obvious,
I don't expect the troops wanted to be there either. But the sight
set me wondering. How long will commandeering outlast its
cause and emergency? Will there ever again be meaning in those
old and comfortable words, "A poor thing, but mine own"?
Civilization. Will it soon be—is it now?—just a word in the dic-

tionaries and in the mouths of canting doctrinaires who think
that knowledge and Mr Gollancz are synonymous terms and who
use Economics as a substitute for God. "Little Old Lady Passing
By". You remember the song? Rather saccharine, perhaps.
Little old lady. With the emphasis on the last word. An unpopular emphasis, maybe, in these days of candour about sex and
reticence about social status. The ladies, spinsters and widows,
do not much interest the Socialist State. Let them live on memory, courage, fruitless queues, and what money is left to them
when their thin investments have been plundered to the bone by
the thief Nationalization. Not long ago I heard a man, supposedly possessed of brain and heart, after a most satisfactory
meal in a men's club, remark—"and do you know, in that one
street alone there are three cottages each big enough for a whole
family and each occupied by one old lady?" At which, a member,
till then silent, leant across and said, "None of those three, I
presume, is your own mother?" There was no answer.

You don't believe these stories of atrocities at home? Well, I
could tell you of an Alderman on the Council of an English
Channel town, a man belonging to no party except that which
was founded by One and carried on by Twelve, nearly two thousand years ago, in Galilee. During War II this man was commissioned to inquire into housing accommodation in his own town
with a view to military billets. And he met these old ladies, many
of them, living in one room, with three or four favourite books;
uncomplaining, and, if they were to complain, in effect unrepre-
sented. He raised this question at a meeting of the Town Council
and a Labour member of it said, "Never mind about them,
they're finished; it's only the children that matter." I seem to
recall very similar words in speeches by Herr Hitler.

A few months later, the *Morning Post* blew up. And so did I.
With other assets and liabilities, Lord Camrose had taken me
over, as Cricket Correspondent of the *Daily Telegraph*. I wrote a
few articles for that journal, as my old would-be instructor Dr
G. B. Grundy would have put it; but illness won a temporary
victory. What had once taken me half a minute was now taking
me half an hour. It was in hospital that I met, and was nursed
by, Elizabeth. Cupid may be blind. But he is a lynx compared
with some of his victims.

XVI

STORM AND RAINBOW

O NE thing about being ill; you get to know who are your friends, during, and immediately after. On returning to life, I settled at the preparatory school, between Pangbourne and Bradfield, which brother Bobs and his partner, H. M. Ward-Clarke had started in the summer of 1934. Haven; and a springboard for another dive. These are debts that cannot be either paid or printed.

The house in which the school began had been built in 1885 by a teetotal member of a brewing family. "Teetotal" is an under-proof word for this autocratic Calvinist and enemy of alcoholic refreshment. He was of that small but regrettable band of cellar-wreckers who, as the hammer cracks the bottle and the wine rushes down the gutter, fancy they hear and see the operative Will of the Almighty. The former Dean of St Paul's, Doctor Inge, learning, on a visit from neighbouring Wallingford, of this fanatic's secession from the family business, remarked, "Ah, but he continued to draw the profits, I suppose." In justice to the Oinoclast, it should be recorded that he did not; also, that he knew how and where to build a house, and that his love of trees has benefited successors of whom, however, he might not have whole-heartedly approved.

While convalescing, I had seen Leonard Hutton bat for 800 minutes and 364 runs for England against Australia at the Oval, and so beat Don Bradman's Test record of 334 made against England at Leeds in 1930. "The death of cricket" was a common verdict on Hutton's innings and that fantastic match. But I enjoyed every stroke of the impeccable Hutton till, in pale weariness, he gave a pale and weary little catch; and I drank in the deep slow draught of that Test match, partly because of long abstinence, but chiefly because I could not humbug myself out of delight in Australia's resounding defeat. I thought of the dismal end of England on that same ground four years before, and I laughed aloud, to the consternation and disgust of a dignified

member of the Surrey County Cricket Club. A little incident
comes back from that match; a comedy, that might have been a
tragedy. On the third morning, when Hutton had been batting
for two days and an hour or so, the head waiter of the Surrey Club
stood in the gangway of the pavilion with a tray of drinks for the
players; a portly, smiling Ganymède. Hutton needed but a few
runs to beat the Bradman record. The very gasometers awaited
the stroke of triumph. The waiter had taken one step down the
stairway, when "Jim" Swanton, then of the *Evening Standard*, put
out a staying hand and, with soothing but potent clarity, explained the nature of the impending crime. A few more minutes,
and all was congratulation and refreshment.

And now, I supposed, I must plan a return to pen-pushing.
But I was still more than half in love with indolence. I had often,
far too often, heard about the boredom that is born from lack of
regular occupation. I had no boredom; only a common bout of
impecuniosity. At last I had time for thought, or what passes for
thought; I could read books, old and favourite, new and pro-
voking. I could write letters without hearing that old nuisance
Time hammering at the brain. I could drowse over a cross-
word, and wake almost in time for an unbolted cup of tea. I could
take a walk with that sweet wasteful companion, Fancy. I could
browse in newspapers and, just as successfully as the hurrying
crazy world, utterly fail to foresee the colossal catastrophe round
the corner.

If, as some tell us, Wars are our punishment from God. never
can mankind have been doing less to avert the Divine sentence
than in the year of so-called Grace 1938-39. Blinding materialism, deafening noise, dumbfounding folly; these with their cour-
tiers reigned. Fear was knocking at the door; death was on his
way to the party; but still the party went on. The Socialists, with
their one-track minds, are fond of the lie that privilege makes and
can prevent war. But the causes of the disease start from below
the line of social or financial distinctions. In the peace as in the
war, everyone was in it; everyone was to blame in the former; in
the latter, everyone to praise. In the Judgement, here or afterwards, the profligate artisan is no better than the profligate stock-
broker. Both waste much of their income; one on beer and
dogs and Blackpool, the other on wine and horses and Le Tou-
quet. Both are parasites. Both want all they can get for as little as

they can do. The churches are empty of one; the chapels of the other.

Gaps fill quickly in Fleet Street. The *Daily Telegraph*, not unnaturally, had made other arrangements for cricket reporting. So I turned my steps, or, in common prose, wrote a letter, to the *Observer*, where my old but ever-young friend, Harold Gale, was then assistant Sports Editor. Their former cricket correspondent, the brilliant and Johnsonian H. J. Henley, had died some months earlier, and I was summoned to the sanctum by the Sports Editor, W. J. McAliece. McAliece was an experienced and competent journalist, but a man of some ceremony and pomp. Very carefully he balanced on the scales a selection of words which could, as it were, have been weighed by eye. At the interview, I adopted an air of sympathetic gravity, and inwardly felt that my qualifications would have been strengthened by a wing-collar and a power to quote from speeches uttered by Lord Harris on solemn occasions. McAliece, after emphasizing the need for avoiding the demon Levity in reports of the ancient game, added the further warning that Mr J. L. Garvin, the Editor, was in the habit of personally reading the cricket column very carefully. I murmured indefinite words of approval and remarked that my former Editor, Mr H. A. Gwynne of the *Morning Post*, had paid his correspondent a similar compliment. Whether at the interruption or at the mention of a newspaper which had committed the indiscretion of expiring, McAliece winced a little. We concluded terms. They were not princely; but I was in the game again. I nurtured hopes, since not unfulfilled, of rising in the batting order. Before we parted, I suggested to McAliece that I might have a word with the Editor. "That," he replied, "would be quite impossible. He is a very busy man. Why, we hardly see him ourselves." And I never did see J. L. Garvin in all the four years that I worked for him. I wish that I had. For he was a great journalist, and reputedly one of the few masters, in a tip-and-run world, of the conversational art. My mother once received a letter from him in answer to some political question which happened to be exercising her already athletic mind; but, as Mr E. Rockley Wilson, the former Yorkshire and England cricketer, would say, that hardly constitutes a touch.

And then the storm; first with caressing, apologetic drops;

almost with stage-effects; next with the real thunder and lightning; last, with the invincible panoply of destruction.

We who knew nothing of the inner works of the War, and that
was only just less than 100 per cent of this country, always
reckoned that Germany would lose. How, when, and where
they'd lose, time and Mr Churchill would decide. There was no
reasoning about it. The biggest beliefs don't run on reasoning.
Never mind about Norway, Dunkirk, and the Nazi flag flying
over Paris. Hitler win? Him? Not bloody likely.

At home, we were all somewhat and magnificently crazy in
that summer of 1940. I remember a half hour, late one night on
the Berkshire hills. There were two of us on Home Guard patrol,
armed with scatter-guns and a little of what we fancied in a
bottle. London was burning forty miles away. It looked about
four miles away, and the Eastern sky was red like blood. For the
only time in the War I was seized with a sudden doubt, and I
found myself wondering what the Germans would look like and
whether a scatter-gun would kill one of them at thirty yards. I
glanced at my companion's face for reassurance, and got it. He
was a gamekeeper, nearly seventy years old, but tough and
stringy. "They can't do that," he said, in a matter-of-fact voice,
"they can't do that and get away with it. We'll burn Germany
from end to end." He didn't live to see it done. He died two years
later, after jesting his way nearly to the end of a terrible illness,
with jokes about men in our platoon, about Bert, who was always
complaining that the tea was cold, and Jack, who slept in gaiters
and a Balaclava helmet, and Eddie, who, on his way to patrol-
duty, had gone to sleep in a ditch.

Jack was a corporal, on the strength of his local knowledge as
forester on a big estate. He had fought in his County regiment
through the first World War, in which one of his two brothers had
been killed. He hated the Germans, simply. "Don't you listen to
anyone," he'd say. "They're the dirtiest fighters in the world.
I know." He always spoke as if one of them might pop up at any
moment from behind a hay-stack or tree. "Shoot 'em," he said,
"whether they put their hands up or not. Someone else can do
the talking afterwards."

No words, not even Churchill's, can ever say what Churchill
meant to us in those first months of compressed emotion, and in
the later times of stolid waiting. He made ordinary blokes feel

great, and anyone's apt to feel pretty ordinary, standing in a
fish-queue or in two feet of a railway-train corridor, or waking
up in a room without any walls to find the world taking an
unaccustomed interest in the bedroom furniture. It wasn't only
Churchill's public speeches and actions that did the trick. His
off-the-record remarks got around, as when he was asked by a
Home Guard Commander on the South Devon beach what to do
if the Germans landed, and the Prime Minister said, "Hit 'em on
the head with broken bottles"; then, aside, as if to an invisible
Ordnance Expert, "It's about all we've bloody well got." Then,
when V.E. Day-plus-something came, Churchill rode round on
the hood of a car in the rain, and called on three Ambassadors for
a drink.

V.E. Day around London was a funny feeling. People were still
suffering from a slight stupefaction at being able to stand in a
pub without a Doodle or Rocket interfering with an argument,
and at going to bed with nothing hanging over them except Income Tax, and the next morning's work. It was pretty different
from the 1914 War, because that War seemed as if it never *could*
end. All mud and blood, and a thousand yards counting as a
victory. It ended with a tremendous bang, and everyone went
hopping mad with joy at the bang. It was like a dam bursting;
but *this* war had a sort of delayed-action victory. It was like a
dam with holes in it. Mighty big holes at the end, but still only
holes.

The full victory won't come till the old homes and the new
homes still unbuilt fill up again, and, when it does come, I suppose we won't notice it, because we'll be so busy dodging cars,
signing forms, and arguing whether our Government should be
blue, pink, or just a neutral tint. The heart has been too full,
larders and cellars too empty, for total thanksgiving.

Security is supposed to be returning to the world, and security
is a nice thing to have; living in peace in your own home, with
enough to pay for it and something over for pleasure. But security on its own is nowhere near enough. Mass security and
mass servility are never far apart. It took a man of the noblest service and the most magnificent individualism to pull us out of the
pit. We have been given another chance. Can we throw it away?

In August 1943, Elizabeth and I were married. She was

wearing a different hat, and I wasn't quite sure of her identity as she began to walk up the aisle. Uncle Patrick Shaw travelled down from York and, with characteristic fervour and kindly eloquence, helped to marry us. We went by foot from church to the modified reception, because we had much to say to each other. At the end of this walk Basil Cameron met us with a bottle of whisky and a musical score.

I end, as I started, with my mother. She died in March of 1946. I am glad that Elizabeth heard her laugh. No one who knew her well could sincerely mourn the parting of a spirit from a body which was utterly tired. It is not easy to be objective about one of whom you are, in every sense, a part. But silence can be miserly as well as golden. She had one friend above all; innumerable and true friends in all walks of life, who enjoyed her candour, her boundless humour and warm intelligence, and loved her for her sympathy. She had a quick and deep appreciation of the troubles of others, for she had learnt by suffering. "Never the spirit was born; the spirit shall cease to be never."

And now, to-morrow.

INDEX